STUDY GUIDE AND WORKBOOK

Ruth W. Yates

Business Law in Canada

Sixth Edition

Richard A. Yates

Prentice
Hall

Toronto

ISBN 0-13-093068-7

Vice President, Editorial Director: Michael Young
Developmental Editor: Suzanne Schaan
Production Editor: Marisa D'Andrea
Production Coordinator: Deborah Starks

1 2 3 4 5   06 05 04 03 02

Printed and bound in Canada.

Contents

Preface

This Study Guide and Workbook is designed to provide support to students taking a course based on the text, *Business Law in Canada*, Sixth Edition by Richard Yates. It provides several aids for students who are approaching the study of law for the first time and contains outlines of textual material as well as exercises to help students assimilate the material in the text.

Each chapter is outlined for quick review and includes a list of key terms with definitions that you should become familiar with in each chapter. Space is provided on the right hand side of the page to allow you to add your classroom notes to the guide. Review questions rated at three levels of difficulty (D.1, D.2 and D.3) are provided for each chapter. The first level questions require the student to recall the facts covered in the chapter. The second level questions are concerned with the application of legal principles. They are typical of the kind of questions a student might expect to find on an examination. The third level questions involve complex fact patterns and are designed to challenge and stimulate. Following the questions, you will find answers to the questions along with the designation for the difficulty level. Included also are the page numbers in the text where more information can be located.

One of the major challenges for a new student of the law is to find legal information. The Study Guide provides information that will assist you in locating cases, statutes and other law-related material in a law library and on the Internet. There is also a list of the abbreviations used in the citation of cases and statutes. Web site addresses for many law-related topics are provided in the text. A section entitled "How to Brief a Case" cites a sample case and then analyses it, demonstrating how to find and gloss the legal principles involved more easily. We have included a few suggestions for how to tackle complex test questions.

I would like to acknowledge the contribution and helpful suggestions of Richard Yates, and of his colleagues at the British Columbia Institute of Technology, D'Anne Davis and Bill Hooker who allowed me to sift through and select from the exam questions they have painstakingly produced.

Chapter 1

Introduction to the Legal System

Learning Objectives

At the end of this chapter you should be able to:

1. Distinguish between natural law theory, legal positivism and legal realism.
2. Compare the sources of civil and common law.
3. Describe the role of precedent in the common law system.
4. Outline the history of the Canadian Constitution from the *BNA Act (1867)* to the *Constitution Act (1982)*.
5. Identify and explain the development of human rights legislation in Canada.
6. Outline the terms of the Canadian *Charter of Rights and Freedoms*.

Key Terms

The following terms are highlighted in the text:

law	the body of rules that can be enforced by the courts or by other government agencies
substantive law	establishes both the rights an individual has in society and also the limits on their conduct
procedural law	determines how the substantive laws will be enforced; the rules governing arrest and criminal investigation, pre-trial and court processes in both criminal and civil cases are examples; law can also be distinguished by its public or private function
public law	includes constitutional law that determines how the country is governed and the laws that affect an individual's relationship with government including criminal law and the regulations created by government agencies
private law	the rules that govern our personal, social and business relations, which are enforced by one person suing another in a private or civil action
civil law	the legal system used in most of Europe based on a central code, which is a list of rules stated as broad principles of law that judges apply to the cases that come before them
common law	the legal system developed in Great Britain based on judges applying the customs and traditions of the people and then following each other's decisions

precedent	in a common law system, judges are required to follow a decision made in a higher court in the same jurisdiction
stare decisis	a principle by which judges are required to follow the decision made in a similar case in an equal or higher court
distinguishing the facts	the process judges use to decide which case is the binding precedent
common law courts	the historical English court of common pleas; the court of king's bench and the exchequer court
Roman civil law	source of civil law; provided the common law with concepts of property and possessions
canon or church law	legal system of the Catholic Church that contributed law in relation to families and estates
law merchant	laws developed by the merchant guilds and source of common laws relating to negotiable instruments such as cheques and promissory notes
Court of Chancery	court developed as a supplement to the common law courts hearing matters not covered under the common law
equity	legal principles developed in Courts of Chancery to relieve the harshness of the common law
Confederation	the process that united the British colonies in North America as the Dominion of Canada in 1867
rule of law	principle inherited from Britain that everyone is subject to the law, including members of parliament and the prime minister
paramountcy	when a matter is covered by both federal and provincial legislation or there is a conflict, the federal legislation takes precedence
parliamentary supremacy	the primary law-making body is parliament or the provincial legislatures in their respective jurisdictions and statutes take priority over the common law
bill	the form in which legislation is introduced into parliament or legislature
royal assent	the final approval of the representative of the British crown for a bill to become law in Canada
Charter of Rights and Freedoms	a document entrenched in the Canadian Constitution in 1982 listing and guaranteeing fundamental human rights
statutes	legislation passed by parliament is law in the form of statutes.

Chapter Outline

Philosophical Basis of Law

Natural law theory - What is law based on prevalent moral code

Legal positivism - What is law is determined by the authority of the source

Legal realism - What is law is determined by what rules the courts are willing and able to enforce
- There are problems applying theories; it is difficult to come up with a workable definition
- Definition of law: Law is that body of rules that can be enforced by the courts or by other government agencies.

Origins of the Law

Civil law - originated in Rome; recodified by Napoleon; used in Quebec

Common law - originated in England; developed under feudal kings
- *stare decisis* - system whereby judges follow each other's decisions (following precedent)

Sources of Law

Courts - (common pleas, king's bench, exchequer) called collectively common law courts because the law was "discovered" in the customs and traditions of the people

Equity - (Courts of Chancery) designed to provide redress for the inadequacies of the common law and common law courts
- As part of the reform movement in English law, common law courts and courts of chancery were replaced by a single system of courts divided into trial divisions and an appellate court under the *Judicature Acts* of 1873-75

Parliamentary statutes - override judge-made law

The Law in Canada

Confederation - *BNA Act* (now *Constitution Act, 1867*)

Parliament - is supreme
- Powers divided between federal and provincial governments (sections 91 and 92)

Statutes - government-made laws summarized and published

Courts - interpret and apply statutes

Constitution Act (1982) - included *Charter of Rights and Freedoms*, which modifies principle of supremacy of parliament and protects fundamental rights of individuals from abuse by governments or their agents.
- All legislation must be compliant with *Charter*.

- Applies to relationships with government.
- Limited by sections 1 and 33

Human Rights

- Federal: protection against abuses by businesses within federal jurisdiction
- Provincial: protects individuals in private relationships

Review Questions

1. Three theories of law have played important roles in the development of a philosophical basis of law. Name them.

   (a) _____

   (b) _____

   (c) _____

2. What tests would an adherent of each of these philosophies employ to determine whether a given rule was a law?

   (a) _____

   (b) _____

   (c) _____

3. Natural law theory defines law in terms of morality.
   (a) True
   (b) False

4. With the approach to the law called legal realism, law and morality are inseparable.
   (a) True
   (b) False

5. What practical definition of law has been determined to be the most workable in modern society?

   _____

6. Our definition of law is affected by which of the following?
   (a) history
   (b) theory
   (c) legal system in place
   (d) social realities
   (e) all of the above

7. The definition of law used in the text is:
   (a) The body of rules set out by a sovereign or government
   (b) The body of rules set out by a divine creator
   (c) The body of rules that can be enforced by the courts or other government agencies
   (d) Whatever the prime minister says it is
   (e) The rules that are consistent with science and nature

8. Which of the following describes procedural law?
   (a) Governs behaviour and sets limits on conduct
   (b) How rights and obligations are enforced
   (c) Regulates our relationship with government
   (d) Regulates personal, social and business relationships
   (e) Controls our private relationships with each other

9. Civil law as used in Quebec is based on which of the following sources?
   (a) the law merchant
   (b) the criminal code
   (c) Napoleon's Code
   (d) Hamurabi's Code
   (e) church law

10. Civil law is the most commonly used system in developing countries.
    (a) True
    (b) False

11. Common law is used primarily in Great Britain and Commonwealth countries.
    (a) True
    (b) False

12. Civil law can be distinguished from common law by its use of a written body of rules, known as the _____.

13. The term "common law" came to identify the legal system because it developed from the customs and traditions common to the people.
    (a) True
    (b) False

14. The most significant characteristic of common law is the doctrine known as _____.

15. Under a common law system people can predict decisions based on prior decisions made in a higher court.
    (a) True
    (b) False

16. In our system, it is more important for judges to decide on the basis of what is fair and just rather than merely applying the law.
    (a) True
    (b) False

17. An Ontario judge is free to ignore a decision made in B.C.
    (a) True
    (b) False

18. Which of the following statements is the most accurate description of common law?
    (a) The common law did not come from the king down to the people but up from the people to the legal system.
    (b) The common law is merely a compilation of all the decisions made in the courts and does not look to any other source of law.
    (c) Judges faced with making new decisions never borrowed from other legal systems.
    (d) The common law is system of law devised by the king and imposed on the people by his judge.
    (e) Common law is based on a central code and is a re-codification of the Roman law.

19. What are two features of the common law courts that gave rise to the need for a method of providing relief from the harshness of that system?

    (a) _____

    (b) _____

20. The most common area of dispute between the Courts of Chancery and the common law courts was the arbitrariness of the chancellors.
    (a) True
    (b) False

21. The Courts of Chancery replaced the common law courts.
    (a) True
    (b) False

22. Which of the following is not an accurate description of the Courts of Chancery?
    (a) The Courts of Chancery have been fraught with as much delay and inefficiency as the common law courts.
    (b) The Courts of Chancery eventually became as formal and as rigid as the common law courts.
    (c) The Courts of Chancery never fell into the trap of basing their decisions on past cases.
    (d) The Courts of Chancery eventually adopted the practice of *stare decisis*.
    (e) The Courts of Chancery provided a supplement to the common law courts and did not replace them.

23. How did the common law courts and Courts of Chancery manage to achieve a workable system?

    _____

    _____

24. Which of the following statements is false with regard to equity?
    (a) The term equity as it is used in our legal system today simply means that body of rules developed by the Courts of Chancery.
    (b) The body of law called equity forms a complete system of law and could function as our legal system if the common law did not exist.
    (c) The practice of paying monetary compensation as a remedy in a court action is a remedy developed in the Common law courts.
    (d) The law of equity was developed to overcome the limitations of the common law.
    (e) The remedy of an injunction is an equitable remedy created by the Courts of Chancery.

25. The *Judicature Acts* amalgamated the Common Law Courts and the Courts of Chancery.
    (a) True
    (b) False

26. The reform movement in the English legal system that took place in the 19th Century resulted in the formation of two distinct systems known as Courts of Equity and the Courts of the Common Law.
    (a) True
    (b) False

27. The common law court system was made up of:
    (a) The Court of Common Pleas, the Exchequer Court and the Court of King's Bench
    (b) The Exchequer Court, the Court of Chancery and the Court of Common Pleas
    (c) The Court of King's Bench, the Chancery Court and the Exchequer Court
    (d) Just the Court of King's Bench
    (e) Just the Chancery Court.

28. Our law with respect to families and estates originated in Roman law.
    (a) True
    (b) False

29. The Exchequer Court developed the law of equity.
    (a) True
    (b) False

30. The executive branch refers to which of the following?
    (a) courts and judges
    (b) members of parliament
    (c) prime minister and cabinet
    (d) departments and agencies of government
    (e) c and d

31. Which of the following statements is false?
    (a) Government is divided into three functions, the executive branch, the legislative branch and the judicial branch.
    (b) Because of parliamentary supremacy in England, the executive and judicial branches are submissive to the legislature.
    (c) The bureaucracy is the embodiment of the executive branch of government.
    (d) Regulations are rules of law made by judges determining how a statute is to be interpreted.
    (e) Regulations are subordinate legislation created under the power vested in someone by statute.

32. Parliamentary statutes override common law.
    (a) True
    (b) False

33. What is the primary significance of the *Constitution Act (1867) (British North America Act)* besides the fact that it created the Dominion of Canada?

    _____

34. Which of the following is not part of the Canadian Constitution.
    (a) *Constitution Act (1867)*
    (b) *Statute of Westminster (1931)*
    (c) *Constitution Act (1982)*
    (d) *Canadian Bill of Rights*
    (e) *Canadian Charter of Rights and Freedoms*

35. What is the effect of Sections 91 and 92 of the *Constitution Act (1867)*?
    (a) To create parliament
    (b) To determine how and when elections would be conducted
    (c) To divide powers between federal and provincial governments
    (d) To determine the powers of the prime minister and cabinet
    (e) To regulate Canada's relations with foreign governments

36. The federal parliament has jurisdiction over the provincial legislatures.
    (a) True
    (b) False

37. Assume that there is valid federal legislation making it a crime for an employer to fire an employee for union activities. Assume also that a new provincial government passes valid provincial legislation making it an offense for an employer to hire or keep in his/her employ anyone associated with a trade union or engaging in union activities. If you found you were the employer of such a person and you operated a small construction business, which law would you obey? (Explain.)

_____

_____

38. What is the legal result of a court holding that a provincial statute is beyond the power of the province?

_____

39. Human rights in Canada are protected by
    (a) conventions found in the common law
    (b) federal statutes
    (c) the rule of law
    (d) provincial statutes
    (e) all of the above

40. Federal human rights statutes are designed to only protect employees of the federal government.
    (a) True
    (b) False

41. Provincial human rights statutes protect every resident of the province in his/her private relationships.
    (a) True
    (b) False

42. The principle of the supremacy of parliament has been modified by the

_____

43. Why was it deemed necessary to entrench the Canadian *Charter of Rights and Freedoms* in the Constitution?
    (a) Canadians had no protection against discrimination.
    (b) The government had the power to pass legislation that infringed on Canadians' rights.
    (c) Personal freedoms were not protected in Canada.
    (d) Trudeau wanted to go down in history as a great civil libertarian.
    (e) Human rights are exclusively a provincial area.

44. Before the *Charter*, how were the rights of Canadian citizens protected?
    (a) Traditionally there was no protection for human rights and individual freedoms.
    (b) Provincial human rights legislation protected citizens from the actions of governments.
    (c) Human rights codes prevented governments from enacting legislation that infringed on human rights.
    (d) Legislation protected individuals against human rights violations in some social and private relationships.
    (e) The Canadian *Bill of Rights* effectively protected individuals from abuses by government.

45. What is the effect of the *Charter of Rights and Freedoms*?
    (a) Entrenches individual rights
    (b) Provides a remedy for an individual who has been discriminated against by his/her landlord
    (c) Protects individuals from infringement on their rights by governments or their agents
    (d) Gives an individual a right to be heard by the Supreme Court of Canada
    (e) a and c

46. Can the federal parliament pass legislation that specifically overrides the Canadian *Charter of Rights and Freedoms*? _____ Explain:

    _____

    _____

47. Section 33 "the notwithstanding clause" means that
    (a) Parliament or the legislatures can pass acts that override Section 24.
    (b) Any notwithstanding legislation must be reviewed every 3 years.
    (c) The courts can override legislation "notwithstanding" the *Charter*.
    (d) Parliament and legislatures can pass legislation that overrides certain sections of the *Charter*.
    (e) The *Charter* applies to all government action.

48. Personal freedoms as referred to in the *Charter* do not include which of the following:
    (a) The right to vote
    (b) The right to move anywhere in Canada
    (c) The right to due process
    (d) The right to own property
    (e) The right to be treated equally

49. Which of the following best describes one aspect of language rights under the *Charter*?
    (a) The *Charter* guarantees that all provinces in Canada are bilingual.
    (b) The *Charter* guarantees that citizens can have a court trial in their native language.
    (c) Citizens of Canada have a right to be educated in either French or English depending on which is their native language.

(d) Citizens of Canada are required to learn either English or French.
(e) Citizens have a right to have government documents printed in their native language.

50. The principles of *stare decisis* and parliamentary supremacy have done much to determine the superior courts' position in Canada that they will not make law but merely apply it. Discuss the advantages and disadvantages of this approach and consider how the passage of the *Charter of Rights and Freedoms* affects this position.

51. Explain the role of equity in the Canadian legal system.

52. The protection of human rights in Canada has had a checkered past. What steps have been taken to remedy that situation?

Answers to Review Questions

1. (a) Natural Law Theory

    (b) Legal Positivism

    (c) Legal Realism

        P. 1   D.1

2. (a) What am I required to do morally?

    (b) Was the rule passed by somebody who had authority?

    (c) Do the courts enforce the rule?

        P. 2   D.2

3. a   P. 2   D.1

4. b   P. 2   D.1

5. The law is whatever the courts are willing to enforce.

        P. 2   D.1

6. e   P. 2   D.2

7. c   P. 1   D.1

8. b   P. 3   D.2

9. c   P. 4   D.1

10. a   P. 4   D.1

11. a   P. 5   D.1

12. Civil Code

        P. 4   D.1

13. a   P. 7   D.1

14. *stare decisis*

        P. 6   D.1

15. a   P. 6   D.1

16. b   P. 6   D.1

17. a   P. 6   D.2

18. a   P. 7   D.2

19. (a) procedural rigidity

    (b) inflexibility and/or limited remedies

        P. 7.   D.2

20. a   P. 7   D.1

21. b   P. 8   D.1

22. c   P. 7   D.1

23. The courts were amalgamated and the principle developed that whenever there was a conflict between law and equity, equity would prevail.

        P. 8   D.2

24. b   P. 8   D.2

25. a   P. 8   D.1

26. b   P. 7   D.1

27. a   P. 7   D.2

28. b   P. 7   D.1

29. b   P. 7   D.1

30. e   P. 9   D.1

31. d   P. 9   D.2

32. a   P. 9   D.1

33. It divides power between the federal and provincial governments.

        P. 9   D.2

34. d   P. 9   D.1

35. c   P. 10   D.1

36. b   P. 11   D.1

37. You would obey the federal legislation if it is not possible to obey both (doctrine of paramountcy).

        P. 11   D.2

38. The legislation will be held to be invalid.

        P.12   D.2

39. e   P. 16   D.1

40. b   P. 17   D.2

41. b   P. 16   D.1

42. Canadian *Charter of Rights and Freedoms*

        P. 17   D.1

43. b   P. 17   D.2

44. d   P. 17   D.2

45. e   P. 17   D.2

46. Yes and no. Under Section 33 of the *Charter* the federal or provincial governments have the power to override certain designated rights under the *Charter*.

        P. 18   D.2

47. d   P. 19   D.2

48. d   P. 22   D.2
49. c   P. 24   D.2

50. In answering this question you should identify that the historical role of the Supreme Court in Canada has been quite different from the role of the Supreme Court in the U.S. The Supreme Court will legislate or create new law whereas in Canada, because of the principle of supremacy of parliament, that role has historically been given exclusively to Parliament and the Supreme Court justices have always been extremely careful not to step into that area. Where it is appropriate to make significant changes to law or make new law in Canada, that has been left to parliament. The advantage to this is that those involved in making new law are directly answerable to the electorate. The disadvantage is that these politicians can be swayed by popular pressure and may not be as zealous as the courts in protecting the interests of minorities and unpopular causes.

D. 3

51. A good answer to this question should trace the development of the law of equity. Because of rigid procedures and other restrictions (e.g., the practice of being bound by precedent and the restriction on the issuance of new writs and the availability of only limited remedies), the common law courts provided an inadequate system of law. The Courts of Chancery were created to provide relief from the harshness of the common law, and common law courts. These Courts of Chancery developed the body of law that is today known as the law of equity. Equity should be viewed as a supplement to the common law. While that body of rules may have been motivated by concepts of justice and fairness it would be inaccurate to think of the law of equity as meaning the same thing as fairness or justice. It is rather that body of rules developed by the Courts of Chancery that may or may not be fair by today's standards. The courts of equity and common law were abolished as separate court systems by the judicature acts of the 19th century. However, the two separate bodies of law developed by them were retained and so today a judge in a modern Canadian court will often be asked to apply rules taken from the common law or rules taken from equity in a given case. The judge may also look to statutes that have been passed if applicable. Such statutes override both common law rules and equity.

D.3

52. In answering this question you should point out instances of past discrimination in Canada such as the way people from Asia and our own natives have been treated and show how the passage of human rights legislation in the provinces first started to overcome that injustice, albeit somewhat late in our development. But that left the problem of government, which had the power to override any such legislation and to determine what areas it was to be applied to or not. The passage of the *Charter of Rights and Freedoms* controlled that government power and gave residents of Canada certain human rights in their dealings with government. Also, since statutes passed by all levels of government had to comply with the *Charter*, those other acts including provincial human rights legislation had to be consistent with the provisions of the *Charter*. A good answer should deal with both the problems that first existed, the passage of human rights legislation and the impact of the *Charter of Rights and Freedoms*.

D.3

Chapter 2

The Resolution of Disputes – The Courts, Litigation and Its Alternatives

Learning Objectives

At the end of this chapter you should be able to:

1. Describe the court structure in your province.
2. Outline the structure and function of the federal courts.
3. Explain how the role of judges has changed since the *Charter of Rights and Freedoms*.
4. Summarize the purpose of the civil courts.
5. Outline the process of civil litigation.
6. List the advantages and disadvantages of the civil litigation process.
7. Describe three alternate dispute resolution processes.
8. Summarize the advantages and disadvantages of each.
9. Determine the best resolution process for a variety of disputes.

Key Terms

The following terms are highlighted in the text:

in camera hearings	part of trial proceedings closed to the public
civil litigation	the process of one party suing another in a private action in a small claims or superior court action
jurisdiction	The *Constitution Act (1867)* delegated responsibility for matters to federal or provincial governments thus giving them jurisdiction to create laws in those areas
conflict of laws	if there is overlapping jurisdiction, federal law prevails and provincial law goes into abeyance; it also refers to the area of law dealing with disputes with those in other jurisdictions
appearance	the document filed by the defendant indicating that the action will be disputed
statement of claim	the document setting out the nature of complaint and facts alleged forming the basis of the action
statement of defense	response to a statement of claim by the defendant

counterclaim	a statement of claim by the defendant alleging that the plaintiff is responsible for the losses suffered and claiming back against the plaintiff for those losses
pleadings	the documents used to initiate the action, including the statement of claim, the statement of defense and counterclaim and any clarification associated with them
chambers applications	interim applications and questions (before the actual trial) are brought before the judge in a more informal setting for a ruling
discovery of documents	documents in the hands of each side that may be used at trial are made available to the other side
examination for discovery	lawyers from opposing sides question the plaintiff and defendant in a civil suit under oath—their responses can be entered as evidence; a method of making all relevant information known to both sides before trial
payment into court	the defendant estimates the true value of the claim and deposits it with the court; if the decision is for less than the deposit the plaintiff must pay the court costs; if more, the defendant pays the costs
affidavit evidence	evidence based on statements made by witnesses out of court but under oath
rules of evidence	courts will only accept evidence gathered according to rules established by the courts
party and party costs	court costs determined by a tariff establishing what opposing parties to a civil action ought to pay
solicitor and client costs	costs based on what a lawyer ought to actually charge his client
punitive damages	compensation for damages in excess of plaintiff's actual losses to deter similar conduct
exemplary damages	same as punitive damages
general damages	compensation for injuries that cannot be calculated (e.g., pain and suffering)
accounting	court order requiring the person found liable to disclose what profits have been made from the violation and pay them to the plaintiff
injunction	court order to stop offending conduct
specific performance	court order to require the completion of the term of a contract without variation
declaration	the court declares the law applicable to a particular case

examination in aid of execution	court ordered review of defendant's finances to arrange for payment of the judgment
seizure of property	court authorizes property of the defendant to be sold to pay the damages and costs of action
garnishment	court orders that a portion of the defendant's wages be directed to payment of the judgment
attachment of debt	court order that monies owed to the judgment debtor (defendant) be intercepted and paid to the plaintiff
limitation periods	rules requiring that legal action be undertaken within a specified time of the offending conduct taking place
negotiation	direct communication between the parties to a dispute in an effort to resolve the problems without third party intervention.
mediation	a neutral third party facilitates discussion between parties to a dispute to encourage and assist their coming to an agreement
mini-trials	corporate executives stage a form of trial to consider the issues, arguments and legal opinions that would influence a judicial decision.
arbitration	parties in a dispute elect or are contracted to submit their claims to a panel which makes a binding decision on their behalf.

Chapter Outline

Notes

The Courts

Criminal and civil functions
Trial and appellate functions
Provincial courts – Small Claims, Traffic, Family and Youth, less serious criminal offenses
Superior Court – Serious Criminal offenses and civil matters over $10 000
Appeal Court – hears matters from both provincial and superior courts
Federal courts - Supreme Court of Canada - appellate function. Deals primarily with Constitutional, Charter and other significant matters and questions from federal government
Federal Court of Canada – Trial and appeal divisions. Deals with federal government areas of jurisdiction)
Administrative tribunals - part of executive branch of government - deal with disputes arising out of implementation of government policy

The Process of Civil Litigation

Pre-trial - writ of summons, appearance, summary judgment, pleadings, discovery process, payment to court, offers and pretrial hearing

Trial
- direct and cross-examination of witnesses
- Decision- jury deals with questions of fact, judge deals with questions of law
- Judgments
- costly process with no guarantee of success

Enforcement provisions
- seizure of property, garnishment of wages

Remedies available before judgment - court order required to seize property, injunction

Limitation periods - court action must take place within a specific time of the offense

Alternate Dispute Resolution (ADR)

Negotiation, Mediation and Arbitration are methods or resolving disputes outside of the courtroom

Advantages of ADR:
- parties maintain control of the problem
- determine the time place and length of process
- matters can be kept private,
- good will between parties can be maintained
- procedural flexibility
- minimizes costs

Disadvantages
- unpredictable; no precedents are set
- cannot deal with complex legal problems
- must be voluntary
- must have a balance of powers between the parties
- parties must cooperate to ensure agreement and resolution

ADR Methods
- Negotiation – direct discussion between parties
- Mediation – neutral third party facilitates discussion
- Arbitration - neutral expert makes a binding decision

Review Questions

1. What are the primary divisions of the trial level provincial courts in your province and what function does each serve?

    _____

    _____

    _____

    _____

2. In which court might a jury participate
    (a) Small Claims
    (b) Court of appeal of the province
    (c) Superior court of the province
    (d) Federal Court (trial division)
    (e) Supreme Court of Canada

3. Juries are most likely to sit in which of the following situations?
    (a) civil action for personal injury
    (b) minor criminal action
    (c) serious criminal matter
    (d) small claims action
    (e) a and c

4. An in camera hearing is one where the media are invited.
    (a) True
    (b) False

5. What is the highest court in Canada? _____

6. To what court are appeals taken from Provincial Courts of Appeal?

    _____

7. A case in which a person is tried for impaired driving would be held in a civil court.
    (a) True
    (b) False

8. A person has an automatic right to appeal a case to the Supreme Court of Canada.
    (a) True
    (b) False

9. Identify the court in your jurisdiction in which each of the following matters would be heard.
    (a) An appeal from a conviction of non-capital murder from the Supreme Court of the Province
    (b) An action for negligence where you allege that the defendant's careless use of his power boat swamped yours and caused $500 damage
    (c) An action for a debt owing in the amount of $1 700
    (d) An appeal from a ruling of the Workers' Compensation Board
    (e) An action for negligence in the construction of an airplane where the damages exceed $100 000
    (f) An action for a debt of $8 000. Could this be heard in any other court? _____ (Explain.)

    _____

10. The federal court includes trial and appellate divisions and hears matters dealing with matters assigned to the federal government under Section 91 of the *Constitution Act (1867)*.
    (a) True
    (b) False

11. On what grounds will a case be accepted for appeal?

    _____

12. What choices does a plaintiff have when deciding in which jurisdiction to sue?

    _____

13. The various documents prepared by the parties in a lawsuit prior to trial and filed with the court registry are called the _____.

14. Name the party who initiates an action at the trial level.

    _____

15. What is the purpose of the discovery stage in pre-trial hearings?

    _____

16. How can the time consuming pre-trial processes be justified?

    _____

    _____

17. Which one or more of the following is or are the purpose(s) of an examination in aid of execution?
    (a) It allows a sheriff to seize enough of the assets of a judgment debtor to satisfy the judgment debt.
    (b) It allows a judgment creditor to have money owed to his judgment debtor paid into court.
    (a) It allows the judgment creditor to ask the judgment debtor about his income, property and debts.
    (b) It allows the plaintiff to learn what happened before trial
    (c) It is the term used to describe the process where each party must disclose to the other the documents they will be using at the trial.

18. Litigants are discouraged from going to small claims court without a lawyer.
    (a) True
    (b) False

19. The process of civil litigation is designed to encourage people to settle their disputes out of court.
    (a) True
    (b) False

20. Which of the following remedies cannot be awarded in a civil court judgment?
    (a) punitive damages
    (b) injunction
    (c) community service
    (d) specific performance
    (e) exemplary damages

21. Limitation periods prevent people from suing others a long time after the action complained of takes place.
    (a) True
    (b) False

22. Which of the following is not an alternative dispute resolution strategy?
    (a) communication
    (b) negotiation
    (c) mediation
    (d) arbitration
    (e) adjudication

23. Negotiation is when a neutral outsider helps the parties settle the dispute.
    (a) True
    (b) False

24. Mediation can be required before a court will hear a case.
    (a) True
    (b) False

25. In an arbitration, parties agree to an independent third party to make a decision that will be binding on them.
    (a) True
    (b) False

26. Which of the following cases would be good ones to mediate?
    (a) A supervisor accused of sexually harassing his subordinate
    (b) A doctor accused of negligence
    (c) Parents in a custody battle
    (d) A customer accused of shoplifting
    (e) An accountant accused of making an error in a financial report

27. Which of the following are advantages for using ADR?
    (a) Cost
    (b) Sets a binding precedent
    (c) Requires personal involvement
    (d) Balances power between disputants
    (e) You can predict the outcome

28. Alternative dispute resolution is a way to avoid penalties imposed by the courts.
    (a) True
    (b) False

29. Parties in a court case maintain control of the dispute.
    (a) True
    (b) False

30. List five reasons for choosing an ADR method over a trial.

    1. _____

    2. _____

    3. _____

    4. _____

    5. _____

31. You can always count on a mediated process to be fair.
    (a) True
    (b) False

32. Arbitrators must rely on records of previous agreements to help them make their decisions.
    (a) True
    (b) False

33. A mediator can protect the interests of a weaker party.
    (a) True
    (b) False

34. Which of the following statements is true?
    (a) ADR preserves the rights of due process.
    (b) The rules of precedent apply to arbitration hearings.
    (c) Mediators have the power to enforce decisions.
    (d) ADR methods are generally less costly than adjudication.
    (e) The public is entitled to know the result of mediated cases.

35. List advantages and disadvantages of arbitration when compared with adjudication.

    Advantages   **Disadvantages**

    _____   _____

    _____   _____

    _____   _____

    _____   _____

36. Which of the following statements is correct?
    (a) The parties to a dispute retain the most control in an arbitration.
    (b) Privacy is respected in an adjudication.
    (c) There is a great deal of flexibility in an arbitration.
    (d) Good will is most likely maintained in a face-to-face negotiation.
    (e) An arbitrator's decision can be appealed.

37. Negotiation only works when both parties are willing to make concessions.
    (a) True
    (b) False

38. Negotiation only works between individuals.
    (a) True
    (b) False

39. In a negotiation, which of the following characteristics would not lead to success?
    (a) patient
    (b) knowledgeable
    (c) communicative
    (d) competitive
    (e) conciliatory

40. A negotiation will most likely lead to agreement when the parties are
    (a) aggressive
    (b) uncommunicative
    (c) coercive
    (d) vulnerable
    (e) equal

41. The object of negotiation is to
    (a) win
    (b) compromise
    (c) agree
    (d) overpower
    (e) boondoggle

42. Which of the following will contribute to the success of a negotiation?
    (a) One party is more powerful than the other.
    (b) The parties rely on outsiders to put forward their cases.
    (c) All relevant information is brought forward by both sides.
    (d) One of the parties uses coercion to get an agreement.
    (e) One party dominates or controls discussions.

43. When would it be advisable to include a lawyer in a negotiation?
    (a) When there are complex legal matters involved
    (b) When it is likely the matter will end up in court anyway
    (c) Wwhen the parties are more comfortable in a competitive environment
    (d) When the parties are anxious to spend a lot of money to settle the problem
    (e) All of the above

44. If parties to a negotiation are worried that the matter will end up in court anyway they will be unwilling to make concessions or bring all the relevant information to the table.
    (a) True
    (b) False

45. A successful negotiation has the potential of enhancing a business relationship
   (a) True
   (b) False

46. Judges would prefer that the parties to a dispute not discuss the matter before coming to court.
   (a) True
   (b) False

47. Mediation is a concept developed in the past decade.
   (a) True
   (b) False

48. Which of the following best describes the role of a mediator
   (a) adjudicator
   (b) facilitator
   (c) decision maker
   (d) intervener
   (e) referee

49. Which of the following best describes the process of mediation?
   (a) rigid
   (b) structured
   (c) flexible
   (d) time-consuming
   (e) controversial

50. The mediator should be an expert in the matter under dispute.
   (a) True
   (b) False

51. When hiring a mediator people should look for which of the following qualities?
   (a) honest
   (b) frank
   (c) talkative
   (d) sympathetic
   (e) skilled listener

52. Which of the following characteristics would not result in an effective mediation?
   (a) ethical
   (b) impartial
   (c) consensus-builder
   (d) skilled communicator
   (e) decision maker

53. People are generally more willing to comply with court decisions than mediated agreements.
    (a) True
    (b) False

54. Mediation is mandated as part of the pre-trial process in some jurisdictions.
    (a) True
    (b) False

55. Which of the following is not an advantage of the mediation process?
    (a) privacy
    (b) cost
    (c) speed
    (d) obtaining redress for injury
    (e) flexibility

56. Mediation is not recommended in which of the following circumstances?
    (a) When blame needs to be established
    (b) When one of the parties is vulnerable
    (c) When there is uncertainty that needed secret or confidential information will be disclosed
    (d) When compensation for injuries is required
    (e) All of the above

57. The job of the mediator is to help the parties come to an agreement not to make a decision for them.
    (a) True
    (b) False

58. Why would it be advisable to get legal advice before signing a mediated agreement?

    _____

    _____

59. Which of the following conditions contribute to a successful mediation?
    (a) Parties participate voluntarily
    (b) There is trust that the other party will act in good faith
    (c) Both parties want a settlement
    (d) Parties are comfortable with an informal process
    (e) All of the above

60. Which of the following is not a variation of the mediation process?
   (a) mini-trial
   (b) sentencing circle
   (c) summary jury trial
   (d) consensus-building

61. Arbitration has been closely associated with the labour movement.
   (a) True
   (b) False

62. Which of the following situations preclude the right to go to arbitration?
   (a) When there is no contract between the parties in dispute
   (b) When one of the parties is the government
   (c) When there is a complex legal relationship between the parties
   (d) When there is a full moon
   (e) None of the above

63. There is no right to appeal an arbitrator's decision.
   (a) True
   (b) False

64. Courts can review an arbitration hearing for all but which of the following reasons?
   (a) The parties are unhappy with the decision.
   (b) The arbitrators were biased.
   (c) One party was not permitted to enter evidence.
   (d) The arbitrators exceeded their jurisdiction.
   (e) An error of law was made.

65. What characteristics does arbitration not have in common with litigation?
   (a) appealable
   (b) adversarial
   (c) costly
   (d) structured
   (e) formal

66. Contracts requiring arbitration are becoming more common.
   (a) True
   (b) False

67. What advantages does arbitration have over litigation?
   (a) privacy
   (b) expertise
   (c) speed
   (d) control
   (e) all of the above

68. Which of the following are disadvantages of arbitration?
    (a) lack of predictability
    (b) adversarial
    (c) hostilities may increase
    (d) no appeal
    (e) all of the above

69. Describe the advantages of private judging.

    _____

    _____

    _____

70. Reforms have been proposed to make the civil litigation process more efficient. Describe some that have been suggested and indicate how ADR strategies could further facilitate litigation and relieve some of the burden on the courts.

Answers to Review Questions

1. This will vary with the province. In B.C., the provincial court has a criminal division dealing with lesser criminal offenses and also playing a role in serious criminal offenses. The family court deals with family disputes (not divorce) and young offenders. A small claims court deals with civil disputes less than $10 000.

2. c   P. 33   D.1

3. e   P. 31   D.1

4. b   P. 31   D.1

5. The Supreme Court of Canada

     P. 32   D.1

6. The Supreme Court of Canada, but there is no longer an automatic right to appeal.

     P. 33   D.1

7. b   P. 32   D.1

8. b   P. 35   D.1

9. These answers will vary from province to province. P.33   D.1

10. a   P. 35   D.1

11. When a judge has made errors in law

     P. 33   D.1

12. Where the defendant resides or where the injurious event occurred.

     P. 36   D.1

13. Pleadings

     P. 38   D.1

14. The plaintiff, generally

     P. 38   D.1

15. To get all the information pertinent to the case out.

     P. 39   D.1

16. It is an attempt to get all the matters out so that the parties can settle it between themselves.

     P. 39   D.2

17. c.   P. 43   D.2

18. a   P. 42   D.1

19. a   P. 42   D.1

20. c   P. 42   D.1

21. a   P. 45   D.1

22. e   P. 46   D.1

23. b   P. 52   D.1

24. a   P. 52   D.1

25. a   P. 56   D.1

26. c, e   P. 53   D.1

27. a, c   P. 46-7   D.1

28. a   P. 46   D.1

29. b   P. 46   D.1

30. Less costly, less time consuming, flexible, private, not bound by precedent. P.46 D.3

     P. 46   D.2

31. b   P. 52   D.2

32. b   P. 56   D.2

33. b   P. 54   D.2

34. d   P. 47   D.1

35. Advantages: Private, not bound by precedent, less costly, tailored decision, easier to enforce an agreement. Disadvantages: Decision not predictable, does not establish legal principal, doesn't deal with underlying issues, does not protect rights of weaker party.

     P. 56   D.2

36. d   P. 56–7   D.2

37. b   P. 50   D.1

38. b   P. 50   D.1

39. d   P. 50   D.1

40. e   P. 50   D.1

41. b, c   P. 50   D.2

42. c   P. 50   D.1

43. e   P. 51   D.1

44. a   P. 51   D.2

45. a   P. 51   D.1

46. b   P. 51   D.1

47. b   P. 51   D.1

48. b   P. 52   D.1

49. c   P. 52   D.1
50. b   P. 52   D.1
51. e   P. 52   D.1
52. e   P. 52   D.1
53. b   P. 54   D.2
54. b   P. 52   D.2
55. d   P. 53   D.2
56. e   P. 53   D.2
57. a   P. 52   D.1

58. A mediated agreement is a binding contract and a party should be certain that it meets all of the requirements of a contract and be in their best interests.

                P. 54   D.2

59. e   P. 52   D.1
60. c   P. 54   D.1
61. a   P. 56   D.1
62. c   P. 56   D.2
63. a   P. 56   D.2
64. a   P. 54   D.2
65. a   P. 56   D.1
66. a   P. 57   D.1

67. e   P. 57   D.2
68. e   P. 57   D.2

69. A former judge hired to hear a case brings legal expertise, experience making decisions, impartiality and can take the time to understand the complex issues unique to the case.

                P. 58   D.2

70. The reforms require that the parties play a greater role in resolving their disputes. Among the recommendations for reform are that judges hearing a case become involved at an earlier stage. Some judges would be assigned a mediation role in disputes where mediation seems feasible. This would enhance settlement possibilities because the judge could let the parties know their likelihood of success. Some cases could be fast tracked, suggesting that the parties would be required to settle minor differences before the judge imposes a decision. The involvement of judges may mean less need for counsel. This might make the process less adversarial and cut down on the number and extent of pre-trial hearings. Judges can become more aware of the issues behind the conflict and that may play a role in the decision.

Chapter 3

Government Regulation and the Environment

Learning Objectives

At the end of this chapter you should be able to:

1. Outline the process by which federal and provincial governments exercise their powers.
2. Outline the duties of administrative tribunals and the rules by which they are regulated.
3. Apply the rules of natural justice to the regulatory process.
4. Discuss the review capacity of courts with respect to decisions handed down by administrative tribunals.
5. List the remedies available when administrative bodies abuse their powers.
6. Identify legislative restrictions on judicial review.
7. Review the legal issues relating to the protection of the environment.
8. Outline the sources of environmental power and regulating legislation.
9. Suggest means by which environmental control is exerted by governments.
10. Discuss the effectiveness of environmental legislation.
11. Outline the effects of de-regulation.

Key Terms

The following terms are highlighted in the text:

legislative branch	Parliament, legislatures including the cabinet and prime minister or premiers constitute legislative branch
judicial branch	courts and officers of the court constitute judicial branch of government
executive branch	the queen acting through the prime minister, cabinet, deputy ministers and all officers, agents and employees of the government
administrative law	the rules and regulations governing the function and powers of executive branch
regulators	government agencies including ministries, departments, boards, commissions, agencies, tribunals and individual bureaucrats at the federal, provincial and municipal levels.
judicial review	power held by the courts to review decisions made by administrative decision makers

ultra vires	beyond the jurisdiction, power or authority of a decision maker
jurisdiction	limitations placed on the power of an officer or agent of the government
regulations	supplementary rules passed under the authority of a statute and having the status of legislation
golden rule	rule for interpreting a statute requiring that the normal meaning of the terms be applied
mischief rule	rule requiring that an ambiguous term be interpreted in the most reasonable way or according to the intention of the act
strict interpretation	courts need only apply legislation where the meaning is clear.
interpretation statutes	statute terms that direct the court to interpret legislation in specific ways
principles of fundamental justice	principles set by tradition and convention that protect the right to a fair hearing by an impartial decision maker acting in good faith
fair hearing	person affected negatively by a decision has a right to receive proper and timely notice of all the matters affecting the case and be given a chance to put forward their side
heard by decision maker	all the evidence must be heard by the individuals making the decision
good faith	the decision maker must act with honesty and integrity
bias	the decision maker must be impartial and have no personal interest in the decision
appeal	a formal process whereby a higher court will reexamine a decision made by a lower court
authority	the right or power to act or to make a decision
procedural fairness	the hearing must follow accepted standards
abuse of power	acting beyond the jurisdiction set out in the legislation or making an unreasonable decision
error of law	incorrectly stating the legal interpretation or effect of the statute or common law
error of fact	making an incorrect conclusion with respect to the facts in the matter in dispute.
prerogative writs	the remedies the court may apply if it finds that an administrator has acted beyond its jurisdiction, made an unreasonable decision or not followed the rules of natural justice
habeas corpus	a court order to release a person being unlawfully detained
mandamus	a court order directing that a specific act be performed

certiorari	a court order overturning a decision making it null and void
prohibition	an order not to proceed with a hearing or other administrative process
declaratory judgment	the power of the court to declare what the law is in any matter brought before it
injunction	an order to stop offending conduct
privative clause	terms in a statute that attempt to restrict the right of judicial review
riparian rights	the common law right to have water flow free and clear of pollutants
devolution of powers	the process of transferring power from one level of government to another
site audit	the process of examining a site to determine its state of environmental contamination
compliance audit	the process of entering, inspecting and investigating private property to ascertain that owners are living up to environmental standards
due diligence	the requirement that a person do all that is reasonably possible to prevent pollution or destruction of the environment
stop orders	an order to stop offending conduct
deregulation	agencies created to monitor and enforce environmental protection standards are dissolved and corporations are encouraged to self-regulate.

Chapter Outline

Notes

Regulatory Role of Government

Executive branch - Ministries overseen by prime minister and members of the cabinet –administered and managed by deputy ministers/executives in departments and agencies and their staff –also known as bureaucrats. This body develops regulations under the authority of statutes passed by parliament. The regulations are administered by government agents and are designed to control such government services as health, welfare, transportation and environment

Administrative Law

Limitations on parliamentary power

Rule of law - although parliament is supreme neither it nor government can act arbitrarily – must trace their authority to some statute

Regulations - Boards and commissions are given powers to create their own rules. The process used by decision maker when arbitrating, can be challenged

Statutory interpretation – rules that govern courts with respect to the interpretation and application of the statutes as they determine the validity and fairness of administrative decisions made under those statutes
- plain meaning
- golden rule
- mischief rule

Administrative Action

Questions to determine validity of decision of administrator:
- (1) Does the legislation or regulation authorize the action?
- (2) Is the legislation or regulation valid?
- (3) Was the regulation authorized by the statute?
- (4) Was the statute passed authoritatively?
- (5) Was the process or decision improper? (Bias or bad faith or error of law)
- (6) Did the decision maker exceed jurisdiction?

Functions of Administrators

Policy creation
Legislative (creating regulations)
Administrative (implementation of policy)
Judicial or Quasi Judicial (adjudicative)

Rules of Natural Justice

May be determined by statute
Fair hearing basic
Heard by decision maker based on evidence
Decision maker must be free of bias
Right to cross examine if necessary
Note: No general right to a lawyer nor is there a need to follow the strict rules of evidence

Judicial Review

Superior court has right to review judicial process
This is not an appeal

Methods of Judicial Review (prerogative writs)
- *Habeas Corpus* - the right of a custodian to hold a person in custody is reviewed by the court
- *Certiorari* - renders a decision of body inferior to the court as having no legal effect
- Prohibition - prevents administrators from making a decision
- *Mandamus* - forces an administrator to make a decision
- Declaratory Judgment - declares the law - compensation can be provided to injured person when unfair decision has been enforced
- Injunction - court order to stop breaking law
- Prerogative writs in some circumstances modified by statute

Privative clauses
- Terms in statutes that attempt to prevent judicial review may not be as effective as would appear at face value
- Contract and tort law may apply
Note: *Charter of Rights and Freedoms* will override

The Protection of the Environment

Environmental pollution and the depletion of natural resources—major concern of government – example of administrative action

Common law offers some protections
- riparian rights to clean water
- private nuisance – protects from interference on private property
- public nuisance – pollution on more general scale
- strict liability

Government statutes at both provincial and federal levels—
controlling such matters as air, land and water pollution, elimination of hazardous wastes and transportation of dangerous goods

Goals of Statute Law - prohibit environmental offenses
- assess damage of proposed projects
- levy fines and penalties for violations
- educate public and encourage good practices
Environmental protection adds substantially to the cost of doing business

Review Questions

1. Name the three major functions of government and describe the role of each.

   _____

   _____

   _____

2. Under which function does administrative law apply?

   _____

3. The doctrine of parliamentary supremacy is limited by the rule of law.
   (a) True
   (b) False

4. Administrative tribunals are quasi-courts that make decisions affecting the rights of others.
   (a) True
   (b) False

5. Only the federal government has the power to create regulatory bodies.
   (a) True
   (b) False

6. A government regulator or administrator is limited in his/her power by the statute and regulations that create the position.
   (a) True
   (b) False

7. The authority of a decision maker may not be challenged on which of the following grounds?
   (a) The fairness of the policy on which it is based
   (b) The authority of the legislation on which it is based
   (c) The procedure by which the decision was arrived at
   (d) The validity of the statute
   (e) That it violates a charter right

8. What is the term that describes a governmental body acting beyond its powers?

   _____

9. Rick had a successful business making custom shoes. He was recently charged with an offence under an environmental protection statute. He is very apprehensive about this matter, but a friend told him that the tribunal hearing had to follow the rules of natural justice. Which of the following is not one of the requirements of natural justice?
   (a) Notice of the nature of the complaint
   (b) A fair hearing
   (c) Adherence to the rules of evidence used in courts
   (d) A decision free from bias
   (e) A decision made by the person who heard the evidence

10. Which of the following is not a rule of natural justice?
    (a) When a person's rights are being interfered with, he is entitled to notice of the hearing.
    (b) The person appearing before the tribunal is entitled to be represented by a lawyer.
    (c) The decision of the tribunal should be made free of bias.
    (d) The decision must be made by the person hearing the evidence.
    (e) The rules require that a person be allowed to put forward his/her side.

11. Which of the following is not included in the rules of natural justice?
    (a) Fair hearing; complainant must have notice and opportunity to be heard.
    (b) Heard by decision maker; the people making the decision must be the same ones hearing the evidence.
    (c) That the strict rules of evidence be adhered to.
    (d) Impartiality; no bias on part of decision makers.
    (e) Must be given a chance to state their side of the problem.

12. Which of the following are not rules of natural justice?
    (a) Person charged must be read his rights.
    (b) Person affected by a decision must be notified that the decision is to be made.
    (c) Person must be given an opportunity to put his/her side forward.
    (d) Person must be allowed to retain a lawyer.
    (e) The decision maker must be impartial.

13. Judicial review is the right of a court to review decisions made by governmental bodies or agents.
    (a) True
    (b) False

14. *Ultra vires* refers to a regulator having the authority to carry out the act in question.
    (a) True
    (b) False

15. The golden rule and the mischief rule are accepted rules of:

_____

16. The mischief rule of statutory interpretation means that an ambiguous statute ought to be interpreted in terms of accomplishing the goal that the statute set out to accomplish.
    (a) True
    (b) False

17. Which one of the following is not a reasonable basis for conducting a judicial review?
    (a) The decision maker has acted beyond his authority.
    (b) Procedural fairness was not followed by the administrative body.
    (c) The decision includes a remedy that was beyond the body's authority to grant.
    (d) The decision maker uses his/her own discretion in making a decision.
    (e) When there has been an error in the law.

18. Sam has just been hired as a bureaucrat working in a provincial government office. He is worried that some of the decisions he makes will be challenged by the members of the public affected by them. He asks another bureaucrat, George, about this, who responds by listing the various reasons for which his decisions can be challenged. Which of the following in that list is incorrect?
    (a) For making a decision not authorized by the statute or regulations.
    (b) Where he enforces a policy a court doesn't like.
    (c) Where he fails to give notice and hold a proper hearing.
    (d) Where he fails to carefully follow the procedure set out in the legislation.
    (e) Where the provincial government didn't have the power to pass the statute in the first place.

19. Under which of the following grounds will a court call for a judicial review?
    (a) The penalty was unreasonable.
    (b) The decision maker's bias affected the decision.
    (c) The tribunal acted beyond its jurisdiction.
    (d) Decision was made by person who did not hear all the evidence.
    (e) All of the above

20. Which of the following is the most accurate description of natural justice?
    (a) Maximum standard of fairness
    (b) Minimum standard of procedural fairness
    (c) Judicial process
    (d) Statutory defined fairness
    (e) Government imposed standard of fairness

21. One of the basic rules of natural justice is that all parties appearing before an administrative tribunal have the right to be represented by a lawyer.
    (a) True
    (b) False

22. The courts will review the decision, but not the process by which it was made.
    (a) True
    (b) False

23. All other remedies must be exhausted before courts will hear the case.
    (a) True
    (b) False

24. Jed feels that his rights have been violated by an administrative tribunal. Read each of the following separately and indicate which is false with regard to this situation?
    (a) He can go to the courts for a judicial review, which is not truly an appeal; rather it is a request for the court to exercise its supervisory jurisdiction.
    (b) If the statute provides for an appeal procedure, he must proceed in that manner before seeking help from the courts.
    (c) Jed could request, in addition to a prerogative writ, a declaration or an injunction.
    (d) A privative "clause" will successfully prohibit the courts from reviewing a decision of a tribunal.
    (e) If the action involves a right protected under the Charter of Rights and Freedoms, the administrator must follow the fundamental rules of justice.

25. When an administrator has exceeded his powers in reaching a decision, which of the following terms is used to describe his conduct?
    (a) *ultra vires*
    (b) *intra vires*
    (c) prohibition
    (d) *res judicata*
    (e) *mandamus*

26. Which of the following challenges will not be heard by the courts when reviewing the decision of an administrative tribunal?
    (a) Challenges to authority of decision maker
    (b) Questions of procedural fairness
    (c) Decision and remedy goes beyond power set out in legislation
    (d) Decisions that involve errors of law
    (e) The merits of the decision itself

27. Which of the following is not a remedy available to the courts when reviewing the decision of an administrative tribunal?
    (a) *certiorari*
    (b) prohibition
    (c) *res ipsa loquitur*
    (d) *mandamus*
    (e) declaratory judgment

28. The process of judicial review of the decision of an administrative tribunal is not an appeal of that decision, but the court exercising its supervisory jurisdiction.
    (a) True
    (b) False

For questions 29 to 34, match the appropriate judicial review with the following statements:
    (1) *habeas corpus*
    (2) *certiorari*
    (3) prohibition
    (4) *mandamus*
    (5) declaratory judgment
    (6) injunction

29. The court exercises its right to declare the law, assess damages and grant compensation. _____

30. The court prevents an administrator from making a decision. _____

31. An order to stop a decision from being implemented. _____

32. An already-made decision is declared to have no legal affect. _____

33. A person being held in custody is ordered to be brought before the court. _____

34. Forces a decision maker to make a decision. _____

35. The decision of an administrative tribunal may be challenged on the basis that the decision maker did not have the authority to make the decision made.
    (a) True
    (b) False

36. *Certiorari* involves the decision of the decision maker being quashed or of no effect
    (a) True
    (b) False

37. *Certiorari* involves the decision of the decision maker being stopped before the decision is made.
    (a) True
    (b) False

38. After the court has conducted its judicial review it may assess damages and grant compensation.
    (a) True
    (b) False

39. When is an injunction an inappropriate remedy?
    (a) When damage has already occurred
    (b) When there is a delay in making the decision
    (c) When the regulations are about to be amended
    (d) When decision makers are out to lunch
    (e) When a wrong decision has been made but the action it authorizes not yet taken

40. Privative clauses always stop the court from interfering in a government agency's decision-making process.
    (a) True
    (b) False

41. Legislators anticipate the judicial review process and attempt to restrict it by incorporating privative clauses into the statute.
    (a) True
    (b) False

42. Privative clauses may not stop the court from reviewing the decision of a decision maker.
    (a) True
    (b) False

43. An effective defense of the court against privative clauses is its right to interpret statutory provisions.
    (a) True
    (b) False

44. Which of the following is a common law tool that is effective in the protection of the environment?
    (a) riparian rights
    (b) nuisance
    (c) strict liability
    (d) trespass
    (e) all of the above

45. Riparian rights refer to an individuals' common-law right to be free of air pollution.
    (a) True
    (b) False

46. What is a statutory tort?
    (a) The right to sue privately for injuries suffered because of the violation of a statute
    (b) An injury caused when a person is affected by the operation of a statute
    (c) Damage caused by a government bureaucrat functioning in his office
    (d) Any tort action brought against the government
    (e) Any action involving Charter rights

47. Which of the following are the most likely torts to be used to protect an individual's environmental concerns?
    (a) private nuisance
    (b) negligence
    (c) trespass
    (d) assault
    (e) defamation

48. The common law action of nuisance allows a person to sue a neighbour interfering with his enjoyment of his property through pollution.
    (a) True
    (b) False

49. Explain what is meant by riparian rights and what role this principle plays in protecting environmental concerns.

    _____

    _____

    _____

50. What level of government has the jurisdiction to pass environmental type legislation?

    _____

51. Which jurisdiction is responsible for passing statutes relating to the protection of the environment?
    (a) federal
    (b) provincial
    (c) municipal
    (d) a and b
    (e) all of the above

52. The only way of enforcing environmental protection regulations is for the victim of the pollution to sue under the statute.
    (a) True
    (b) False

53. Victims of environmental pollution are responsible for policing and so must seek their own remedy.
    (a) True
    (b) False

54. Which of the following areas is not a responsibility of the federal government?
    (a) international
    (b) interprovincial matters
    (c) federal lands
    (d) coastal waters
    (e) forests

55. Provincial statutes create government departments that are responsible for which of the following
    (a) research and development
    (b) granting permits
    (c) inspect and enforce regulations
    (d) develop prevention programs
    (e) all of the above

56. Federal legislation affects provincial programs by virtue of:
    (a) national presence
    (b) helping to finance provincial programs
    (c) the federal government is the senior government and is supreme
    (d) the federal government controls the queen and she must approve all provincial law
    (e) The federal government appoints the provincial officials

57. Indicate five types of environmental degradation that might be controlled by environmental protection legislation.

    (1) _____

    (2) _____

    (3) _____

    (4) _____

    (5) _____

58. The federal government is responsible for the handling and disposal of hazardous wastes.
    (a) True
    (b) False

59. Where federal and provincial legislation conflict, the federal legislation overrides provincial.
    (a) True
    (b) False

60. Statutes allow for governments to enforce environmental regulations without involving individuals.
    (a) True
    (b) False

61. Which of the following is not within provincial jurisdiction?
    (a) use of natural resources
    (b) elimination of industrial wastes
    (c) air pollution
    (d) toxic substances
    (e) fisheries

62. Which of the following are enforcement provisions allowed for in provincial or federal legislation?
    (a) enter premises
    (b) inspect
    (c) seize documents
    (d) set penalties
    (e) all of the above

63. The *Environmental Assessment Act* requires most new business proposals to include environmental risk assessment.
    (a) True
    (b) False

64. The *Environmental Assessment Act* established the federal environmental review agency that has which of the following responsibilities.
    (a) administering and promoting environmental assessment process
    (b) encouraging research
    (c) promote uniformity throughout Canada
    (d) education
    (e) all of the above

65. Jones operated a local movie theatre in a small town that had fallen on hard times. As a last ditch effort to attract customers he decided to show pornographic movies. From the week the change was made, the theatre had to turn away customers on a regular basis. The local town council was quite upset, however, especially since a number of them represented a conservative and religious constituency. They decided to take away the license of the theatre but were quickly informed that they did not have the power to do that. They then decided to increase the license fee from the regular $50 per year to $50 000 per year. Jones was notified of the fact that this course of action was being considered and he was given a chance to appear before the council to state his case. He did so, but the council decided to go ahead with the decision in any case. This, of course, would force Jones out of business. After exhausting all local remedies and appeals, Jones took the matter to court. Which of the following accurately indicates the legal position of the parties?
    (a) Jones will be successful and will seek an order of *mandamus*.
    (b) Jones will be successful since this is an attempt to pass criminal law, which is federal.
    (c) The municipal council's decision will stand since this is a proper use of their licensing power.
    (d) Jones will be successful and will seek an order of prohibition.
    (e) Jones will not be successful since the decision has been made and he has exhausted his remedies.

66. A provision in the *Consumer Protection Act* prohibited door-to-door sales activities within the limits of a particular town. Maslov was a manufacturer's representative, selling soap products. He called on Green's Grocers Ltd. and in the process of talking to Green about carrying his products in his stores, he was interrupted by a constable who gave him a citation for committing an offense under the legislation. Explain the arguments available to Maslov.

    _____

    _____

67. The Town Clerk was authorized under the *Municipal Act* to grant business licenses within the town. Smith applied for a license to sell ice cream novelties from a mobile vending cart. This would not have created a problem except that Smith's name appeared on a list compiled by the Department of Human Resources which identified people in the town that seemed to fit the psychological profile of potential child abusers. None of these people had been charged or convicted; the list was merely an attempt to identify possible problems. The clerk, relying on this list, refused to give Smith the license and also refused to tell Smith why he was being turned down. Explain the legal position of the two parties and any remedies that would be available to Smith.

    _____

    _____

    _____

68. Jones was assigned as the arbitrator in an employment contract dispute between Ace Manufacturing Ltd. and their employees in Bargaining Unit #3 of the Pipe Fitters Union. Ace had fired one of their employees for refusing to carry out instructions to climb a metal tower to fix a loose segment of the tower. The employee, who was a member of the Bargaining Unit, had refused because of the danger involved. Jones was called to arbitrate the ensuing dispute. After hearing the evidence from both sides, Jones announced that he would have a decision within several days. He then contacted Black, a labour lawyer, and asked for his advice on the matter. Black indicated that the law was very clear, and that an employee was entitled to refuse a request to do something that was unreasonably dangerous, but in this case climbing a tower was precisely the kind of thing that a pipe fitter was expected to do and, therefore, the refusal was not justified. He also stated that he thought that dismissal was a rather harsh penalty and that Ace should have suspended the employee for 15 days. Jones accepted this advice, reconvened the hearing and announced his decision to the parties stating that he had had legal advice on the matter. Explain what complaints the parties would have about this procedure. How would your answer be affected if there was a provision in the labour code which prohibited the decision of the arbitrator from being reviewed by any court of law?

69. Outline the various ways (direct and indirect) that environmental concerns can impact Canadian business.

70. Henderson, under the powers given him in the *Airport Improvement Act*, a federal statute that empowered him to "make all regulations necessary to improve the quality, safety and efficiency of Canadian international airports," acted under a provision which said, "the Minister shall have power to delegate the authority necessary to accomplish the purpose of this Act to other levels of government." Some time later, he was also given the responsibility of seeing that a local airport in Saskatchewan was improved to international standards. Relying on this provision, Henderson contacted the city involved and instructed them to improve the road access to the airport, arranging to provide federal funding for the project. The city was instructed to expropriate any property necessary under the authority of this regulation and the legislation that authorized it.

    The municipality set up a special airport commission to hear proposals for the routing of the new roads. This commission consisted of three people and they were given the authority to make a final decision on the route. Gordon, a local homeowner, was served with notice to appear before the committee but he was not told what would be decided at that time. In fact, he was shocked when he appeared and was asked that he show cause why his property should not be expropriated for the purposes of putting in a new road to the airport. There were two alternate routes, but the three-man commission had decided that the route through Gordon's land was the most appropriate. Gordon did mention at the hearing that he thought that this was odd, because, although the route chosen was the most direct one, it also meant crossing the meandering Saskatchewan River twice, making the construction much more costly. Gordon was thanked for his input. Two days later the commission published its written decision, which stated, "The route chosen was the most economical and direct route to the airport." Gordon was then informed that his property would be expropriated and was given 60 days to vacate.

After some investigation, Gordon discovered that along one of the alternate routes, one of the three members of the commission had several pieces of property that would have been expropriated had that route been chosen. Gordon exercised his right under the *Municipal Act*, under which the commission had been appointed, to appeal to the Municipal Council. The *Act*, however, provided no time within which that appeal had to be heard, but did state that the decision made by a decision-making body would be in effect until overturned at the appeal level. Gordon could see that he would be forcefully evicted and that his house would be demolished so he went to his lawyer to see what could be done about the matter. There was also a clause in the *Municipal Act* that created the power to run such a commission, that any appeals must go through the municipal council and that the decision of the commission and the decision of the council were final and not reviewable in any court by way of any prerogative writs. Explain the legal rights of Gordon in this situation and indicate any remedies that may be available to him.

Answers to Review Questions

1. (1) Legislative - passes laws in form of statutes

   (2) Judicial - adjudicates the law (courts)

   (3) Executive - implements the law

   P. 64 D.1

2. Executive

   P. 65   D.1

3. a   P. 65   D.1

4. a   P. 66   D.1

5. b   P. 66   D.1

6. a   P. 66   D.1

7. a   P. 67   D.1

8. ultra vires   P. 67   D.1

9. c   P. 72   D.2

10. b.   P. 72   D.2

11. c   P. 72   D.2

12. a and d (Note that being read your rights is a right established in the Charter associated with criminal conduct and the right to a lawyer is restricted to those matters where a criminal charge may result.)

   P. 72   D.2

13. a   P. 67   D.2

14. b   P. 67   D.1

15. statutory interpretation P. 69   D.1

16. a   P. 69   D.1

17. d   P. 78   D.1

18. b (Note that where a decision maker has been given discretionary power, the proper exercise of that power is appropriate.)

   P. 78   D.2

19. e   P. 77   D.2

20. b   P. 71   D.2

21. b   P. 73   D.2

22. b   P. 67   D.1

23. a   P. 67   D.1

24. d   P. 82   D.2

25. a   P. 67   D.2

26. e   P. 67   D.2

27. c   P. 79   D.2

28. a   P. 79   D.1

29. (5)   declaratory judgment

   P. 80   D.1

30. (3)   prohibition

   P. 80   D.1

31. (6)   injunction

   P. 81   D.1

32. (2)   *certiorari*

   P. 79   D.1

33. (1)   *habeas corpus*

   p. 79   D.1

34. (4)   *mandamus*

   P. 80   D.1

35. a   P. 70   D.2

36. a   P. 79   D.1

37. a   P. 79   D.1

38. a   P. 80   D.1

39. e   P. 81   D.1

40. b   P. 82   D.1

41. a   P. 82   D.1

42. a   P. 82   D.2

43. a   P. 83   D.2

44. e.   P. 87   D.1

45. b   P. 87   D.1

46. a   P. 87   D.2

47. a, b, c P. 87   D.2

48. a   P. 87   D.1

49. Riparian rights bestow on a downstream owner of property the right to have water flow to that property of undiminished quality and quantity. Where pollution or degradation takes place, that downstream owner can sue relying on this common law protection.

   P. 87   D.2

50. Both the federal and provincial governments have the power to deal with environmental matters in the areas of their jurisdiction. Municipalities derive their power from the province.

    P. 89   D.1

51. e   P. 89   D.1

52. b   P. 89   D.1

53. b   P. 92   D.1

54. e   P. 90   D.1

55. e   P. 90   D.2

56. b   P. 93   D.2

57. damage to land; depletion of water, air and other resources; pollution; contamination of fish and animal habitat; use of dangerous products and materials.

    P. 94   D.2

58. b   P. 94   D.1

59. a   P. 92   D.1

60. a   P. 91   D.1

61. e   P. 93   D.1

62. e   P. 91   D.2

63. a   P. 97   D.1

64. e   P. 77   D.2

65. b (Note that a and d are incorrect because the decision has already been made.)

    P. 79   D.3

66. Maslov would claim that this was an ordinance that was intended to cover only consumer sales to residential people and could not have been intended to apply to normal business operations where agents must call on businesses to perform their duties. The legislation is obviously ambiguous, as it places no limitations on the application of the provisions and so would cause business in general to come to a halt if given its literal interpretation. P. 70

67. Even though this was an administrative action by the town clerk, he is required to follow the basic requirements of fairness and so would have to at least give Smith a chance to respond to the reasons for the refusal. This was not done and so Smith would have grounds to challenge the decision. This also may be a violation of the *Charter of Rights and Freedoms*. P. 72

68. (a) Either the decision was not made by Jones (the arbitrator) and this is a reason to overturn the decision, or there was additional input to the arbitrator after the hearing that Smith was not given a chance to respond to so that the decision was not made on the evidence disclosed in the hearing. This is also grounds to challenge the decision. Smith would apply for an order of *certiorari* and have the arbitrator's decision quashed. It is also arguable that the arbitrator was not authorized to substitute his decision for the employer's, but simply to decide whether the decision of the employer was correct or not.

    (b) The arbitrator has gone beyond what he was authorized to do or has done it incorrectly. The court would likely hold that the privative clause was never intended to take away their power to review in such circumstances and would grant their remedy in any case. P. 72

69. This discussion should include a summary of the direct involvement such as the environmental regulations and their enforcement, the environmental assessment process, pollution permits and the costs associated with these matters. The discussion should also include an examination of the indirect effects such as the attention of environmental activists, boycotts, the image of a polluting business and the costs associated with these factors. P. 86

70. There are two main procedural problems here. Gordon was not given proper notice of the hearing and was not told what he had to answer to. Second, one of the decision makers was biased because he had property that could have been affected if they didn't choose the route over Gordon's property for the road. Both of these are reasons to challenge the decision and I think the court would entertain an application for judicial review despite the privative clause because of the blatant violations of the rules of natural justice. Normally, Gordon would have to exhaust all local remedies before going to the courts, but here the expropriation and destruction of his home can proceed before his appeal before the

municipal council would take place. This would likely be reason enough to convince the court to hear the matter. The best remedy here would be for an order of *certiorari* or a declaratory judgment making the decision of the commission of no effect and void. Another major avenue of attack would be to challenge the power of the commission itself. If the municipality set up this commission acting under the power given to Henderson, Henderson only had power to deal with international airports and the one in question here is local. It could be argued then that Henderson exceeded his powers in instructing the municipality to set up the commission and therefore the commission itself has no power to expropriate the land. A court likely would listen to this argument despite the presence of a privative clause in the *Municipal Act*. P. 68–81

Chapter 4

Torts and Professional Liability

Learning Objectives

At the end of this chapter you should be able to:

1. Define a tort and explain its role in our legal system.
2. Differentiate and explain the various categories of torts.
3. Summarize the basic requirements needed to start a tort action.
4. Explain in some detail the concept of negligence including the elements needed in a negligence action, the methods used to determine whether these elements are present and several situations in which these rules may be modified.
5. Demonstrate an understanding of the principle of vicarious liability.
6. List the duties on manufacturers of products.
7. Describe the special concerns business people regarding professional liability.
8. Explain the remedies available in tort actions.

Key Terms

The following terms are highlighted in the text:

tort	an action that causes harm or injury to another person
negligence	an unintentional or careless act that results in injury to another
special damages	monetary compensation awarded by court to cover actual expenses and calculable losses
general damages	compensation for incalculable losses such as pain and suffering
punitive damages	costs awarded to punish the wrongdoer in a tort action
exemplary damages	same as punitive damages
vicarious liability	an employer can be held liable for the tortious acts of their employees commit while at work
assault	an action that makes a person think he/she is about to be struck
battery	the actual unwelcome physical contact
consent	a defense to an assault charge can be either expressed or implied
self-defence	a person can respond to an assault with as much force as is reasonable in the circumstances
trespass	being on another's property without permission or legal right

false imprisonment	holding someone against his/her will and without lawful authority
private nuisance	the use of property in such a way that it interferes with a neighbour's enjoyment of theirs
defamation	a published false statement about a person
innuendo	an implied statement that is detrimental to another
libel	written or broadcasted defamation
slander	spoken defamation heard by one or more other people
defense of justification	when defamatory statement is the truth
absolute privilege	some settings statements are protected (legislature or court)
qualified privilege	statements made in relation to a duty
fair comment	statements made about public figures
privacy	the right to protect private personal information
reasonable person test	establishes the judicial standard of acceptable behaviour
duty	an obligation to live up to a reasonable standard
reasonable foreseeability test	determines what a person should have anticipated would be the consequences of his/her action
misfeasance	wrongful conduct
nonfeasance	failure to help when situation required it
res ipsa loquitur	the facts speak for themselves
prima facie case	on the face of it
negligent misstatement	careless words that cause economic loss
strict liability	responsibility imposed even when there is no fault
causation	determining whether the act actually caused the injury
"but for" test	had it not been for the act of the defendant, the injury would not have occurred
remoteness	determining whether the damages were too far removed from the original negligent act
thin skull rule	you take your victim as you find them
crumbling skull rule	not responsible for inevitable loss
last clear chance doctrine	the last person capable of avoiding the accident is responsible

volenti non fit injuria	voluntarily assuming a clear legal risk
product liability	manufacturers owe a duty when users are injured by their products
privity of contract	contract terms apply only to the actual parties to the contract
circumstantial evidence	breach of duty can be applied from circumstance
professional liability	a person who puts him-/herself forward as an expert must live up to the standard expected of such an expert
reasonable standard of performance	implied term of contract with a professional that he/she can be held to the standards of the profession
fiduciary duty	an obligation to act in the best interest of a business associate
errors and omissions insurance	insurance to protect holder in the event of causing injury by their negligence
inducing breach of contract	encouraging someone to break his/her contract with another
deceit	deliberately misleading another causing injury
conversion	intentionally taking another's goods to use for own purposes
passing-off action	claiming that your product is another's
injurious falsehood	attacking the reputation of another's product or business

Chapter Outline

Notes

What Is a Tort?

A tort is a social or civil wrong - contrasts with a crime, which is conduct that threatens society generally and with a breach of contract which is a violation of an agreement
Intentional tort - a deliberate act which causes another harm
Negligence - inadvertent or careless act that harms another

Intentional Torts

Assault and Battery - intentional physical interference with another
Assault - a threat that causes fear of contact
Battery - actual physical contact that is unwelcome
Defenses:
1) contact accidental or unintentional
2) consent - doctors escape liability by obtaining consent of patient
3) self-defense - reasonable force can be used to defend oneself from attack

Trespass to Land - Being on another's land without authority
  Damage is not necessary
  Customer becomes trespasser when rules of establishment
    are violated
  Occupier can use reasonable force to eject trespasser
  Minimal duty owed to take care of trespasser
  Continuing trespass remedied by injunction
False Imprisonment - a person unlawfully restrained against
  his or her will
  Restraint must be total with no reasonable means of escape
  Submission through recognition of authority or a threat
  Must not have done anything illegal
Nuisance
  Private nuisance - interference with another's use of their
    property
  Strict liability for inherently dangerous situations
Defamation - a false statement about someone to his detriment
  Must be communicated to a third party
  Innuendo (hidden meanings) may also be defamatory
  Mistake is no defense
  Libel - written defamation - no necessity to prove specific
    loss (actionable per se) - general damages available to
    victim
  Slander - spoken defamation - must prove special damages
    (amount must be specifically calculable (but note
    exception)
  Defenses:
  1) If the statement is true, there is no defamation
  2) Absolute privilege - statements made in certain defined
    situations
  3) Qualified privilege - remarks made pursuant to a duty
  4) Fair comment - opinion expressed about published work
    or public figure

Negligence
  Careless conduct falling below a standard which causes another
    injury
  Duty of care must be established
  Injury must be reasonably foreseeable
  Reasonable Person Test - standard for measuring socially
    acceptable behaviour
    - conduct expected from a reasonably prudent person who
      is being careful
    - better than average but not perfect
  If it were reasonably foreseeable that injury would result from
    conduct then duty of care is owed.

Damage or injury must result from failure to live up to duty
Occupiers owe special duty to people using their property
Standards of care often modified by statute
Higher standards expected of experts
Negligent misstatement - victims can seek compensation for economic loss resulting from negligent misstatement even when there is no contract, no fiduciary duty and no fraud.
Strict Liability - imposed when dangerous substances escape
Vicarious Liability - Liability without fault imposed on employers
Damages - damage or some material loss must be present
Causation - injury must be direct result of careless conduct ("but for" test)

Defenses

Remoteness - whether a reasonable person would have anticipated the general nature of the injury suffered - but this is usually a policy decision made by the judge. In personal injury cases the "thin skin rule" determines that we take our victims as we find them
Contributory negligence - historically if victims did anything to contribute to their own loss, they bore the whole responsibility. This has been modified by "last clear chance doctrine" and statutes that allow liability to be apportioned.
Voluntarily assuming the risk - when a person voluntarily puts him/herself in a dangerous situation he/she may be held responsible for his/her own injury. A person who creates a dangerous situation may be held liable for injuries to someone who attempts to rescue another from that situation.

Product Liability

Manufacturers owe a duty to those who use their products to insure that they are safe and suitable for their intended use. They will be liable to compensate for injuries caused by their defective products.

Professional Liability

Professionals must live up the standard of care of a reasonable member of their profession and owe a duty to all those who could be affected by their actions. A fiduciary duty is owed in some circumstances. Insurance helps to bear the burden of such risk and activities are often regulated by professional bodies.

Other Business Torts

Inducing breach of contract
- Deceit – fraudulent misleading of another person causing damage
- Conversion – wrongful possession or handling of goods belonging to another
- Passing off action when products are wrongfully copied
- Injurious falsehood – wrongfully harming another's reputation

Review Questions

1. Which of the following phrases does not describe a tort?
    (a) A social wrong
    (b) A civil wrong
    (c) When an intentional or careless act harms another
    (d) An apple and hazelnut cake
    (e) When an injured party sues the person who harmed them for monetary compensation

2. A breach of contract is a failure to live up to an agreement.
    (a) True
    (b) False

3. Which of the following is not a tort?
    (a) Intentional or deliberate act that causes injury or loss
    (b) Being on another's property without authority
    (c) Careless or negligent acts that cause injury or loss
    (d) Negligent use of words
    (e) Failure to live up to a promise

4. Which of the following statements is correct in relation to tort law?
    (a) An act must be intentional to be classified as a tort.
    (b) The main purpose of tort law is to impose punishment on a wrongdoer.
    (c) Sometimes a wrongful act will be both a crime and a tort.
    (d) Tort law compensates victims of wrongful conduct.
    (e) c and d above

5. Name four separate intentional torts.

    (1) _____

    (2) _____

    (3) _____

    (4) _____

6. A person injured by careless conduct is out of luck as far as the courts are concerned.
    (a) True
    (b) False

7. Which of the following actions constitute(s) an assault?
    (a) Bumping into another in a crowded hallway
    (b) An offensive or threatening gesture from another motorist
    (c) A bystander struck by a ball during a baseball game
    (d) Pointing an unloaded gun at another who does not know

8. A kiss can be considered a battery.
    (a) True
    (b) False

9. A person sued for assault and battery cannot claim which of the following as a defense?
    (a) It was an accident.
    (b) I didn't mean to do it.
    (c) The injured person consented.
    (d) I was only defending myself.
    (e) I was provoked by what he said.

10. In which of the following situations has a battery taken place?
    (a) An uninvited kiss
    (b) A doctor amputating a badly infected foot
    (c) A youth smashes a window of a parked car
    (d) The attempt to stop a thief from stealing your purse by striking him with your umbrella
    (e) Punching an opponent in a boxing match

11. Trespass is being on another's land without permission.
    (a) True
    (b) False

12. It is necessary to establish that damage has been incurred in order to succeed in action for trespass.
    (a) True
    (b) False

13. It is not necessary to completely physically restrain a person against his/her will in order for there to be false imprisonment.
    (a) True
    (b) False

14. A customer becomes a trespasser when he/she violates the rules of the establishment and refuses to leave when asked.
    (a) True
    (b) False

15. The occupier of property only owes a duty not to intentionally harm a trespasser.
    (a) True
    (b) False

16. Which of the following will not support a claim of false imprisonment?
    (a) Complainant was detained after shoplifting
    (b) Complainant could have escaped by going out an open window
    (c) Complainant submitted to perceived authority
    (d) Complainant was forced to comply
    (e) Complainant had not done anything he/she could be arrested for

17. When a person finds that the normal use and enjoyment of his/her land is being interfered with by fumes, soot, noise or vibration, he/she may be able to sue the offending neighbour for the tort of _____.

18. Which of the following would not be considered a private nuisance?
    (a) A ghetto blaster played loudly by a neighbour
    (b) Fumes from a diesel generator
    (c) Noxious odours from a nearby farm
    (d) Pollution of a river from a pulp mill
    (e) Noise from a neighbour's pool party

19. Libel is easier to prove and usually causes more harm than slander.
    (a) True
    (b) False

20. _____, also known as libel or slander, generally consists of an unjustified injury to the reputation of another.

21. Truth is one type of complete defense to this tort, but there are several other defenses that may be successful. What are they?

    (1) _____

    (2) _____

    (3) _____

22. Which of the following is not a defense to defamation?
    (a) Truth
    (b) Only repeating what someone else had said
    (c) Absolute privilege
    (d) Qualified privilege
    (e) Fair comment

23. Identify three types of damages available to victims of torts.

    (1) _____

    (2) _____

    (3) _____

24. Negligence is careless conduct falling below a standard that causes another injury.
    (a) True
    (b) False

25. The essential elements of a negligence action do not include which of the following?
    (a) A duty of care existed
    (b) There was a failure to help someone in need
    (c) Injury or damage was reasonably foreseeable
    (d) The act caused the injury
    (e) There was no contributory negligence

26. To win an action in negligence a plaintiff must prove, among other things, that the defendant's conduct was below an acceptable standard. Which of the following has developed as the test to determine that standard?
    (a) That a person act to the best of his/her ability
    (b) That a person act with sincerity and goodwill
    (c) That a person act with reasonable care and prudence
    (d) That a person act flawlessly

27. Reasonable conduct falls somewhere between careless and average.
    (a) True
    (b) False

28. The reasonable foreseeability test is used to determine if a duty is owed?
    (a) True
    (b) False

29. Which of the following is the test used by the court in a negligence action for personal injury to determine if the defendant owed the plaintiff a "duty of care"?
    (a) Would a reasonable person have foreseen that type or kind of injury?
    (b) Would a reasonable person have acted like that in the circumstances?
    (c) Would a reasonable person have foreseen that the plaintiff would have been affected by the action of the defendant?
    (d) Would a careful person have acted like that in the circumstances?

30. Which of the following does not describe a principle established in the Anns Case?
    (a) Further refined the test to determine duty of care in a negligence case.
    (b) Determined where the standard of care in a negligence case could be reduced.
    (c) There must be no social policy reason to deny claim.
    (d) There must be a demonstrated injury to the victim.
    (e) None of the above

31. What is the essential difference between negligence and other torts such as assault or defamation?

    _____

    _____

32. Which of the following was not established in the case, *Donoghue v. Stevenson*?
    (a) Set several precedents in the law of negligence.
    (b) The test to determine the existence of a duty.
    (c) The manufacturer of a product is strictly liable for injury caused by it.
    (a) The manufacturer owes a duty to customers.
    (b) Privity of contract may not defeat an action for negligence in product liability cases.

33. Misfeasance is the failure to prevent an injury when it was possible to do so
    (a) True
    (b) False

34. The courts are reluctant to provide a remedy for malfeasance.
    (a) True
    (b) False

35. "What would a reasonable person have done in the circumstances?" is the question the court responds to when trying to assess liability in a negligence action.
    (a) True
    (b) False

36. A person driving a bus is subject to a higher standard of conduct than a person driving a car.
    (a) True
    (b) False

37. The fact that it was an accident excuses a person from the injury caused to another.
    (a) True
    (b) False

38. Strict liability in U.S. means that a plaintiff need not produce proof of the defendant's negligence.
    (a) True
    (b) False

39. Which of the following does not attract an action in negligence?
    (a) F inserted a coin in a Pepsi Cola vending machine at the Red Lion Inn and received an electrical shock that caused him immediate pain and disabled him permanently.
    (b) A hemophiliac was infected with contaminated blood supplied by the Red Cross.
    (c) A customer opened the can and drank a soft drink with a toxic substance.
    (d) A bar patron asked an "exotic dancer" to sit on his lap. When she did as he asked, he bit her on the back.
    (e) An accountant, who knew that some potential investors would rely on the financial statements, accidentally made a mistake that caused the man who did rely on them to lose $20 000.

40. Actions that fall below socially acceptable standards, even when they are accidental, create liability for damages.
    (a) True
    (b) False

41. To which of the following groups of people does an occupier of property not owe a special obligation?
    (a) invitees
    (b) licensees
    (c) trespassers
    (d) guests
    (e) none of the above

42. Which of the following is not a duty of an innkeeper required by law?
    (a) Safeguard property of guests
    (b) Post the appropriate section of Innkeepers/Hotelkeepers Act
    (c) Return goods left by guests
    (d) Provide protection from the wrongful acts of others
    (e) None of the above

43. Courts will award compensation to anyone who suffers financial loss because of negligent statements because of the principle established in *Haig v. Bamford*.
    (a) True
    (b) False

44. Children are held to the same standard as adults when they have committed a tort.
    (a) True
    (b) False

45. It is not necessary for a plaintiff to show injury to self or loss of property as a result of defendant's negligence.
    (a) True
    (b) False

46. In an action for negligence, for which of the following will the courts not award compensation?
    (a) loss of income
    (b) mental disorder
    (c) punishment of wrongdoer
    (d) property loss
    (e) unusual damages because of preexisting weakness of victim

47. Causation in a negligence action means that the injury must be a direct result of the careless conduct.
    (a) True
    (b) False

48. The "but for" test is best described by which of the following:
    (a) But for the conduct of the plaintiff, no injury would have resulted
    (b) But for the poor driving conditions, the accident wouldn't have happened
    (c) But for the phone call, I wouldn't have been on that road that night and there would have been no accident.
    (d) But for the actions of the pedestrian, there would have been no accident.
    (e) But for my inattention, the accident would have been avoided.

49. The court found the plaintiff 40% at fault and the defendant 60% at fault in a motor vehicle accident. What portion of the damages suffered by the plaintiff can the plaintiff collect from the defendant? Would your answer be different if it was determined that the defendant had the last opportunity to avoid the accident?

    _____

    _____

50. Which of the following is not a defence to a negligence action?
    (a) No duty was owed
    (b) No damage
    (c) The driver was being reasonably careful
    (d) Thin Skull Rule
    (e) *Volenti non fit injuria*

51. When a person negligently puts another into a dangerous situation and a rescuer is injured in an attempt to help that person, who is liable for the rescuer's injury?

    _____

52. A person who volunteers to enter a situation where the risk of injury is obvious can never recover damages
    (a) True
    (b) False

53. The *Occupier's Liability Act* establishes that there must be clear intention on the part of the volunteer to absolve occupier of legal responsibility in order to avoid liability.
    (a) True
    (b) False

54. A person who keeps a dangerous animal on his/her property would be responsible for any damage it causes, even if someone else wrongfully releases it.
    (a) True
    (b) False

55. *Rylands v. Fletcher* established the principle of strict liability.
    (a) True
    (b) False

56. When a dangerous situation is created by the normal use of property, the owner/occupier is liable for all damages when it escapes.
    (a) True
    (b) False

57. A lawyer had to have stitches after a parrot bit him while he was in a pet shop. Which of the following is a true statement about the liability of the shopkeeper?
    (a) The owner of the shop is subject to strict liability (i.e., liability without fault) for any injury suffered by a customer in the shop.
    (b) The obligation of the shopkeeper is set out in a federal statute and therefore is the same for all the provinces.
    (c) The shopkeeper has a duty of care to his staff, but not to customers.
    (d) The standard of care is set by provincial statute.
    (e) If the shopkeeper is a tenant, he cannot be liable; only the owner of the building can be sued.

58. Which of the following is not a tort?
    (a) inducing breach of contract
    (b) deceit
    (c) conspiracy
    (d) passing off action
    (e) injurious falsehood

59. Which of the following statements with regard to the tort of negligence is false?
    (a) Case law has established that a manufacturer owes a duty of care to the ultimate consumer if the product is meant to reach the consumer as it left the manufacturer, without being inspected by the consumer.
    (b) Although the plaintiff usually has to prove his case, in some negligence cases the court will find that "the thing speaks for itself," and on the basis of this circumstantial evidence will find a *prima facie* case and then the defendant must prove he was not negligent.
    (c) If the court finds that the plaintiff was 60% and the defendant 40% responsible for the loss suffered by the plaintiff, the plaintiff can recover 40% of his loss from the defendant.
    (d) The *Occupiers' Liability Act* sets the standard of care owed by the occupier, namely to take reasonable care that a guest is reasonably safe.
    (e) If you hurt someone and are sued for negligence, a possible defense is that you did not intend to hurt the person.

60. Three years after graduating from college, Josh learned that his main competitor in selling computer programs designed for inventory control was a former classmate, Len. Time and again when talking to potential customers, Josh would be told about Len's latest improvements, ads and offers. Josh approached Ron, one of Len's employees, and offered to hire him at $10 000 more a year if he would break his employment contract with Len and come work with him. Ron did just that. When Len found out he went around to Josh's customers and told them a falsehood, namely, that there was a serious flaw in Josh's program that would cause them trouble in time. Josh countered this tactic by going to Len's office and calling Len some very colourful names and threatening to punch him in the face. Only Len heard his words. Read the following potential lawsuits and indicate which, on these facts, could not succeed.
    (a) *Len v. Josh* for inducing breach of contract
    (b) *Len v. Josh* for assault
    (c) *Josh v. Len* for injurious falsehood
    (d) *Len v. Josh* for defamation
    (e) *Len v. Ron* for breach of contract

61. Sam and Jed worked together on a construction site. Sam accidentally hit Jed with a long board. Jed thought Sam did it on purpose and threw a hammer at Sam. Luckily, Sam saw it coming and ducked. Neither Sam nor Jed was hurt at all. On these facts

    (a) What tort could Jed sue Sam for? _____

    (b) What tort could Sam sue Jed for? _____

62. Bill goes to a restaurant and orders roast Peking duck. When the meal arrives, the duck is still frozen in the middle, the vegetables are hard and the rice is overcooked. Bill complains and, after some discussion, is presented with a bill which he refuses

to pay. When he attempts to leave, the manager and waiter prevent him from leaving and call the police. He is arrested, but later released. Bill sues the manager, the waiter and the restaurant.

(a) What tort will he sue for?

_____

(b) If he is successful who can be held liable?

_____

(c) Would the restaurant have any recourse for the unpaid bill?

_____

63. Although there was no carelessness on the part of Mr. Jones and although he had no intention of harming anyone, he could still be sued by someone harmed by dangerous substances which escaped from his property. This is an example of what principle of tort law?

_____

64. Greene had been troubled by vandals breaking into his prize garden and destroying his precious plants and flowers. To stop this he dug a ditch and covered it with canvas and dirt. He also erected a tall fence to keep people out of his property and put up signs reading "NO TRESPASSING." White climbed over the fence and in the process of picking one of the flowers fell into the ditch and broke his leg. He sued Greene for compensation for the injuries he suffered. What would be the nature of White's tort action? Explain the likely outcome. Would your answer be different if the ditch were there as the excavation for a new concrete retaining wall to be built the next day? Explain.

_____

_____

_____

65. In the following situations, indicate whether there is a case for a negligence action and what the grounds for such an action would be.
   a. A man looking out his dining room window saw his eighteen-year-old neigbour trying to impress some friends by zooming his car toward them in reverse. He lost control of the car and went up onto the plaintiff's driveway. The young man then drove away as if nothing had happened. No one was hurt and no damage was done. Because this wasn't the first stupid thing he had seen the neighbour do, the man thought he'd teach him a lesson by suing him.

_____

b. A ship, improperly docked in a river, broke loose, drifted downstream and collided with a bridge, which fell into the river. As a result the river flooded and damaged some farmland along the banks. The farmers sued the owner of the ship.

_____

_____

c. A farmer bought some sealed, pre-packaged cattlefeed from the manufacturer. The farmhand, hired by the farmer, fed the cattle and suffered a skin disease because a chemical had been carelessly mixed with the feed by the manufacturer. The farmhand sued the farmer for negligence.

_____

_____

d. An accountant prepared financial statements for a client who owned a small business. The client used the financial statement to prepare his tax returns. There was an error on the statements that was detected when Revenue Canada audited his books and the business owner was assessed a penalty for the incorrect declaration of his earnings.

_____

_____

66. Narinder went to Lee's restaurant with his friend Sam. After eating his meal, he suddenly remembered that he had left the burner on in his art studio. Fearing a fire, he quickly made arrangements with Sam to pay for the meal and ran out of the restaurant. Seeing him leave, the waiter thought he was trying to avoid paying for the meal and ran after him shouting, "Stop, thief." Still running, Narinder heard this turned to look back. He ran into Bob, who unwittingly walked into Narinder's path. Narinder and Bob fell to the ground. Narinder got up and tried to continue to his studio but Bob caught his foot and held him until both Lee and Bob forcibly took Narinder back to the restaurant despite his protestations. When they got back Sam had already come forward to pay the bill. Explain what torts have been committed, what defenses may be raised in each instance and the legal liability of the parties in the above situation.

67. Ramos, a local politician, read a newspaper article by Bronsky, an influential columnist, in which Bronsky mistakenly associated Ramos with some well-known people recently charged with illegal drug distribution. Bronsky had been given the information by a reliable source who had given him accurate information in the past, but the source had Ramos, the politician, mixed up with another person of the same name. Unaware that an honest mistake had been made, Ramos was so infuriated by the article that he immediately went to the newspaper and forced his way into the office where Bronsky worked, kicked in the door to his office, went over to the desk, pointed his finger at him and yelled, "If you weren't such a rotten little runt, I'd smash your face in." Bronsky, in panic, grabbed a heavy paperweight off his desk

and when Ramos had his head turned as the other people in the office rushed in, Bronsky hit him over the head with the weight. Ramos was seriously injured. Explain any torts that have been committed, any defenses that can be raised and the legal liability of each of the parties.

68. James was operating his cabin cruiser with his family a kilometer off the coast when he needed to go below to prepare a meal. He left his twelve-year-old son to drive the boat. While James was below the cruiser struck a small, dark-coloured rubber dinghy which contained Ned, a diver in a wet suit, who was resting between dives that he had been making in the area. There were no marker buoys, and the dinghy was difficult to see in the swells. (Ned's diving companions had taken their boat to the nearest settlement to refill their tanks.) Ned suffered a leg injury in the collision and as soon as James heard the screams, he came up from below, stopped the boat and rescued Ned. It was clear that the leg was broken and James took Ned as quickly as possible back to the town where he was immediately transferred to the local hospital. Ned was admitted and examined by Dr. Green. The doctor noted and treated Ned for a broken ankle, but failed to notice that the leg had also been injured above the knee where a small bone protruded from the skin. Because of this failure the wound became infected and it became necessary to amputate the leg. Green was not a surgeon and so gave clear instructions to Dr. Blade, the local surgeon, as to what was required. In the operating room Blade got mixed-up and amputated the wrong leg. When the error was discovered, Blade then amputated the correct leg. Ned then sued the owner of the boat, his son who was driving at the time of the accident, Drs. Green and Blade, and also the hospital for the injuries he suffered. Explain what torts had been committed, the arguments that can be used as defense and the likely liability which will be imposed on each of the parties.

Answers to Review Questions

1. d   P. 109   D.1
2. a   P. 109   D.1
3. e   P. 109   D.2
4. e   P. 109   D.2
5. Assault, Battery, Trespass, False Imprisonment, Defamation

     P. 110   D.2
6. b   P. 109   D.2
7. a   P. 110   D.1
8. a   P. 111   D.1
9. e   P. 111   D.1
10. a   P. 111   D.2
11. a   P. 112   D.1
12. b   P. 112-3   D.1
13. a   P. 113   D.1
14. a   P. 112   D.1
15. a   P. 113   D.1
16. e   P. 113   D.2
17. private nuisance

     P. 114   D.1
18. d   P. 114   D.1
19. b   P. 115   D.1
20. defamation

     P. 116   D.1
21. (1) absolute privilege

     (2) qualified privilege

     (3) fair comment

     P. 118   D.2
22. b   P. 118   D.1
23. (1) general damages

     (2) special damages

     (3) punitive damages

     P. 110   D.2
24. a   P. 122   D.1
25. b   P. 122   D.1
26. c   P. 122   D.1
27. b   P. 122   D.1
28. a   P. 122   D.1
29. c   P. 123   D.2
30. b   P. 123   D.2
31. Negligence involves inadvertent or careless conduct whereas assault and defamation involve intentional conduct.

     P. 122   D.2
32. e   P. 123   D.2
33. b   P. 124   D.1
34. b   P. 124   D.1
35. a   P. 125   D.1
36. a   P. 125   D.1
37. b   P. 125   D.1
38. a   P. 130   D.2
39. d   P. 127   D.2
40. a   P. 126   D.1
41. c   P. 127   D.2
42. e   P. 128   D.2
43. b   P. 125   D.1
44. b   P. 126   D.1
45. b   P. 132   D.1
46. c   P. 131   D.1
47. a   P. 132   D.1
48. c   P. 132   D.1
49. The answer will vary from province to province. Where a contributory negligence is in place, the complainant could collect 60% of his loss. P. 134

     P. 133   D.2
50. c   P. 133   D.1
51. The person responsible for creating the dangerous situation in the first place.

     P. 133   D.2
52. b   P. 135   D.2
53. a   P. 127   D.1
54. a   P. 130   D.1

55. a   P. 130   D.1

56. b   P. 130   D.1

57. d   P. 127   D.1

58. c   P. 147   D.2

59. e   PP. 122–147 D.2

60. e   P. 148   D.2

61. (a) Nothing, as a negligence action requires some form of injury.

P. 122   D.2

(b) Assault , since damage is not required for this tort.

P. 110   D.3

62. (a) false imprisonment

(b) the manager , the waiter, the restaurant and maybe the police

(c) Yes. Breach of contract action, but there is a question as to who breached the contract.

P. 113   D.3

63. This is an example of strict liability, sometimes referred to as the rule in *Rylands v. Fletcher*

P. 130   D.3

64. He would sue for assault and battery since this was a trap set out to injure him. However, if the excavation were there for a different purpose, he would take the property as he finds it and would be unsuccessful, but note that this may vary with the jurisdiction.

P. 112   D.3

65. (a) There is no negligence because there is no damage.

PP. 122–147 D.3

(b) There is no negligence because the damage suffered was too remote. The flooding was not reasonably foreseeable as a result of an improperly docked ship.

PP. 122–147 D.3

(c) Note that the farmhand is suing the farmer. The farmer was not negligent because it was pre-packaged cattle feed that caused the injury.

PP. 122–147 D.3

(d) An accountant has a duty to live up to the standard of a reasonable accountant and since it is reasonable to expect that financial statements would be used for tax purposes then accountant would likely be held responsible for the penalty assessed to the client.

PP. 122–147 D.2

66. When the waiter saw Narinder leaving and yelled, "Stop. Thief," this was defamation in the form of slander. As such, it is not actionable without proof of special damages suffered by Narinder. Since there is little likelihood of the words causing any actual damage, it is likely that little would come from a defamation action unless it could be argued that all of the ensuing events were caused by the statement. When Narinder ran into Bob, knocking him down, that was negligent since he was not looking where he was going. But again, there could be no action unless Bob suffered some sort of injury or damage. When Narinder tried to continue and Bob caught his foot this was a battery and it was also an imprisonment. And when Lee and Bob forcibly took Narinder back to the restaurant, it was also battery and false imprisonment. The battery was not justified and the imprisonment was false because Narinder had done nothing wrong and, in fact, no crime for which a person could be arrested had taken place. Only if Narinder had gone back voluntarily or an actual crime had been committed would the action taken by Lee and Bob have been justifiable.

PP. 110–114 D.3

67. The article published by Bronsky in the evening paper is defamatory in the form of libel and the mere fact that Bronsky got this information from a normally reliable source and its publication was therefore an honest mistake is no defense. Bronsky and the paper are liable for defamation. The defense of fair comment may not be relied upon because what is involved is a false allegation of fact rather than an opinion or conclusion based on a correct fact. There is no special privilege, either qualified or absolute, available to media people and so a defamation has occurred. When Ramos, the subject of the article, came onto the premises and forced his way into the office this was an actionable trespass and the fact

that he was provoked to do it would be no defense, though it may be taken into consideration when assessing damages. It was not an assault when Ramos went over to Bronsky's desk, pointed his finger at him and yelled, "If you weren't such a rotten little runt, I'd smash your face in," because Ramos was saying in effect that he had no intention of assaulting Ramos. The words take away the threat of the action. Ramos said that he had no intention of smashing his face in. Bronsky's response in grabbing the heavy paperweight and hitting Ramos with it as his head was turned was an act of battery rather than self-defense. In fact, there was no amount of force needed by Bronsky to defend himself in this situation.

PP. 110, 116–119   D.3

68. In these circumstances, Ned, the injured party, would sue the 12-year-old son James for negligence. The son would be negligent in his own right in that he failed to keep a reasonable watch while operating the boat. It should be noted however that the standard of care required would be that of a reasonable 12-year-old in the same circumstances. James also could be sued not for vicarious liability but for negligence in his own right for allowing his 12-year-old son to run and be in charge of such a potentially dangerous vehicle. It could be argued that a reasonable boat operator would not have done this. Whether James and his son were careless is important, but more important is whether the presence of Ned in the dingy could have been reasonably anticipated by either of them. If not, there is no duty owed to be careful. I would argue that when Ned was admitted to the hospital a separate series of events took place for which James and his son could not be held responsible. Doctor Green carelessly treated Ned in that he failed to examine him closely enough to discover the other break in his leg. This became infected and caused the loss of that leg. Doctor Green would be sued for negligence for this carelessness. Blade, the surgeon, on the other hand, was again responsible for his own conduct. He carelessly took off the wrong leg and so Blade would bear responsibility for this. It should be noted that since, in the end, both legs had to be amputated, the damages would be much higher than if just one leg had been taken. The hospital would be vicariously liable for the negligence of both doctors.

PP. 109–147 D.3

Chapter 5

Formation of Contracts

Learning Objectives

At the end of the chapter you should be able to:

1. Explain the nature of a contract and how a breach of contract differs from a tort or a crime.
2. Summarize the elements necessary for the formation of a contract.
3. Discuss the characteristics of an offer.
4. Explain what constitutes acceptance of an offer.
5. Define consideration and give examples of valid consideration.

Key Terms

The following terms are highlighted in the text:

contract	a voluntary exchange of promises creating obligations, which if defaulted on can be enforced and remedied in the courts
formal contract	an agreement under seal
simple contract	written or verbal agreement
express contract	clear verbal or written statement of an agreement
implied contract	an agreement inferred from the conduct of the parties
valid contract	a legally binding agreement
void contract	not a legally binding agreement because an essential ingredient is missing
voidable contract	one of the parties has the option to end the contract
illegal contract	one that is unenforceable because it has an unlawful purpose
bilateral contract	a contract in which both parties assume an obligation
unilateral contract	a promise that becomes binding only when someone voluntarily completes the required act
consensus	when both parties understand and agree to the terms of a contract
offer	A tentative promise to do something if another party fulfils what the first party requests
invitation to treat	invitation to engage in the bargaining process

counteroffer	a new offer is proposed before acceptance of a standing offer
option agreement	a subsidiary contract putting a condition on an offer
acceptance	when one party agrees to the terms of the offer made by another
postbox rule	mailed acceptance is effective when and where it is dropped into a mailbox
revocation	withdrawal of an offer before acceptance (must be communicated to the offeree)
consideration	the price one is willing to pay for promise set out in the offer
gratuitous promise	a one-sided deal that the courts will not enforce
past consideration	something completed before an agreement is made is not valid consideration
illegal consideration	a promised payment to commit an unlawful act is not valid consideration and will not be enforced by a court
promissory estoppel	or equitable estoppel; when a gratuitous promise to do something in the future causes a person to incur an expense, the promisor may be held liable for those expenses if they fail to live up to the promise

Chapter Outline

Notes

A contract is a voluntary exchange of promises creating obligations which, if defaulted upon, are enforceable in court.

Ingredients of a Contract

Consensus - both parties to an agreement must have a common will in relation to the subject matter of their negotiations.
  (a) Offer - tentative promise
    Must contain all essential terms (may be inferred from conduct)
    Must be distinguished from invitation to make an offer
    Must be communicated to the offeree
    An offer lapses:
    (1) after reasonable time (according to nature of subject matter)
    (2) after specified time (if not revoked before expiration of that time)
    (3) upon death or insanity of offeror (whether or not offeree is aware of it)
    (4) after revocation (offer may be revoked any time before acceptance)
    (5) after rejection or counteroffer

(b) Acceptance - offeree communicates intention to be committed

Must be complete, unconditional

Must be communicated (if the offeror stipulates a specific method of acceptance, it must be complied with)

Silence will only be taken as acceptance when there has been a long history of dealings between the parties.

Postbox Rule - an acceptance is effective when and where it is dropped in a mailbox if response by mail is appropriate (does not apply to revocation)

A unilateral contract is accepted by performance of the act specified in the offer

Consideration - the price one is willing to pay for the promise of another

- Not necessarily money (can be anything the parties think is of value)
- Can be a benefit or a detriment to either party
- Must be specific
- Need not be fair (courts will not release parties from a bad bargain)
- An existing duty to the other party cannot be used as consideration
- Past consideration is no consideration (when the bargain is struck after the consideration has been paid)
- Paying less to satisfy a debt has become permissible in some jurisdictions
- Out-of-court settlements - the consideration is the giving up of the right to have the case tried
- Must be legal
- Reasonable amount must be paid where services requested without agreement of specific price.

Promissory estoppel-where the expectation that a gratuitous promise will be fulfilled causes the promissee to incur expenses (can be used as shield but not as a sword)

Documents under seal cannot be challenged on the basis of lack of consideration

Review Questions

1. A contract is a voluntary exchange of promises, creating obligations, which if defaulted on, can be enforced and remedied by the courts.
   (a) True
   (b) False

2. In what forms may a contract be found to exist?

   _____

   _____

   _____

3. What approach do the courts take when dealing with a contractual relationship?

   _____

4. The primary concern of the courts is to enforce the reasonable expectations of the parties.
   (a) True
   (b) False

5. What are the elements necessary for an agreement to be enforceable in the courts?

   (1) _____

   (2) _____

   (3) _____

   (4) _____

   (5) _____

6. Which of the following is not an element of a contract?
   (a) consensus
   (b) consideration
   (c) accounting
   (d) legality
   (e) intention

7. A formal contract is one under _____.

8. Simple contracts are also referred to as

   _____ contracts and may be either

   _____ or in

   _____ form.

9. A contract must be evidenced in writing before it is a binding agreement.
   (a) True
   (b) False

10. Which of the following does not describe the element of consensus?
    (a) A meeting of the minds of contracting parties.
    (b) Parties share an understanding of the bargain struck.
    (c) Parties are willing to commit themselves to terms.
    (d) The written terms of the agreement are clear and concise.
    (e) Parties have read the contents of documents describing the agreement.

11. A valid contract must be based on a fair bargain.
    (a) True
    (b) False

12. A voidable contract is one that can be ended by either party.
    (a) True
    (b) False

13. A void contract may be legally binding if only an unimportant term is missing.
    (a) True
    (b) False

14. Which of the following is false with respect to offers?
    (a) Must contain all essential terms of the contract
    (b) Must be a communication of willingness to be bound
    (c) Terms of offer must be clear
    (d) Must not contain uncertainties
    (e) Must be in writing

15. Parties wishing to enter into a contract must come to a/an

    _____ before a valid contract can be struck.

16. How does an offer differ from an invitation to treat?

    _____

    _____

17. An invitation to treat is another term for an offer.
    (a) True
    (b) False

18. An invitation to treat can be described as
    (a) An invitation to the general public to engage in the process of a contract
    (b) Advertisements or sales promotions
    (c) Articles displayed for sale
    (d) All of the above
    (e) None of the above

19. Which of the following is generally not an acceptable means of communicating an offer?
    (a) A signal to an auctioneer
    (b) A person hailing a cab
    (c) A sign indicating a public parking lot
    (d) A reward notice posted on a bulletin board
    (e) An ad in a newspaper

20. An offer can be communicated by:

    (a) _____

    (b) _____

    (c) _____

21. Which of the following is false with regard to contract law?
    (a) If an ad in the paper offers $100 for the return of a certain computer disk and you find that disk and return it, the owner won't have to pay because the ad isn't an offer, just an "invitation to treat."
    (b) An exchange of promises can be consideration adequate to form a contract.
    (c) To form a contract there must be an offer that is accepted unconditionally.
    (d) The terms of a contract must be brought to the attention of the offeree before or at the time of contract.
    (e) If the offeror mails a revocation at the same time that the offeree mails his acceptance and it is reasonable to accept by mail, the offeror would be bound in contract.

22. What is usually the acceptable mode of acceptance?

_____

23. What rule governs acceptance of an offer over a distance?

_____

24. During a lecture on contract law, Jeff sent a note over to Azar, offering to sell him a ticket to the Rolling Stones concert, First Night, for $100. The note stated "This offer to remain open until noon tomorrow, October 20". Read each of the following separately and indicate which is false.
    (a) If Jeff received no response from Azar, the offer would lapse at noon, October 20.
    (b) If Jeff receives no immediate response from Azar and wants to sell it to someone else, he can revoke the offer to Azar even before noon, October 20.
    (c) This offer could be ended by a counteroffer from Azar.
    (d) This offer would be ended if Azar wrote back "Sorry, I have mine already. Thanks."
    (e) If Azar makes an inquiry, "Would you consider anything less?" the offer would be ended.

25. Which one of the following situations will not cause an offer to lapse?
    (a) Insanity of the offeree.
    (b) The offeror has not stipulated a time limit and the offeree does not accept within a reasonable time.
    (c) The offeror sells the subject matter of the intended contract to someone else before hearing from the offeree.
    (d) Death of the offeror.
    (e) The offeree has not accepted within a stipulated time.

26. As long as a disclaimer is in writing it will relieve the issuer of responsibility.
    (a) True
    (b) False

27. A disclaimer must be posted in plain sight or printed on back of tickets in order to relieve the issuer of responsibility.
    (a) True
    (b) False

28. Which of the following is not an acceptable time for ending an offer?
    (a) At a specified time
    (b) When the subject matter of the offer is sold to another
    (c) At the death or insanity of offeror

(d) When it is revoked before acceptance and the revocation is communicated to offeree

(c) When offer is rejected and counteroffer is put forward

29. In which of the following circumstances is it possible to withdraw an offer?
    (a) When an option agreement is in place
    (b) When an offer has been accepted
    (c) When a subsidiary contract exists to hold the offer open
    (d) When an error has been made and the offer not yet accepted
    (e) None of the above

30. The law assumes that parties to a contract are in equal bargaining positions whether that is, in fact, the case or not.
    (a) True
    (b) False

31. Exculpatory clauses are intended to limit the liability of one of the parties to a contract.
    (a) True
    (b) False

32. Which statute regulates exculpatory clauses?
    (a) *Statute of Frauds*
    (b) *State Immunity Act*
    (c) *Frustrated Contracts*
    (d) *Sale of Goods Act*
    (e) None of the above

33. Courts have a tendency to interpret exculpatory clauses very liberally.
    (a) True
    (b) False

34. A standard form contract is restricted to use between large business operations.
    (a) True
    (b) False

35. When an offeror puts his offer in the following terms, "If I don't hear from you in two weeks, I will consider this offer as accepted." What is the effect of the offeree's failure to reply?

_____

_____

36. When an offeree places a condition on the acceptance, it does not change the validity of the offer.
    (a) True
    (b) False

37. If an offer is ambiguous, the courts will apply a reasonable interpretation of the terms.
    (a) True
    (b) False

38. An offer can only be accepted verbally or in writing.
    (a) True
    (b) False

39. A unilateral contract can best be described as:
    (a) A contract in which the person making the offer determines all the terms.
    (b) A contract that can be revoked by the offeror.
    (c) A contract that is valid only when the offeree performs the act specified in the offer.
    (d) A contract that binds a party without his/her being aware of it.
    (e) All of the above

40. A failure to respond to an offer can never be interpreted as an acceptance.
    (a) True
    (b) False

41. Which of the following is incorrect with respect to acceptance?
    (a) Must be unconditional
    (b) Is effective only when communicated
    (c) Must not specify any new terms
    (d) Will be effective when sent if use of mail is reasonable
    (e) Will not overcome the defect of an incomplete or defective offer

42. Which of the following is not an acceptable means of communicating the acceptance of an offer
    (a) Sometimes by conduct
    (b) By performance of the act stipulated in offer
    (c) Silence between strangers
    (d) By phone when offer sent by mail
    (e) By mail

43. The postbox rule applies to revocation of an offer as well.
    (a) True
    (b) False

44. The rule for establishing the place of formation of a contract is which of the following?
   (a) The place where the offeree receives an offer that he/she decides to accept
   (b) The place where the offeror makes the offer
   (c) Always the place where a letter of acceptance is posted
   (d) Always the place where a letter of acceptance is received
   (e) The place where the acceptance becomes effective

45. After a storm, Ken, who owned a business offering home care services, went through the neighbourhood to solicit work. He approached Ms. Klein, who was picking up branches and raking leaves. He offered to clean the gutters for $150. She answered that $150 was $50 more than she had paid in the past and said she would pay the $150 if he would clean the gutters and spray clean the front steps. He answered, " I'll clean the gutters and spray clean the front steps, but for $175." She rejected that offer saying "No, I don't think we can do business today," and continued to rake. He then said "Okay. I accept your last offer. I'll clean the gutters and spray-clean the front steps for $150." On these facts, which of the following is true?
   (a) There is no contract because Klein's offer was revoked.
   (b) There is no contract because Klein's offer had been rejected by a counter-offer, and Ken's offers had been rejected or left unanswered.
   (c) There is no contract because Klein's offer had lapsed after a reasonable time.
   (d) There is a contract because at one point in the conversation Klein was willing to pay $150 and Ken was willing to take $150 to clean the gutters and spray-clean the steps.
   (e) There is no contract because there is a presumption in law that in these circumstances, the parties did not intend to a legally binding agreement.

46. What effect, if any, does a counteroffer have on an existing offer?

   _____

47. When an option is purchased, what is the position of the offeror?

   _____

   _____

48. An exchange of promises must have some _____ before they can form a binding contract.

49. Consideration in a contract means that both parties have agreed to abide by the terms of the contract.
   (a) True
   (b) False

50. The promises must be of equal value in order to be binding.
    (a) True
    (b) False

51. The benefit that each party derives from the contract is called the consideration.
    (a) True
    (b) False

52. Can an act performed in the past be valuable consideration? _____

53. A promise not to do something is good consideration.
    (a) True
    (b) False

54. A gratuitous promise is
    (a) A gift that creates contractual obligations
    (b) An arrangement that the courts will enforce
    (c) A legal obligation to do what is promised
    (d) A promise where there is no legal obligation created
    (e) All of the above

55. Consideration is the price one is willing to pay for a promise.
    (a) True
    (b) False

56. Consideration need not be
    (a) specific
    (b) not necessarily money
    (c) legal
    (d) reasonable
    (e) all of the above

57. It is possible to hold a person to an agreement to pay for a service provided gratuitously.
    (a) True
    (b) False

58. In an out-of-court settlement, it is presumed that there is consideration.
    (a) True
    (b) False

59. An agreement to perform an illegal act is regarded as a failure of consideration.
    (a) True
    (b) False

60. The courts are sometimes willing to enforce an implied promise to pay a reasonable amount.
    (a) True
    (b) False

61. There is a requirement to pay a reasonable price when no specific price for a service has been agreed upon.
    (a) True
    (b) False

62. Promissory estoppel means:
    (a) People cannot be bound to promises to do something in the future.
    (b) Parties to a contract cannot later deny the terms of the agreement.
    (c) Gratuitous promises are not enforceable.
    (d) A person can use another's refusal to live up to his/her promise as a defense.
    (e) None of the above

63. Which of the following is not an exception to the requirement of adequate consideration?
    (a) past consideration
    (b) paying less to satisfy a debt
    (c) settlement out of court
    (d) request for services
    (e) sealed documents

64. Assume that all the other requirements for a valid contract are present and indicate which of the following would not be a binding agreement because of a problem with consideration.
    (a) Although a travelling antique show told May her statute was worth $500, she later agreed to sell it for $100.
    (b) Mr. Ng promises to give $50 to a local theatre association and makes that promise under seal.
    (c) Laura promises to pay a carpenter an additional $100 if he will build an extra second cabinet for her files.
    (d) John, back from a month in Ottawa, promises to give Sam, a neighbour, $50 for having kindly shoveled his walks while he was away.
    (e) Jones agrees to accept $800 as full payment of a $1000 debt if Kahn, the debtor, agrees to pay the $800 a week before the due date.

65. Key:
    (a) invitation to treat
    (b) offer
    (c) gratuitous promise
    (d) bilateral contract

(e) unilateral contract
(f) none of the above

The following are examples of which of the above?
(a) Mrs. Wright pledged to give Planned Parenthood Association a $200 donation during its annual fund raising campaign. _____
(b) An announcement in the newspaper read as follows: "$200 reward for the return of two lost Brittany spaniels." _____
(c) After having read the announcement given in (b) above, Mr. Hong found and returned the two lost dogs. _____
(d) An ad in the morning paper read "Brand New 1998 Ford Escorts $9 499. No payment until January, 1999. We make your first payment." _____
(e) "I'll give you $7.00 for your tennis racquet." _____

66. Mr. Holmes, a wholesale nursery operator, offered to sell 20 pine trees at $10.00 each to Mr. Parmar, a retail nursery owner. The offer was to remain open until noon on Friday. On the Monday following, Mr. Parmar had finally determined that he could use the trees and accepted the offer. Mr. Holmes had sold them on Sunday. What would be Mr. Holmes' defense if Mr. Parmar sued for breach of contract?

_____

67. Which of the following statements about consideration is/are incorrect?
(a) In a bilateral contract, the exchange of promise for promise provides consideration for both parties.
(b) The common law holds that consideration must be "adequate" to insure that contracts are fair bargains.
(c) Consideration is "the price for which the promise (or the act) of the other is bought."
(d) An altered course of action, even though it brings no direct benefit to the promisor, may be good consideration.
(e) In a unilateral contract, the act of the promisee provides consideration to the promisor.

68. A is indebted to B, C and D for $10 000 each.
(a) B agrees to accept $5 000 in full satisfaction for the debt. Before A delivers the $5 000 to B, B sues A for the full amount of the debt. What difficulties, if any, does A have in avoiding full payment? Explain.

_____

(b) C agrees to accept A's offer to pay the sum of $5 000 plus some shares in a mining company valued at $100 in full satisfaction of the debt. Before the cash and shares are delivered to C, C sues A for the full amount of the debt. What defense, if any, does A have?

_____

(c) D agrees to accept the sum of $5 000 in full satisfaction for the debt. After D has received the $5 000 he learns that A has just won the provincial lottery and decides to sue A for the remaining $5 000 owed to him. What defense, if any, does A have?

_____

69. Which of the following is a correct statement about the effect of promissory estoppel on a promisor:
   (a) Promissory estoppel has no effect on a promisor because it only relates to statements of fact, not to promises.
   (b) Promissory estoppel is also known as unjust enrichment.
   (c) Promissory estoppel can only be used as a defense against a promisor who has failed to live up to a promise.
   (d) Promissory estoppel is known as injurious reliance in the United States and has the same affect in both American and Canadian law.

70. Indicate the correct statement(s) concerning the use of a seal.
   (a) A seal is taken to indicate a serious intention to be legally bound and, therefore, the court will not require consideration.
   (b) A seal converts an otherwise illegal contract into a valid one.
   (c) A court will always refuse to enforce a promise for which there is no consideration even if it is given under seal.
   (d) Almost any method that makes an identifiable mark will do as a seal.
   (e) It does not make any difference when or by whom a seal is placed on a document, just so long as it is placed before the document is brought to court as evidence.

71. Frank Dogood's service station was located near the parking area of the local college. Jane, an impoverished student, parked her car and rushed off to class

without realizing that she had just driven over some glass left on the road after an accident and that her tires were going flat. Frank had been kept busy that morning repairing other tires that had met the same fate on the road near his station. He noticed that Jane's tires were also in need of repair and decided to take it upon himself to fix them. He left a note on Jane's window to tell her what he had done and that he was charging $20 for the service. After some discussion with Frank, Jane was happy to agree to pay Frank but arranged to have a week to raise the money. After several weeks, Jane still had not paid and eventually told Frank she would not. Frank was angry and decided to sue her. Explain the likely outcome of the action.

72. Jones, a car dealer, owned a 1957 Ford Thunderbird and put the following ad in the newspaper: "1957 Ford Thunderbird, good shape, $10 000," accompanied by his phone number. Smith, a regular customer of Jones, saw the ad and went to Jones' car lot to see the car. After some discussion, Smith said that he would pay $5 000 for it, but Jones said it was not enough. Jones said that he would sell it for $8 000 and include financing. Smith said that he would need some time to think about it. Accordingly, Jones wrote on a sheet of paper as follows: "I, R. Jones, agree to sell to J. Smith my 1957 Ford Thunderbird automobile for $8 000, usual financing terms apply. In exchange for Mr. Smith's promise to give this offer due consideration, I agree to hold the offer open until Friday noon, September 24" (signed) R. Jones (dated) Monday, September 20.

Smith took this document home with him and on Tuesday morning Jones was offered $10 000 for the car by Brown, which he accepted. He immediately wrote Smith a letter revoking the offer. In the meantime Smith decided to accept the offer and sent Jones a letter to that effect on Monday evening. This letter was addressed to Jones and stated, "After due consideration of your offer to sell me a 1957 Ford Thunderbird I hereby accept, delivery to be at my home, Friday, September 24 at 5:00pm" (signed) J. Smith. Smith received the letter of revocation on Wednesday morning. Jones received the letter of acceptance on Thursday afternoon. On Thursday morning Jones discovered that Brown was bankrupt and thus could not go through with the deal. Jones phoned Smith and told him to ignore the letter of revocation. Smith responded that while he had already sent his letter of acceptance, he had changed his mind since he had lost his job that morning and could no longer afford to purchase the car. Jones insisted that Smith go through with the deal and hung up. He received the letter of acceptance about three hours after this telephone call.

Jones then took the vehicle on the specified Friday with the intention of delivering it to Smith, but on the way he fell asleep at the wheel and the car was destroyed in the resulting crash. In the meantime Smith had discovered that he could resell the car for $10 000 and so was looking forward to the delivery. When the car was not delivered, he sued Jones for breach of contract.

Smith comes to you, his lawyer, asking you to explain the legal positions of the parties. How would you respond?

Answers to Review Questions

1. a   P. 157   D. 1

2. written, verbal or implied

     P. 157   D.1

3. They enforce the bargain whenever possible. The courts have adopted a hands-off approach

     P. 157   D.2

4. a   P. 157   D. 1

5. consensus, consideration , capacity, legality, intention

     P. 157   D.1

6. c   P. 157   D.1

7. seal

     P. 158   D.1

8. parol; verbal or in written form

     P. 158   D.2

9. b   P. 158   D.1

10. e   P. 160   D.1

11. b   P. 158   D.1

12. a   P. 158   D.1

13. b   P. 158   D.1

14. e   P. 160   D.1

15. bargain

     P. 157   D.1

16. An invitation to treat is just part of the pre-bargaining negotiations, whereas the offer creates a legal power in the offeree to accept the contract.

     P. 160-2   D.2

17. b   P. 162   D.1

18. d   P. 162   D.1

19. e   P. 162   D.2

20. writing, verbally, by conduct

     P. 162   D.2

21. a   P. 161   D.2

22. By communication of acceptance to the offeror verbally or in writing (usually in the manner in which the offer was made.

     P. 168   D.1

23. Postbox Rule

     P. 169   D.1

24. e   P. 164   D.2

25. c   P. 165   D.2

26. b   P. 163   D.2

27. a   P. 163   D.1

28. b   P. 164   D.1

29. d   P. 164-5   D.2

30. b   P. 166   D.2

31. a   P. 163   D.1

32. d in B.C., e in other provinces

     P. 167   D.1

33. a   P. 166   D.1

34. b   P. 166   D.1

35. Generally silence will not be regarded as acceptance unless there is an on-going business relationship between the parties. P.163 D.3

36. b   P. 167   D.2

37. a   P. 167   D.1

38. b   P. 167   D.1

39. c   P. 168   D.1

40. b   P. 168-9   D.1

41. b   P. 169   D.1

42. c   P. 170   D.2

43. b   P. 171   D.2

44. e   P. 170   D.1

45. e   P. 170   D.2

46. It causes the original offer to lapse.

     P. 165   D.1

47. An option will prevent the offeree from revoking the offer before acceptance. It is, in effect, a contract to hold the offer open.

     P. 165   D.2

48. Material value

     P. 174   D.1

49.	b	P. 174	D.1
50.	b	P. 174	D.1
51.	a	P. 174	D.1
52.	No	P. 177	D.1
53.	b	P. 175	D.1
54.	d	P. 174	D.1
55.	a	P. 174	D.1
56.	d	P. 175	D.1
57.	b	P. 174	D.1
58.	a	P. 178	D.1
59.	a	P. 178	D.1
60.	a	P. 178	D.1
61.	a	P. 178	D.1
62.	d	P. 178	D.2
63.	a	P. 175-180	D.2
64.	d	P. 177	D.2

65. (a) c

(b) b

(c) e

(d) a

(e) b

P. 159-174   D.2

66. Since the offer had ended at the end of a specified time, there was no offer to accept and, therefore, no contract.

P. 164   D.2

67. b   P. 175   D.2

68. (a) This will vary from province to province.

(b) A has paid off the debt because the mining shares are extra consideration referred to as accord and satisfaction.

(c) It is too late. D has accepted less and he cannot recover the rest of the money. (This can vary with the jurisdiction.)

P. 176   D.2

69. c   P. 179   D.1

70. a, d   P. 180   D.3

71. Had Jane requested Frank to repair her tire, she would have been required to pay a reasonable price and since she later agreed that the $20 was appropriate, she would have to pay this amount. In this case, however, she only agreed to pay the money after the repair had been made and she in no way requested or authorized the repair. When she agreed to pay the $20.00 she was promising to pay for something that had already been done. This is past consideration, and past consideration is no consideration. Jane is not obligated to pay and Frank would lose if he sued her for breach of contract.

P. 177   D.3

72. The original offer to sell the Ford Thunderbird for $10,000 by Jones ended as a result of Smith's $5 000 counteroffer. That counteroffer similarly ended when Jones made his counter offer to sell the car for $8000, "usual financing terms apply." The problem with this statement is whether it is capable of being an offer since the financing term is not specific. If it is too vague to be an offer, it of course cannot be accepted and there would be no contract. If it is an offer, then the offer will remain open until Friday noon unless it is revoked earlier. There is no option agreement here since the consideration given to hold the offer open, "the promise to give the offer due consideration," is not specific enough to be any form of consideration which would be necessary in order to have an option. If there is no option then the offer can be revoked before the Friday deadline, and this is just what Jones tried to do. But his letter of revocation would not be effective until received since the postbox rule does not apply to a letter of revocation. Since Jones used a phone to tell Smith to ignore the letter of revocation (but after it was received) that revocation would be effective unless it had been accepted before. This could only happen if the postbox rule applied, since the letter of acceptance was received well after the letter of revocation was received.

When Jones mailed his letter of acceptance, he did so within the stipulated time and before any revocation. So if the postbox rule applied that acceptance would be effective when mailed or on Monday evening. Note that it could be argued that this is not an acceptance but a counteroffer because another term is added (i.e., delivery to Jones' home on Friday). If the acceptance is valid and the postbox rule applies, Jones' attempt to revoke his acceptance would likely not be effective since the acceptance was effective when the letter was mailed. By the time of the phone conversation the contract was already in effect. If the acceptance is effective only when received, however there is no contract because the letter of revocation has already been received and the acceptance letter has been repudiated before it was received. Whether the contract is binding then depends on whether postbox rule applies or not and whether the offer was really an offer capable of being accepted to form a contract and whether the acceptance is really an acceptance or another counteroffer.

P. 165,
169-71,
175   D.3

Chapter 6

Formation of Contracts (Continued)

Learning Objectives

At the end of the chapter you should be able to:

1. Explain who is affected by the requirement of capacity.
2. Create a list of contracts that would be considered illegal or against public policy.
3. Describe the relationships where intention to enter into a contract is presumed.
4. Explain what kinds of contracts are affected by the *Statute of Frauds*.

Key Terms

You should be able to define the following terms:

capacity	the freedom to enter into a contract is sometimes limited by a person's ability to understand or fulfill its terms
infants	a person under the age of majority
necessaries	the essential needs required to function in society
service contracts	an agreement to perform a beneficial service
executory contract	when an agreement has been made but there has been no performance
partially executed contract	when one party has performed and the other has not
executed contract	when both parties have performed their obligations under the contract
unenforceable contract	one party cannot enforce the contract because of limited capacity of other party
insanity	when a person cannot understand the nature of his/her acts
legality	the object of the contract must not be against the law
public policy	although some acts may not be illegal, the court will not encourage them by enforcing contracts that are socially distasteful
insurable interest	a real and substantial interest in specific property
intention	parties must intend to assume the obligations of the agreement
evidence in writing	any document that provides information relating to the contract

Chapter Outline

Capacity

Some categories of people have had their freedom to enter into contracts restricted

(a) Infants - an infant is not bound by the contracts it enters into except for the purchase of necessaries and for beneficial contracts of service

- Age of majority differs in various jurisdictions
- Must pay fair price only for necessary goods and services
- Adults bound but infants may escape contracts at their option (voidable contract)
- Infants may ratify on reaching age of majority
- Executed contracts- when infant has obtained some benefit under the contract, he/she cannot avoid obligations unless what was obtained was of no value

Parents not responsible for infant's contract

Seller can't sue for tort instead

Note: *Infants Act* in B.C. declares *all* contracts with infants to be unenforceable

(b) Insane - Persons claiming insanity must show:
  (1) They didn't understand what they were doing
  (2) Other person knew or ought to have known of the insanity

(c) Intoxicated - treated like insanity
  - Must repudiate as soon as sober

(d) Native Indians - right to contract restricted when living on the reserve
  - Restricted in using property as security

(e) Corporations - capacity depends on method of incorporation
  - Crown bodies limited by legislation

(f) Enemy Aliens - contracts void *or* suspended in event of outbreak of war

(g) Married Women - No longer incapacitated

(h) Unions - Not incapacitated if contract relates to union activities

(i) Bankrupts - Before discharge must notify
  After discharge - full capacity

Legality (Public Policy)

Objective of the agreement must be legal and not contrary to public interests

May be void - i.e. there is no contract and parties returned to
original position or if contract is illegal and void - court
won't assist either party

Note statutes may set out what happens

Examples of illegal contracts:
- to commit a crime or tort
- to commit an immoral act
- to obstruct justice
- to injure the state
- bets and wagers - (note special treatment of agreements in
restraint of trade and to restrict competition)
- promote litigation
- injure public service
- restrain marriage

Intention

Parties must have intended legal obligations to flow from their
agreement

Protects reasonable expectations of the person being promised
something

Courts will honour stated intention

Intention presumed in contracts where parties have an
established commercial relationship

Lack of intention presumed where parties have domestic or
social relationship

Reasonable person test where relationship in question or where
claims exaggerated

Form of the Contract

Generally verbal contracts are binding

Must be evidenced in writing when *Statute of Frauds* involved:
(a) contracts for longer than one year
(b) for title to land
(c) guarantees
(d) promises in consideration of marriage
(e) promise of an executor
(f) where value of goods exceeds specified minimum

Written evidence of contract must contain all essential terms
- May arise after agreement
- Signed by defendant
- May be surmised from a compilation of documents
- Part performance may satisfy the need for written
evidence of contract

Review Questions

1. The age of majority in this jurisdiction is:
   (a) 18
   (b) 19
   (c) 20
   (d) 21
   (e) none of the above

2. An infant under the law is:
   (a) a baby under two
   (b) a child under 12
   (c) an adolescent
   (d) anyone under the age of majority
   (e) all of the above

3. The law of infancy tries to balance the protection of infants against harm resulting to merchants when infants abuse this protection.
   (a) True
   (b) False

4. An infant will be held responsible for what types of contracts?

   _____ and

   _____

5. What two things must be established in order for a purchase to be deemed a necessity?

   (a) _____

   (b) _____

6. Infants are not protected in which of the following circumstances?
   (a) For the purchase of necessaries
   (b) When they have agreed to pay a fair price
   (c) When they have purchased goods on credit
   (d) When they have completed all the terms of the contract
   (e) None of the above

7. Which of the following would not be considered a necessary?
   (a) food
   (b) clothing
   (c) bus fare

(d) an engagement ring
(e) tools for a trade

8. A contract in which an infant agrees to do something for someone else is binding if it is beneficial to the infant.
   (a) True
   (b) False

9. If a contract is determined to be prejudicial to the interests of the infants the contract is void.
   (a) True
   (b) False

10. An executory contract is one in which:
    (a) The infant has completed his/her side of the bargain but the adult has not.
    (b) The infant has neither performed nor received a benefit under the contract.
    (c) The infant has paid but not yet obtained anything from the deal.
    (d) An infant changes his mind after the deal has been completed.
    (e) None of the above

11. An infant bought a very expensive bicycle from a merchant that he used during the summer. The bike was destroyed in a cycling accident. The infant had purchased the bike on credit and had paid half the installments at the time the bike was destroyed. Which one of the following accurately describes the legal position of the parties?
    (a) The infant will be able to sue the merchant for the return of any monies already paid since the contract was void.
    (b) The merchant will be able to sue for any unpaid balance even if it was used for pleasure.
    (c) The merchant will be able to sue the infant in tort for negligently damaging the bicycle.
    (d) The infant will have to pay the balance if the bike was used as transportation.
    (e) None of the above.

12. Which of the following is not correct with respect to the law of infancy?
    (a) A contract made by an infant will bind him if he affirms it after reaching the age of majority.
    (b) A contract made by an infant will bind him if he fails to repudiate it upon reaching the age of majority.
    (c) A contract made by an infant for housing or food will binding on him.
    (d) Even if a contract may not be enforceable against an infant, it is enforceable by the infant against the adult.
    (e) All contracts involving infants are unenforceable against them.

13. Parents must pay for debts incurred by their minor children.
    (a) True
    (b) False

14. Parents are liable for their children's contracts.
    (a) True
    (b) False

15. A contract made by an infant with the parents' personal guarantee is binding on the parents.
    (a) True
    (b) False

16. British Columbia has changed its legislation making all contracts with infants enforceable against the infant and unenforceable against the adult.
    (a) True
    (b) False

17. An infant can be sued for tort but not generally for breach of contract.
    (a) True
    (b) False

18. List three other types of legal incapacity.

    (1) _____

    (2) _____

    (3) _____

19. A person claiming insanity must show that
    (a) He/she no understanding of what the deal was about.
    (b) The other person knew or should have known of insanity.
    (c) He/she repudiated the deal when sanity returned.
    (d) a, b, and c
    (e) a and c

20. People in psychiatric institutions are deemed incapable of entering into any form of contract.
    (a) True
    (b) False

21. A person intoxicated by any form of drug is treated like the insane.
    (a) True
    (b) False

22. What three things must a drunk demonstrate in order to escape liability for a contract on the basis of incapacity?

    (1) _____

    (2) _____

    (3) _____

23. Which of the following is correct with respect to a person wanting to get out of a contract.
    (a) The law with relation to insane people applies to drunks as well.
    (b) If Jones can show he had been drinking he can get out of the contract.
    (c) If Jones can show that he was drunk he can get out of the contract
    (d) Jones can only get out of the contract if he can show that he was drunk and the other person knew it.
    (e) a and d

24. A person who, on becoming sober, hesitates to repudiate a contract entered into while intoxicated will be bound by the contract.
    (a) True
    (b) False

25. Status Indians have their capacity to contract limited when living off a reserve.
    (a) True
    (b) False

26. Government agencies or crown corporations may have their capacity to contract limited by legislation.
    (a) True
    (b) False

27. Representatives of foreign governments are immune from prosecution while in Canada, but this does not affect their capacity to enter into commercial or personal contracts.
    (a) True
    (b) False

28. The capacity of married women to enter into contracts is no longer limited.
    (a) True
    (b) False

29. With respect to the capacity to enter into contracts which of the following statements is not true.
    (a) Union contracts must relate to union activities.
    (b) Bankrupts must notify potential contracting parties.
    (c) Government bodies and crown corporations always have the capacity to enter contracts.
    (d) Women have the same legal capacity to enter into contracts as men.
    (e) An intoxicated person must repudiate a contract immediately upon becoming sober.

30. When a contract is deemed illegal, what is the likely response of the court?
    (a) The contract is declared void and the parties are returned to their former positions.
    (b) The contract is voidable and the innocent party can get their money back.
    (c) The court will treat the contract as if it had never existed and will not assist the parties.
    (d) The parties will be required to return anything taken under the contract.
    (e) The courts will treat a breach like any other contract.

31. If a contract is illegal or against public policy the court will deem the contract void and refuse to enforce it.
    (a) True
    (b) False

32. Give two examples of an illegal contract.

    (1) _____
    _____
    (2) _____
    _____

33. Which of the following statements is false with respect to the legality of contracts?
    (a) A judge can refuse to enforce a contract that involves conduct that is not prohibited by law but which the court considers morally unacceptable.
    (b) A contract that provides for one party to commit a crime or a tort is illegal.
    (c) Insurance taken out on a stranger's life is illegal because you would have no "insurable interest" in his life.
    (d) A non-competition clause in an agreement between a seller and of a business is legal so long as it is reasonable between the parties (e.g., to protect goodwill) and not against the public's interest.
    (e) The court would enforce a contract between a boxer and his promoter (which requires the approval of the provincial boxing commission), even without that approval if it were signed by both parties.

34. Contracts that place undue restrictions on a person's right to conduct his business activities have been deemed against public interest.
    (a) True
    (b) False

35. Which of the following would not be considered against public policy?
    (a) Bets and wagers
    (b) Contract for services of an escort
    (c) Contract that unduly restrains trade
    (d) Contract that unduly restrict competition
    (e) Contract that promotes litigation

36. Except when one of the parties is innocent of any wrongdoing, the courts refuse to deal with the parties to an illegal contract.
    (a) True
    (b) False

37. What is the significance of a court determining that a contract is not only void, but illegal as well?

    _____

    _____

    _____

38. The courts are bound to enforce contracts that are not illegal but are merely against the public's best interest.
    (a) True
    (b) False

39. List five types of contracts that have been determined to be against public policy.

    (1) _____

    (2) _____

    (3) _____

    (4) _____

    (5) _____

40. Which of the following is not true with regard to intention to enter into a contract?
    (a) Protects reasonable expectations or intentions of the parties
    (b) Intention presumed in commercial relationships
    (c) Intention presumed in social or domestic relationships
    (d) Will give effect to the clearly-stated intention in the contract
    (e) Reasonable person test applied in cases of exaggerated claims.

41. Courts will enforce the reasonable expectations of the parties even when one of the parties was kidding.
    (a) True
    (b) False

42. Two parties enter into a contract containing a term that requires one of the parties not to compete with the other. Explain under what circumstances, if ever, the term will be enforceable.

    _____

    _____

43. What must the purchaser of an insurance policy demonstrate about the insured person or thing to avoid the contract being declared void as a wager?

    _____

44. In a business relationship, the courts will presume that the parties to an agreement intended to be legally bound.
    (a) True
    (b) False

45. An agreement is only legally binding when it can be demonstrated that both parties intended to be bound.
    (a) True
    (b) False

46. If companies with a history of doing business together agree to change an aspect of their relationship, there must be evidence in writing of the agreement before the courts will enforce it.
    (a) True
    (b) False

47. The courts will presume an intention to be bound in contracts between family members.
    (a) True
    (b) False

48. The reasonable person test is used to determine whether the parties intended to be bound.
    (a) True
    (b) False

49. When dealing with exaggerated claims by an advertiser, the court will apply _____ test to determine its validity.

50. Is it safe to assume that a contract not evidenced in writing is unenforceable?

    _____

51. What determines whether or not a contract must be in writing?

    _____

    _____

52. Verbal contracts are normally binding.
    (a) True
    (b) False

53. The *Statute of Frauds* required written evidence of contracts that were:
    (a) To be performed longer than one year
    (b) For land transactions
    (c) Guarantees
    (d) Promises in consideration of marriage
    (e) All of the above

54. In some provinces legislation stipulates that when the value of goods exceeds specified minimum, the sale must be evidenced in writing.
    (a) True
    (b) False

55 The importance of a written document is that it provides evidence of the terms of the contract when memories fail, but it is generally not essential to prove a contract exists.
    (a) True
    (b) False

56. List four kinds of contracts that must be in writing.

    (1) _____

    (2) _____

    (3) _____

    (4) _____

57. When writing is required, what will satisfy the requirement?

_____

_____

58. If a contract for the sale of land is not in writing, what other evidence would be sufficient to make the contract enforceable?
    (a) An affidavit by the purchaser that there was such an agreement
    (b) Evidence of the fact that the purchaser started to make renovations on his new home
    (c) A letter written after the fact referring to the purchase agreement and signed by the seller
    (d) A receipt for a $5,000 down payment signed by the seller
    (e) b, c and d.

59. Which of the following would not be considered evidence in writing?
    (a) A cash register receipt
    (b) A description of the deal written after the fact
    (c) A recorded telephone message
    (d) A letter of congratulations on the deal from a distant relative
    (e) c and d

60. According to provincial legislation, which of the following contracts should be evidenced in writing?
    (a) Sale of assets with a value of over $10
    (b) A two-year lease
    (c) Employment contract
    (d) Sale of land
    (e) Domestic agreements

61. Which of the following agreements has to be in writing in order to be enforceable?
    (a) An agreement to sell a car
    (b) An agreement by a creditor to accept $800 in full satisfaction of a $900 debt
    (c) A lease of a warehouse for a term commencing on November1, 1997, and expiring November 1, 2001
    (d) All of the above
    (e) None of the above

62. The *Statute of Frauds* contains the same provisions in all jurisdictions.
    (a) True
    (b) False

63. The courts will assist a party who has performed his/her side of the bargain to get out of a contract for which there is no evidence in writing.
    (a) True
    (b) False

64. The courts will waive the requirement of writing if the parties can produce evidence that the contract has been partially performed.
    (a) True
    (b) False

65. Read the following and indicate which of these contracts most likely would be enforced by the courts.
    (a) A restrictive covenant in a buy-sell agreement for the sale of a grocery store that reads: "the seller promises not to open a competing business in Canada."
    (b) A contract between a boxer and a promoter which was not approved by the boxing commission contrary to statute
    (c) A contract between a newspaper journalist and a businessman in which the businessman promised to pay the journalist's legal fees if the journalist would print a defamatory story
    (d) An insurance policy bought by your neighbour on your life shortly after you purchased a motorcycle
    (e) None of the above

66. Jerry, who was 17, went to his girlfriend, Jan, who was 21, and borrowed $5 000 for his college education. However, Jerry used the money to take a new girlfriend to Las Vegas for a week of fun and returned with nothing left. Jan learned of this, but waited until the next summer when Jerry had earned some money from a summer job and then sued for breach of contract and for the return of the $5 000. Explain the likely outcome.

    _____

    _____

67. An infant bought a very expensive bicycle from a merchant and used it during the summer. The bike was then destroyed in an accident. The infant had purchased the bike on credit and had paid half the installments at the time the bike was destroyed. Which one of the following accurately describes the legal position of the parties?
    (a) The infant will be able to sue the merchant for the return of any monies already paid since the contract was "absolutely void."
    (b) The merchant will be able to sue for any unpaid balance because this was an "executed contract."
    (c) The merchant will not be able to sue the infant because the contract is unenforceable.
    (d) The merchant will be able to sue the infant in tort for negligently damaging the bicycle.
    (e) None of the above.

68. Jones entered into a contract for the sale of his barbershop to Harry Cutter. One of the terms of the contract was that Jones would not open up a similar business within 25 miles of the location of the barbershop being sold. About two weeks after the sale, Cutter noticed a new barbershop opening across the street with brand-new facilities and equipment. When he learned that the owner of the new shop was the very Jones who sold the business to him, he sued for breach of contract. Explain the likely outcome.

_____

_____

_____

69. Old Mr. Greely had been a bachelor all his life and was intensely opposed to the institution of marriage. He put under seal a promise to pay his niece $100 000 if she promised never to marry. She agreed to this, but before the payment was made he died and his executor refused to honour the agreement. She sued. Explain the likely outcome.

_____

_____

70. Mr. Straight operated an import business and one day caught his employee, Louis Lightfingers, stealing goods from a new shipment of expensive electronic goods from Japan. After some questioning he discovered that Louis had been stealing merchandise for six months to the tune of about $20 000. Straight told Louis he wouldn't turn him in if he agreed to work for less money and return the value of the goods taken. Louis agreed to this, but six months later quit, leaving a substantial amount yet unpaid. Mr. Straight sued him for breach of agreement. Explain the likely outcome.

_____

_____

71. Negotiations between Dave and Mary resulted in the following agreement: Dave would sell his property to Mary for the sum of $300 000, closing date to be March 4, 1987. When the two completed their discussion, Mary paid Dave $40 000 as a partial payment of the purchase price. The contract was not in writing. On March 4, 1987 Mary tendered the money, but Dave refused to convey the property. Mary sued Dave for breach of contract and asked for the equitable remedy of specific performance instead of damages. According to these facts which of the following is true?

(a) Mary cannot enforce this contract because the contract was not in writing.

(b) Mary cannot enforce this contract because the contract was not evidenced in writing.

(c) Mary can enforce this contract and if she were granted an order of specific performance and Brown did not obey the court order, Brown would be in contempt of court.

72. One day Joe, 17, and his 19-year-old brother, Sam, began to talk about Joe's future after a visit to the pub where Sam had consumed several beers. Although Sam was somewhat intoxicated he was capable of carrying on a rational conversation and was trying to persuade Joe to go to university. Joe was complaining that he didn't have any money. After about an hour of this conversation, Joe finally said that if Sam felt that strongly about it, why didn't he help. Sam, rising to the challenge, said that if Joe enrolled himself in college he would support him to the tune of $5 000 per year until he graduated. Since this discussion took place in August, at the time when registration usually takes place, the next day, Joe went out and registered at his local college, purchased his books and quit his job. The immediate expenses were $500 and, of course, the loss of a job eliminated any income which he had been bringing in. When he presented a claim for funds to his brother, Sam was shocked, since he had forgotten the whole agreement. He said, "You didn't think I was serious did you" and refused to pay. Sam had a drug addiction problem and said to Joe that he would be willing to pay these bills and be willing to support him if Joe could get a supply of cocaine for him from the supply that was available through the student body at the campus. Joe at first agreed to do this and then later changed his mind and sued his brother for the amount owing on the original deal. Explain the legal position of the parties and the obligations they have to each other.

Answers to Review Questions

1. b   P. 186   D.1

2. d   P. 186   D.1

3. a   P. 186   D.1

4. Necessities and beneficial contracts of service (but not in B.C.)

   P. 187   D.1

5. (a) That it was the type of good that could be classified as a necessity and

   (b) That it was in fact needed by the infant in the sense that he didn't already have a sufficient supply.

   P. 187   D.1

6. a   P. 186   D.1

   (In B.C. the answer is d.)

7. d   P. 186   D.1

8. a   P. 186   D.1

   (In B.C. the answer is b.)

9. a   P. 187   D.1

10. b   P. 188   D.2

11. d   P. 188   D.2

12. e   P. 187   D.2

    (In B.C. the answer is c.)

13. b   P. 189   D.1

14. b   P. 189   D.1

15. a   P. 189   D.1

16. b   P. 189   D.1

17. a   P. 190   D.1

18. (1) insane

    (2) drunk

    (3) enemy aliens

    (4) Native Indians

    (5) unions

    (6) government bodies, crown corporations, and limited companies

    P. 190   D.2

19. d   P. 190   D.2

20. a   P. 190   D.1

21. a   P. 191   D.1

22. (1) That he was so intoxicated he didn't understand what he was doing.

    (2) That the other person knew or should have known of the intoxication.

    (3) Repudiation within a reasonable time of regaining sobriety.

    P. 191   D.1

23. e   P. 191   D.2

24. a   P. 192   D.1

25. b   P. 192   D.1

26. a   P. 192   D.1

27. b   P. 192   D.1

28. a   P. 195   D.1

29. c   P. 192   D.2

30. c   P. 194   D.2

31. a   P. 194   D.1

32. (1) A contract to unreasonably restrict competition.

    (2) A contract to commit a crime.

    P. 194-7 D.2

33. e   P. 194   D.2

34. a   P. 196   D.1

35. b   P. 197   D.2

36. a   P. 194   D.1

37. If it is illegal to the extent of being immoral, the courts will not help either party to regain what they have lost.

    P. 193-4 D.1

38. b   P. 194   D.1

39. Contracts: to obstruct justice, to injure the state, to promote litigation, to restrain marriage, to commit crimes.

    P. 194-7 D.1

40. c   P. 200   D.2

41. a   P. 199   D.1

42. Such a term in a contract will be enforceable if it is a reasonable restraint of trade and one that will not injure the public interest.

    P. 197   D.2

43. An insurable interest (i.e., he will lose something if the event insured against takes place)

    P. 195-6 D.2

44. a   P. 200   D.1

45. b   P. 199   D.1

46. b   P. 201   D.1

47. b   P. 200   D.1

48. a   P. 199   D.1

49. The reasonable person test.

    P. 200   D.1

50. No   P. 201   D.1

51. The *Statute of Frauds* and in some provinces other legislation   (Note B.C.'s *Law and Equity Act*.)

    P. 202   D.1

52. a   P. 201   D.1

53. e   p. 202   D.1

54. a   P. 203   D.1

55. a   P. 201   D.1

56. This varies with the jurisdiction.

    (1) Contracts dealing with interests in land

    (2) Leases over three years

    (3) Contracts involving the promise of an executor to pay the debts of an estate out of his own pocket

    (4) Guarantees

    (5) Promises given in consideration of marriage

    P. 202-4 D.2

57. All important terms of the contract must be evidenced in writing, but that evidence need not arise at the time of the contract, or even be in the contract, and it may be a compilation of several documents.

    P. 204   D.1

58. e   P. 202-3 D.2

59. e   P. 204   D.2

60. d   P. 202   D.2

61. c   P. 202-4 D.2

62. b   P. 202   D.1

63. b   P. 205   D.1

64. a   P. 205   D.1

65. e   P. 194-7 D.2

66. Although the money was loaned for a necessity (education), it was not used for education; consequently it cannot be classified as a necessity, and therefore she cannot recover it.

    P. 187   D.2

67. c (assuming that the bicycle was not a necessity)

    P. 186   D.2

68. He'd lose his action because the contractual term prohibiting competition is void. There is a 25 mile limitation on the location but no limit on the time; therefore, it is an unreasonable restraint of trade.

    P. 196-7 D.2

69. Such an agreement would be void because any contract that attempts to prevent or restrict marriage is against public policy.

    P. 195   D.2

70. Such an agreement is against public policy since it is an attempt to interfere with the process of justice, i.e. an agreement to withhold information from the police about a crime.

    P. 194   D.2

71. b (An exception to the requirement of evidence in writing [*Statute of Frauds*] is where part performance is present. The payment of money alone, however, is usually not adequate to satisfy this requirement of part performance except in B.C.)

    P. 202-3 D.2

72. Sam would have two arguments for claiming he was not bound by the agreement to support his brother at school. He would first claim that there was no contract because of his incapacity due to drunkenness. But in order to escape the contract he would have to establish that his brother knew, or ought to have known, of the drunkenness and that he repudiated it upon becoming sober. He could also argue that since this was an arrangement between brothers, there was a presumption that there

was no intention to be legally bound. If there was a contract Joe's failure to supply his brother with cocaine would not alter his brothers obligation to support him in school since Sam was already obligated to do so. If there was no contract for one of the reasons stated above, Joe's promise to

supply cocaine to his brother does nothing to cure it. This new agreement is clearly illegal and so there would be no contractual obligation on Joe to supply the cocaine or on Sam to supply the funds to support Joe in school.

P. 191, 200   D. 3

Chapter 7

Factors Affecting the Contractual Relationship

Learning Objectives

At the end of this chapter you should be able to:

1. Show the difference between the types of mistakes and the significance of those differences.
2. Explain the courts' approach toward the interpretation of contracts.
3. Set out the principles involved in misrepresentation, undue influence and duress.
4. Define privity of contract and explain the exceptions to that rule (such as assignment).

Key Terms

You should be able to define the following terms:

mistake	a misunderstanding about the nature of an agreement that destroys consensus
shared mistake	both parties make the same mistake
unilateral mistake	only one of the parties is mistaken about the terms of the contract
rectification	courts correct the mistake
non est factum	"it is not my act"—a party is unaware of the nature of the contract
parol evidence rule	courts will not permit outside evidence to contradict clear wording of a contract
misrepresentation	a false statement of fact that persuades someone to enter into a contract
non-disclosure	silence constitutes misrepresentation only when there is a duty to disclose
rescission	both parties to the contract are returned to their original positions
duress	force or pressure to enter into a contract
undue Influence	a special relationship that induces a person to enter a contract
unconscionable transaction	one of the parties to a transaction is under extreme disadvantage

privity	contract only affects immediate parties to it
novation	when a party to a contract is substituted by another
assignment	rights to a contract can be transferred to another party
chose in action	the thing or benefit that is transferred in an assignment
champerty	a party to a contract cannot sell the right to sue
vicarious performance	another qualified person may perform the obligations under the contract
negotiable instruments	substitutes for money that bestow unique benefits

Chapter Outline

Notes

Consensus

Essential to any binding agreement. A lack of consensus may be indicated by any of the following forms of mistake:

Mistake
- error that destroys consensus
- Results in void contract (as if there had been no contract)
- Must go to the nature of agreement, not the effect of the agreement
- Must be a fundamental mistake of fact

Shared Mistake (Common Mistake)
- Fundamental shared mistake about subject matter voids contract
- When the result of negligence the careless party is responsible
- Courts will rectify mistake in document when it does not reflect the real intention of the parties

Mutual Mistake
- Misunderstanding between parties about the nature of the agreement
- If misunderstanding is serious enough it may void contract; otherwise court may enforce most reasonable position

Unilateral Mistake
- One-sided, fundamental mistake
- Contract may be void
- "Let the buyer beware" (*caveat emptor*); if the identity of one of the parties is in question
- "It's not my act" (*non est factum*) where one of the parties is unaware of the true nature of the document being signed

Rules of Interpretation
Reasonable person test (an objective test)
Literal or liberal meanings imposed on written terms
Outside evidence will not change clear wording (parol evidence rule)
Courts or statutes may imply terms not included by parties
Equity - courts may impose new terms in the interests of fairness

Misrepresentation
False statement of fact which persuades another to enter into a contract
Silence, unless there is a duty to disclose, is not misrepresentation
Must be no effort to hide the facts important to the contract
A statement about the law, even if misleading, is not misrepresentation
If the statement becomes a term of the contract then normal rules for breach apply

Innocent Misrepresentation
When a false statement is made with the honest belief that it is true, the victim can ignore the misrepresentation and affirm the contract or have the contract rescinded (return both parties to their original positions)

Fraudulent Misrepresentation
- intentional misrepresentation that induces another to enter into a contract
- Rescission and reimbursement for expenses are available as remedies to the victim
- Victim can sue for damages (monetary compensation)
- Voids contract when consensus destroyed

Negligent Misrepresentation
- a person making a statement should have known it was false
- Victim may claim remedies available in tort law including damages
- Where negligent statement becomes term of contract, victim must seek remedy available in contract law

Duress
Contract made under threat of violence or imprisonment is voidable at the option of the victim of duress
Victim's remedy can't jeopardize position of third party

Undue Influence

Where free will to bargain not possible, contract voidable

- Presumed in certain relationships - must be proven in others
- Must be exerted by a party to the contract, not an outsider

Unconscionable Transactions

Where one party has been taken advantage of because of inherent weakness that makes bargaining positions unequal

- such contracts are voidable

Privity of Contract

Contract only affects parties to it - its terms cannot bind outsiders

Exceptions

Original party can enforce contract when benefits are to be bestowed on an outsider

Novation - a new agreement which changes the terms of the original contract--usually the substitution of one party for another

- Contractual rights run with land and thus affect new owners
- Contracts created through agents are really contracts between a principal and third party (apparent exception)
- Trusts and insurance policies allow people to bestow benefits on third parties

Assignment

Contracting party can assign rights (benefits only) to a third party

Statutory Assignment

- Where certain qualifications are met, the assignee has right to enforce the claim directly
- Must be absolute and unconditional
- Must be in writing with parties properly identified
- Proper notice must be given to original debtor
- Some things cannot be assigned (maintenance, right to sue)
- Only the rights and benefits can be assigned, not the obligations
- Assignee takes subject to equity at time of assignment - i.e. the assignee gets no better rights than were held by the original parties

Involuntary Assignment
E.g. after death, rights and obligations are automatically
transferred to the administrator of the estate

Negotiable Instruments
- Can be freely transferred and they carry with them all the
rights associated with the original agreement between the
parties.
- They are inconsistent with the rule of privity and an
exception to it.
- Can assign better rights to third parties since they are not
bound by previous agreements concerning the instrument.

Review Questions

1. What kind of mistake voids a contract?

    _____

2. The courts may relieve the parties to a contract of their obligations on the basis of a mistake.
    (a) True
    (b) False

3. When both parties make the same mistake it is called

    _____ or

    _____ mistake.

4. If either party misunderstands the legal effect of the agreement, he or she will not be able to escape the contract on the basis of mistake.
    (a) True
    (b) False

5. If two people enter into a contract involving a shipment on a particular boat without knowing that the boat had sunk the previous night, what kind of mistake is it?

    _____

6. A person can use mistake as a defense only when:
    (a) An error destroys consensus
    (b) An error was made as to the subject matter or the identity of the parties
    (c) Both parties simply change their mind about going through with the contract
    (d) a and b
    (e) a and c

7. A shared mistake is a fundamental mistake about subject matter of contract that is common to both parties.
    (a) True
    (b) False

8. If I were to agree to sell my house to you for $100 000 but inadvertently sign an agreement that reads $10 000, what will the courts do?

    _____

9. A unilateral mistake is made when each party makes a different mistake about the nature of the contract.
   (a) True
   (b) False

10. If you agreed to buy my 1979 Chrysler for $5 000 but when it was delivered you discovered it was a boat rather than a car, what rule would the courts apply to determine the validity of the contract?

    _____

11. If the contract read boat but you had your mind fixed on car, how would the court respond?

    _____

12. Could you introduce outside evidence to prove you intended to buy a car?

    _____

    What is the name of the rule that would be applied in this instance? _____

13. If the written document does reflect the common intention of the parties to the contract, the courts will not rectify the document.
    (a) True
    (b) False

14. Which of the following situations give(s) rise to the application of the equitable remedy of rectification?
    (a) Both parties to a contract agree that they want to change some of its terms and thus apply jointly to the court to have the relevant terms altered.
    (b) The two parties to a contract have made a mutual mistake and one of these parties is asking the court to choose the more reasonable meaning of the terms in question.
    (c) The defendant has a justifiable defense of *non est factum*.
    (d) A written instrument because of an obvious mistake does not embody the unchanged terms of an original oral agreement.
    (e) The contract is one requiring "utmost good faith."

15. If the misunderstanding between parties to a contract is serious and both interpretations are equally reasonable, there is a question of the existence of intention and therefore there is no contract.
    (a) True
    (b) False

16. One-sided or unilateral mistake is where one of the parties makes a mistake in relationship to the contract and the other party is not aware of it.
    (a) True
    (b) False

17. Which of the following does not apply to a one-sided mistake?
    (a) One party intentionally misleads the other.
    (b) Mistake in the identity of one of the parties.
    (c) Often involves innocent misrepresentation.
    (d) Often involves fraudulent misrepresentation.
    (e) When more is paid than was owed.

18. When one of the parties is unaware of the nature of the contract, the agreement may be void on the basis of *non est factum*.
    (a) True
    (b) False

19. The finding of a court that a one-sided mistake has resulted in a void contract usually involves the victim being intentionally misled into making that mistake.
    (a) True
    (b) False

Key to next four questions:
    (a) mistake
    (b) illegality of object
    (c) rescission
    (d) *non est factum*
    (e) rectification

20. Mr. Frank, a foreman supervising some 43 employees, was asked by his secretary to sign a form requesting additional supplies needed on the factory floor. He was not careless when he examined the form but his secretary had cleverly arranged the signature line so that instead of signing a request for supplies he signed a cheque payable to his secretary. What plea, if any, would be used to defend against her action on the cheque? _____

21. A and B entered into a contract for the purchase and sale of three grams of cocaine. B delivered the goods but A didn't pay. If B sued for payment, the court would not enforce the contract because of which of the above? _____

22. If Mr. Jay took out a life insurance policy on a stranger, Mr. Wilde (known for his rough and dangerous habits), on which of the above grounds would the insurance company refuse to pay Jay if Wilde did die in one of his wild escapades? _____

23. What remedy would the courts award if a buyer were induced to enter into a contract because of an innocent misrepresentation by the seller? _____

24. Jones owned a rare painting that Smith desperately wanted. Smith threatened to shoot Jones if he didn't sell the painting to him. In fear of his life, Jones agreed to sell it for $50 000, which was a fair market value for the painting. After acquiring the painting Smith regretted his tactics and, before skipping the country, sold the painting to Brown for $30 000. When Jones discovered that Brown had the painting he sued for its return. Will Brown be able to keep the painting?

_____

25. Normally only the parties to a contract can bring an action for breach of contract. Which one or more of the following are legal exceptions?
    (a) The beneficiary named in an insurance contract
    (b) Son or daughter of one party to the contract
    (c) An employee of one of the parties
    (d) None of the above

26. Rules of interpretation include which of the following applications?
    (a) Reasonable person test
    (b) Literal or liberal meanings imposed on written terms
    (c) Parol evidence rule
    (d) Applicable statutes
    (e) All of the above

27. Company A contracted to sell to Company B 400 barrels of Chemical C for $1 200. Company A assigned the entire $1 200 in writing to Mr. Long, who sent a letter informing Company B of the assignment and directing Company B to forward money to him instead of Company A. Unbeknownst to both Company A and Company B at the time of the contract the ship carrying the chemical had sunk and all cargo was lost. Which of the following is true?
    (a) Mr. Long, the assignee, will receive $1 200 from Company B.
    (b) The assignment to Mr. Long would fail to be a statutory assignment.
    (c) Mr. Long will receive nothing from Company B because nothing is owed to Company A.
    (d) Mr. Long will receive part payment.
    (e) a and b

28. Misrepresentation is usually false statement of fact that persuades someone to enter into a contract.
    (a) True
    (b) False

29. Which of the following is an example of misrepresentation?
    (a) False statement of fact that persuades someone to enter into a contract.
    (b) The person making the statement must have known it was false.
    (c) The statement must be an allegation of fact.
    (d) Silence cannot be misrepresentation.
    (e) The misrepresentation must be in a term of the contract.

30. Which of the following is not true with regard to innocent misrepresentation?
    (a) The person making it honestly believes it to be true.
    (b) Person making the misrepresentation is not at fault.
    (c) The victim can ignore or rescind the contract.
    (d) Remedies are limited to rescission.
    (e) When the other party knew of the mistake but went ahead with the contract.

31. Rescission puts both parties back into original positions.
    (a) True
    (b) False

32. In which of the following circumstances is rescission not available?
    (a) When the contract has been affirmed
    (b) When it is impossible to restore the parties to their original position
    (c) When a third party is involved
    (d) When both parties have completed their obligations under the contract
    (e) All of the above

33. An innocent misrepresentation must be rectified when discovered.
    (a) True
    (b) False

34. Which of the following is not a civil remedy for fraudulent misrepresentation?
    (a) rescission
    (b) contract may be considered void
    (c) fine or imprisonment
    (d) monetary compensation
    (e) punitive damages

35. What is the meaning of the phrase *caveat emptor*?

    _____

36. The same remedies available for innocent misrepresentation are available for negligent misrepresentation.
    (a) True
    (b) False

37. An incorrect statement that persuades a person to enter into a contract is called

_____.

38. Which of the following statements is true with regard to the law of misrepresentation?
    (a) A statement of opinion by a non-expert cannot be a misrepresentation.
    (b) The court can award the equitable remedy of rescission for fraudulent misrepresentation but not for innocent misrepresentation because in the latter there is no wrong.
    (c) Misrepresentations are written or oral misstatements of fact; silence cannot be a misrepresentation.
    (d) To avoid a contract on the basis of misrepresentation, a party has to show the court that the misrepresentation was about a term of the contract.
    (e) Misrepresentation cannot be used to overcome the obligations set out in a written contract.

39. With regard to the law concerning misrepresentation, which of the following is false?
    (a) A misrepresentation can be made by words, conduct and even by silence.
    (b) A statement of opinion cannot be a misrepresentation.
    (c) A misrepresentation can be a false assertion of fact which induces (persuades) the party to contract.
    (d) For fraudulent misrepresentation, the court can order the equitable remedy of rescission.
    (e) a and c above.

40. What is the significance of finding that a misrepresentation is fraudulent rather than innocent?

_____

41. When a false statement becomes a term of the contract what rule applies?

_____

42. Which of the following is true of a misrepresentation?
    (a) An opinion of an expert can be a misrepresentation.
    (b) A misrepresentation that induces a person to enter a contract can result in an award of the equitable remedy of rescission.
    (c) A misrepresentation can be a term of a contract and result in an award of the remedy of damages.
    (d) All of the above

43. In *Haig v. Bamford* the courts found that because the accountants honestly believed what they had stated on the audit was true, they were not liable for the damages they caused.
    (a) True
    (b) False

44. Only when the misrepresentation is truly innocent and without fault is the victim restricted to the remedy of rescission.
    (a) True
    (b) False

45. When two parties are involved in a misunderstanding as to the meaning of a term of the contract, which of the following is usually applied by the court to settle the matter?
    (a) The court will find that there is no contract because there is no meeting of the minds.
    (b) *Non est factum*
    (c) *Caveat emptor*
    (d) The reasonable person test
    (e) The equitable remedy of rectification

46. What recourses are available to a victim of innocent misrepresentation?

    _____

    _____

47. A misrepresentation can be made by words, conduct and even by silence.
    (a) True
    (b) False

48. A contract made under the threat of violence is void.
    (a) True
    (b) False

49. Which of the following is false with regard to contract law?
    (a) The court can presume the intention of the parties to be legally bound, but a party to the contract can bring forward contrary evidence to rebut the presumption.
    (b) A life insurance policy bought by Harvey insuring the life of his wild neighbor Joe, without Joe's consent, would be illegal and therefore would not be binding.
    (c) Although all the elements of a contract are present, a party to the contract may successfully avoid his obligations if he were forced to enter the contract because of threats of physical violence.
    (d) To escape a contract on the basis of insanity, the insane person need only show that he did not know what he was doing at the time the contract was formed.
    (e) Independent legal advice given to a person who wants to give a gift to a dominant person (e.g., his doctor) is good evidence to rebut a presumption of undue influence.

50. Neither the person who exercised duress nor the injured party can get out of the contract.
    (a) True
    (b) False

51. Undue influence which reduces free will to bargain makes a contract voidable.
    (a) True
    (b) False

52. In which of the following relationships is undue influence not presumed?
    (a) Adult contracting with child
    (b) Salesperson contracting with senior citizen
    (c) Solicitor contracting with client
    (d) Trustee contracting with beneficiary
    (e) Doctor contracting with patient

53. It is up to the dominant contracting party to overcome the presumption of undue influence.
    (a) True
    (b) False

54. Unconscionable transactions are voidable at the request of the person claiming undue influence.
    (a) True
    (b) False

55. How can parties in a relationship where undue influence might be presumed overcome the problem?
    (a) Write a disclaimer in the contract.
    (b) Get witnesses to the bargain.
    (c) Follow documented independent legal advice.
    (d) Make sure that the terms of the agreement are reasonable.
    (e) Make sure the agreement is under seal

56. Unconscionable transactions are dealt with under a principle of equity which allows the courts to set aside a contract in which one party has been taken advantage of because of which of the following factors?
    (a) A person's failure to read the small print
    (b) A person believing that the contract was a joke
    (c) A party who is mentally impaired
    (d) A party who is made desperate because of poverty
    (e) c and d

57. If a contract is simply unfair, the courts will consider applying the principle of an unconscionable transaction.
    (a) True
    (b) False

58. The courts will presume undue influence in certain circumstances that may include a spouse assuming the indebtedness of their partner.
    (a) True
    (b) False

59. The judge in the case of *Stevenson v. Hilty* determined that a contract could be set aside if:
    (a) One party is ignorant, in need or in distress
    (b) One party uses position of power to achieve an advantage
    (c) The agreement is substantially unfair to weaker party
    (d) All of the above
    (e) b and c

60. The principle that a contract cannot bind an outsider or stranger to it is known as privity.
    (a) True
    (b) False

61. Name two exceptions to this principle.

    (1) _____

    (2) _____

62. Exculpatory clauses cannot be used to limit the liability of employees in breach of contract or for negligence.
    (a) True
    (b) False

63. Which one or more of the following is/are true?
    (a) A right to exercise contractual rights may be assigned without consent of the promissor (debtor).
    (b) Contractual obligations, like contractual rights, can always be assigned.
    (c) The receiver for value of a negotiable instrument may acquire better rights than the person who gave it to him had.
    (d) All assignments must be in writing to be enforceable.
    (e) All of the above are true.

64. The assignment of contractual rights allows the benefits received under a contract to be assigned or transferred to another.
    (a) True
    (b) False

65. A chose in action is a term that describes which of the following:
    (a) A limitation period
    (b) A right to make a claim on a contract
    (c) A term of the contract limiting the rights of the parties
    (d) The right of a contracting party to opt out of a term of the agreement
    (e) None of the above

66. Which of the following is not a qualification for a statutory assignment?
    (a) Assignment must be absolute.
    (b) Assignment must be unconditional.
    (c) Assignment must be witnessed by the party affected by it.
    (d) Assignment must be in writing and complete.
    (e) Assignor must give proper notice to the debtor.

67. What elements of a contract can be assigned to a third party?

    _____

68. What conditions are placed on assignments?

    _____

    _____

69. Which of the following things cannot be assigned?
    (a) The right to sue
    (b) When contract involves the personal performance of a particular skill
    (c) The right to collect money's owing on the contract
    (d) a and c
    (e) a and b above

70. Novation is a term describing the right to collect money owing on a contract.
    (a) True
    (b) False

71. Subsequent claims on a contract destroy the claim of an assignee.
    (a) True
    (b) False

72. Which of the following is correct with respect to the distinction between statutory and equitable assignment?
    (a) A statutory assignment must be in writing.
    (b) A statutory assignment must be of all the claim.
    (c) Notice in writing must have been given to the debtor of the assignment for it to be a statutory assignment.
    (d) A statutory assignment is easier to prove than an equitable one.
    (e) All of the above

73. Which of the following is/are false about the law governing privity of contract and assignment?
    (a) A party to a contract for services can assign both his contractual obligations and his contractual rights.
    (b) Novation refers to the ending of the original contract and entering into a new contract with changes in terms, such as substituting one party for another.
    (c) Assignments are modifications of the privity of contract rule since they do allow a stranger to the contract to receive benefits from the contract.
    (d) An employee sent by his/her employer to do a routine job for one of the employer's customers is not in a contractual relationship with the customer.
    (e) A contract to sell land between A, the seller, and B, the buyer, could contain a term which would bind a third party who subsequently purchased the land from B.

74. Contractual rights are assigned automatically in case of death or bankruptcy.
    (a) True
    (b) False

75. John was hired by his doctor to investigate several billing programs and give him a report on his opinion as to which would be the best buy. John's fee was $1000. John was in debt to Mr. Hutton for $2000. When Hutton pressed for payment, John, with a cash-flow problem, made an oral assignment of his $1000 fee to Hutton. At the time of the assignment and at the time of the notice of the assignment (Hutton gave written notice immediately), John had done half the work but owed the doctor $200 for dental work done the week before but not yet paid for. Which of the following is true?
    (a) This assignment is a statutory assignment, Hutton is entitled to receive $1000 on the day of the assignment.
    (b) If the doctor refused to pay, even after John had completed the contract to the doctor's satisfaction, Hutton could not enforce the assignment even with John's help because Hutton is a stranger (3rd party) to the contract between John and the doctor.
    (c) There is no assignment here at all because the doctor had not given permission to John to make the assignment.
    (d) Hutton is entitled to receive from the doctor whatever John is entitled to receive after John's contract is completed.
    (e) None of the above

76. Negotiable instruments bestow unique rights when they are assigned. What are they?

_____

_____

77. What is the significance of the court finding that an assignment is a statutory assignment rather than an equitable assignment?

_____

78. Jerry Sharp, a lawyer, entered into an agreement with his client, Sloe, to sell his car for $5 000. Jerry had quite a few cars and he thought he was selling Sloe a 1975 Ford Thunderbird and this is what Sloe thought he was buying, but it was a 1975 Lincoln Continental that was delivered to Sloe. Sloe thought the car was in good shape since it looked and sounded good and Jerry had made no representation as to the condition of the car. But two days after he got it home, Sloe had to spend $2 000 to replace the engine. On his way home from this repair, another problem became apparent. The idler arm of the steering became disconnected (through no fault of either party). The car went out of control, hit a tree and was destroyed.

The contract between Jerry and Sloe required that Sloe pay the $5 000 on regular $100 monthly installments. Jerry needed the money immediately and so went to his friend Harry and sold him the $5 000 claim against Sloe for $4 500. Harry then demanded payment from Sloe, who refused to pay. Sloe sued both Jerry and Harry. Explain the legal relations among the parties.

Answers to Review Questions

1. A mistake that goes to the very nature of the agreement rather than its effect.

    P. 212   D.1

2. a   P. 211   D.1

3. shared or common mistake

    P. 211   D.1

4. a   P. 211   D.1

5. shared mistake

    P. 212   D.1

6. d   P. 211   D.2

7. a   P. 212   D.1

8. rectification

    P. 212   D.1

9. b   P. 215   D.1

10. A reasonable interpretation under the mutual mistake rule.

    P. 213   D.1

11. Enforce the contract

    P. 215   D.2

12. No. (Contract is not ambiguous.) Parol evidence rule prohibits evidence of contrary intention.

    P. 217   D.2

13. a   P. 212   D.1

14. d   P. 212   D.2

15. a   P. 214   D.1

16. b   P. 215   D.1

17. c   P. 215-7 D.2

18. a   P. 216   D.1

19. a   P. 215-6 D.1

20. d   P. 216-7 D.1

21. b   previous chapter D.1

22. d   P. 216-7 D.1

23. c   P. 223   D.1

24. This is an example of duress. The contract is voidable, but good title was transferred and, therefore, Brown is the owner. Jones must go after Smith for a remedy.

    P. 226   D.2

25. a (exception to privity rule)

    P. 232   D.2

26. e   P. 217   D.2

27. c   P. 212   D.2

28. a   P. 220   D.1

29. a   P. 220   D.2

30. e   P. 223   D.2

31. a   P. 223   D.1

32. e   P. 223-4 D.2

33. b   P. 223   D.1

34. c   P. 224   D.2

35. Let the buyer beware. D.1

    P. 215

36. b   P. 225   D.1

37. misrepresentation

    P. 220   D.1

38. a   P. 220   D.2

39. e   P. 219-220   D.2

40. Damages are available in addition to rescission.

    P. 219-223   D.2

41. Misrepresentation resulting in breach of contract.

    P. 222   D.2

42. d   P. 220, 222-3   D.2

43. b   P. 218   D.1

44. a   P. 223   D.1

45. b   P. 216-7 D.2

46. Rescission and/or compensation for out-of-pocket expenses but not damages.

    P. 223   D.2

47. a   P. 220-1 D.1

48. b (it's voidable)

    P. 226   D.1

49. d   P. 191   D.2

50. b   P. 226   D.1

51. a   P. 226   D.1

52. b   P. 227   D.2

53. b   P. 228   D.1

54. a   P. 229   D.1

55. c   P. 228   D.2

56. e   P. 229   D.2

57. a   P. 229   D.1

58. a   P. 227   D.1

59. d   P. 229   D.2

60. a   P. 231   D.1

61. insurance and trust contracts; contracts dealing with land

P. 231-3   D.2

62. b   P. 232   D.1

63. a, c   P. 233-6 D.2

64. a   P. 233   D.1

65. b   P. 233   D.2

66. c   P. 235   D.2

67. benefits

P. 233   D.2

68. Assignee is in no better position than the assignor. Assignee is subject to the equities between the parties.

P. 234   D.2

69. e   P. 235   D.2

70. b   P. 232   D.2

71. b   P. 235   D.1

72. e   P. 235   D.1

73. a   P. 235   D.2

74. a   P. 236   D.2

75. d   P. 233-6 D.1

76. (1) The holder of the negotiable instrument need not give notice to the original debtor to acquire rights.

(2) A holder in due course will acquire better rights than the person who gave the instrument to him.

P. 236   D.2

77. In a statutory assignment, the assignee can sue under the contract directly rather than having to go through the original assignor.

P. 235   D.2

78. In fact no mistake as to the subject matter of the contract has taken place here. Sloe got the car that he thought he was purchasing even though both were under the impression it was a Thunderbird when in fact it was a Continental. If the car that was delivered had been different from the one they had been bargaining over, that would have been different. Also if the contract describes the car as a Ford Thunderbird, then there would be a breach of a term of the contract. Since Jerry referred to the car as a Thunderbird and it was not, a misrepresentation has taken place. But since this was done believing it to be true, this is an example of innocent misrepresentation only. If there were no negligence involved the only remedy available would be rescission. Since the car was destroyed, this remedy is not available. If Sloe can prove negligence or if it has become a term of the contract that a Thunderbird is being sold, only then will damages be available as a remedy. Since there have been no representations as to the quality of the car, this is an example of *caveat emptor* as far as the repairs on the engine are concerned and Sloe is out of luck.

Harry's position is the same as Jerry's. Harry is the assignee of contractual rights and takes subject to the equities between the parties. Any defenses that Sloe would have against Jerry would be available against Harry as well. Unfortunately, unless it was a term of the contract that the car be a Thunderbird or unless the misrepresentation was negligent, Sloe would have no defense against Jerry and so would have no defense against Harry either. Sloe would have to pay.

Passim   D.3

Chapter 8

The End of the Contractual Relationship

Learning Objectives

At the end of this chapter you should be able to:

Discuss what constitutes performance of a contract.
Explain what is required for a contract to be discharged or modified by agreement.
3. Define the principle of frustration of a contract.
4. Show the effect of a breach of contract on the rights and obligations of the parties.
5. Summarize the remedies that are available when a contract is breached.

Key Terms

You should be able to define the following terms:

performance	when both parties have completed the terms of a contract
substantial performance	the parties have performed all but a minor term of the contract
tender of performance	one of parties attempts to perform but is prevented by the other party
conditions	major terms of a contract
warranties	minor terms of a contract
exemption clause	an attempt to limit liability under an agreement (also exclusion or exculpatory clause)
bailment	goods are being cared for by someone other than the owner
breach	failure to live up to conditions of a contract
repudiation	one party indicates to the other that there will be a failure to honour the contract; expression can be expressed or implied
bilateral discharge	both sides agree to disregard a term of the contract
unilateral discharge	non-binding agreement to discharge that only benefits one of the parties
accord	both parties in agreement on some change in the contract
satisfaction	a substitute in consideration accepted by both parties
conditions precedent	conditions under which the obligations will begin
conditions	conditions under which the obligations will end

subsequent

frustration	some outside event makes the performance of the contract impossible
self-induced frustration	when a frustrating event is caused by one of the parties it is a breach
rescission	returning the parties to the position they were in before the contract
rectification	court corrects the wording of a mistake in the contract
acceleration clause	a contractual term that comes into effect when there is a failure to make an installment
liquidated damages	a remedy requiring party responsible for a breach to pay a stated amount
deposit	money held in the event of a breach
down payment	money that must be returned to the purchaser in the event of a breach
remoteness	a breaching party is only responsible for reasonably expected losses
mitigation	victims of a breach must make effort to lessen the loss
specific performance	court orders the breaching party to live up to the terms of the agreement
injunction	court orders breaching conduct to stop
accounting	court orders a determination of the injuries suffered
quantum meruit	court orders payment for part performance

Chapter Outline

Notes

Performance

Each party satisfactorily performs its part of the bargain

Substantial performance - when most of the obligation has been performed, the contract is discharged. Damages may be available to compensate for an unfulfilled portion of agreement

Performance tendered - when a willing party is prevented by the other from performing, the obligation is considered fulfilled except when money is owed, in which case the creditor becomes responsible for collecting the debt

- Payment must be in legal tender and delivery must be at reasonable time and place

Independent obligations - in some instances failure to perform on the part of one party does not relieve the other of the obligation to perform (i.e. landlord/tenant)

Payment by installment - failure to deliver a single installment on a contract does not relieve the other from obligations under the contract

Breach

The failure to perform a contractual obligation

Conditions - terms essential to the substantial performance of the contract - when breached, victim is relieved of obligations

Warranties - minor terms of contract - when breached, performance is still required but damages are available

Exemption clauses attempt to limit liability, but are strictly interpreted by courts

Fundamental breach - some obligations are so basic that failure to perform is a breach regardless of exemption clauses

Repudiation (anticipatory breach) - when it is clear that one party has no intention of performing or has repudiated the contract, the victim can treat the contract as discharged or go through with his/her part of the obligation and then, if there is a failure, sue for breach

Discharge by Agreement

Contracts can be modified or ended by agreement

Bilateral discharge - occurs when there is consideration to support an agreement to discharge an old agreement, while both parties still have obligations under the original agreement

Unilateral discharge - discharge cannot be one-sided
  - parties must agree on some additional consideration (accord and satisfaction)
  - all rules of contract formation must be met
  - terms in the contract may provide for its own discharge

Conditions precedent - conditions which must be met before the obligations of the contract must be fulfilled

Conditions subsequent - an event or condition that ends the obligation to fulfill the contract after they are in process

Frustration

When an outside, unforeseen event makes performance impossible or essentially different than originally intended, it is discharged through frustration
  - when frustrating event is caused by one of the parties - it is a breach

Effect of frustration - relieves the harshness of the common law doctrine of "let the loss lie where it falls"
Legislation modifies case law

Remedies for Breach of Contract

Rescission - available when parties can be returned to their original positions and when the breach has been significant

Rectification - only available when there has been a defect in the recording of the contractual agreement

Remedies - provided in contract:
- Liquidated damages - a term in the contract states that in the event of breach, the victim will be entitled to a certain sum - must be a reasonable attempt to provide compensation. The intention to forfeit must be clear at outset (e.g. deposit)
- Down payment - a prepayment that will be returned in the event of breach

Damages - courts assess loss and order breaching party to compensate victim for that loss
- limitations on recoverable damages
- the damages must have been reasonably foreseeable (remoteness)
- victim must mitigate losses (keep losses as low as possible)

Equitable Remedies may be applicable in special situations
- Specific performance - courts order defaulting party to go through with contract
- Injunction - a court order that an offending action be stopped
- Accounting - offending party required to disclose finances to aid injured party in recovering damages
- *Quantum meruit* - amount of compensation is dependent on the value of the work already performed (part performance)

Review Questions

1. Contractual obligations are discharged when each party satisfactorily performs its part of the bargain.
   (a) True
   (b) False

2. Which of the following is an exception to the rule that a contract must be fully performed before any payment for the performance is due?
   (a) substantial performance
   (b) incapacitation
   (c) refused tender of performance
   (d) a and b
   (e) a and c

3. What does substantial performance of a contract mean?

   _____

   _____

4. Independent obligations sometimes require a party to make at least a partial payment on the contract despite the breach.
   (a) True
   (b) False

5. Tender of performance is when one party is ready, willing and able and attempts to perform his/her part of the contract.
   (a) True
   (b) False

6. Which of the following is not a requirement when tendering performance?
   (a) Legal tender
   (b) Delivery at reasonable time and place
   (c) To persist when performance is refused
   (d) To seek out the creditor to make payment
   (e) To make payment even after a refusal to take it.

7. Leonard attempted to pay Robinson the $500 he owed him by tendering payment in legal tender at the proper time and place but Robinson refused to accept payment then. Leonard refused to make another attempt to pay Robinson. Which one of the following is true with regard to this situation?

(a) Leonard must pay interest at a "reasonable rate" from the date of his attempt to pay.

(b) Robinson can sue Leonard successfully for breach of contract.

(c) Leonard can sue Robinson successfully for rescission of the contract.

(d) Robinson can sue on the basis of *quantum meruit*.

(e) None of the above

8. Which of the following is false with regard to the law governing tender of performance:

(a) If Fred attempts to deliver the goods contracted for at the time and place designated in the contract but the buyer refuses delivery, Fred doesn't have to attempt to deliver again; he can just sue for breach of contract.

(b) If Sam attempts to pay the $600 debt owed to Chris in $2 bills on the date and at the place designated in the contract and Chris refuses the payment, Sam will have to seek out Chris and attempt to pay another time.

(c) If Sam attempts to pay the $600 debt owed to Chris with a cheque on the date and at the place designated in the contract, Chris would not have to accept that cheque unless payment by cheque was expressly or implicitly provided for in the contract.

(d) If Joe attends the premises of XYZ Co. to repair a computer on the date and at the time designated and XYZ Co. prohibits him from doing the services contracted for, Joe has no further obligations under the contract and can sue for breach of contract.

9. In some contracts, one party's failure to perform may not relieve the other of obligations under the contract.

(a) True

(b) False

10. When the contract is based on a series of installments, at what stage is a contract likely to be considered ended when there is a failure to make an installment?

(a) When each installment is vital

(b) When it is the first installment

(c) When a number of installments have been missed

(d) all of the above

(e) a and b

11. A contract is breached when there is improper or incomplete performance or refusal to perform.

(a) True

(b) False

12. The requirement "it takes a contract to end a contract" would not be met in which of the following circumstances?
    (a) Both parties to a contract agree to call off the contract before either party performed his contractual obligation.
    (b) The parties to a contract agree to call off the contract under which one had paid $200 for the work to be done but the other, although he had not done the work, promised to return the $200.
    (c) Both parties to the contract agree to call off the contract but one has already performed.

13. Which of the following describes a condition of a contract?
    (a) A warranty
    (b) A term essential to substantial performance
    (c) Where breached, victim relieved of obligations
    (d) Where breached, victim must continue to perform
    (e) b and c

14. Terms in a contract are either _____ or _____.

15. When a condition is breached, the victim is relieved of the contractual obligations to the person responsible for the breach.
    (a) True
    (b) False

16. Which one of the following combinations indicates three types of breach of contract?
    (a) Breach of condition, breach of warranty, frustration
    (b) Anticipatory breach, fundamental breach, substantial performance
    (c) Failure of performance, incapacitating conduct, express repudiation
    (d) Inadequate notice, anticipatory breach, strict construction
    (e) Breach of the fundamental term, contempt of court, breach of peace

17. A fundamental breach may occur when the failure to perform is so basic it leaves one party without any benefit in the contract.
    (a) True
    (b) False

18. The courts justify their interference with a contract because of fundamental breach on the basis that it is not clear that the exculpatory clause was intended to exclude liability to such an extent.
    (a) True
    (b) False

19. A properly worded exclusionary clause can overcome a fundamental breach.
    (a) True
    (b) False

20. Courts require parties to a contract to adhere to a standard of conduct based on good faith.
    (a) True
    (b) False

21. Another term for anticipatory breach is
    (a) consideration
    (b) repudiation
    (c) discharge by agreement
    (d) fundamental breach
    (e) b and c

22. A party to a contract must indicate an intention to repudiate in writing.
    (a) True
    (b) False

23. By a contract dated January 17, Lipset, a noted sociologist, agreed to present a two-hour lecture on the differences between Canadian and American cultures. When Lipset called to repudiate the contract 6 days before the performance date, Mr. Lo, the other party to the contract, pressed him to perform. Which of the following could not result in an action by Lo against Lipset for breach of contract? (Read each separately.)
    (a) Lipset repudiates a second time before the performance date and Lo acknowledges the breach and gets another, less well-known speaker.
    (b) Lipset has a heart attack four hours before the lecture was supposed to begin and went in for surgery.
    (c) Lipset shows up but talks a half-hour on the mating habits of Amazon Indians, much to the displeasure of Lo and the audience.
    (d) When Lo went to the airport to pick up Lipset two hours before the lecture time, he sees Lipset board another plane to Hawaii.
    (e) Lipset calls Lo on the night of the performance and say he is definitely not showing up, but that he'll give a three-hour lecture next week. Lo refuses to accept the substitute.

24. The victim of a repudiation has no recourse if the repudiation occurs before performance of the contract.
    (a) True
    (b) False

25. XYZ Co. continued to press for performance from John Brown who had expressly repudiated his obligations. What might happen that would prevent XYZ Co. from suing Brown for breach?
    (a) Brown may never perform.
    (b) Brown may breach a condition of the contract.
    (c) The contract may be discharged by frustration.
    (d) Brown may expressly repudiate a second time.

26. The victim of repudiation can make a choice.
    (a) To ignore it and insist on performance
    (b) To refuse to perform their side of the agreement
    (c) Accept it and treat the contractual obligations as ended
    (d) To continue to perform their side of the contract
    (e) All of the above

27. What possible responses are available to the victim when the other party repudiates a contract?

    _____

    _____

28. Contracts can be modified or ended by agreement even when some of the elements of the contract are missing.
    (a) True
    (b) False

29. One party to a contract cannot impose a change in the contract on the other.
    (a) True
    (b) False

30. When there is an agreement to discharge a contract, which of the following must be in place?
    (a) consensus
    (b) consideration
    (c) legality
    (d) intention
    (e) all of the above

31. A bilateral discharge occurs when both parties agree to end the contract.
    (a) True
    (b) False

32. A unilateral discharge is binding on the parties.
    (a) True
    (b) False

33. Accord and satisfaction is when the parties agree to end contract based on some other consideration.
    (a) True
    (b) False

34. When part payment is accepted early as full payment, the creditor cannot sue for any deficit.
    (a) True
    (b) False

35. A term in a contract which says that on the occurrence of an event, the parties obligations will end prematurely is an example of
    (a) condition subsequent
    (b) condition precedent
    (c) discharge by frustration
    (d) tender of performance

36. When the parties specify conditions in their agreement under which their obligations will begin they are called
    (a) contractual conditions
    (b) conditions of repudiation
    (c) conditions subsequent
    (d) conditions precedent
    (e) a and d

37. Conditions subsequent mean the contract is binding only if some pre-existing conditions are met.
    (a) True
    (a) False

38. Conditions subsequent bring those obligations already resting on the parties to an end.
    (a) True
    (b) False

39. A contract for the sale and purchase of land valued at $250,000 included the following clause: "This contract is subject to the purchaser buying an option on the adjoining lot within one month from the date of this agreement." Which of the following is false with regard to this "subject to" clause?
    (a) The legal term for this "subject to" clause is "condition subsequent."
    (b) The effect of this clause is to make the parties' obligations conditional upon the happening of the event, namely the purchaser buying an option on the adjoining lot.

    (c) This clause may be ignored by either party unilaterally.
    (d) It refers to a term in the contract that provides for the ending of a contract that is in full force and effect.
    (e) None of the above

40. Which one of the following statements is false?
    (a) Three types of breach of contract are express repudiation, incapacitating conduct and failure to perform.
    (b) Anticipatory breach refers to a situation in which a party may be able to sue for breach of contract even though the time for actual performance has not yet arrived.
    (c) A carefully drawn exemption clause may fail for any one of the following reasons: a strict construction approach by the court, inadequate notice or a breach of the fundamental term of the contract.
    (d) Incapacitating conduct refers to voluntary frustration of a contract.
    (e) Whether a breach of contract amounts to a breach of the fundamental term of the contract depends on the presence or absence of an exemption clause.

41. What is the term used to describe the effect of an outside, unforeseen event making the performance of a contract impossible?

_____

42. Frustration of a contract occurs when one of the parties is unable to perform his/her obligations under the agreement because of:
    (a) An avoidable event
    (b) The subject of the contract being destroyed
    (c) An outside, unforeseen event
    (d) A deliberate action on the part of one of the parties that makes performance impossible
    (e) b and c

43. A frustrated contract can occur when the nature of the contract has changed, making performance impossible.
    (a) True
    (b) False

44. When unforeseen interference makes performance of a contract impossible even where that interference has been caused by one of the parties, the courts will find frustration.
    (a) True
    (b) False

45. The common law principle that the party providing the service before the frustrating event occurred would bear the loss was called:
    (a) "It is not my act."
    (b) "He who laughs last..."
    (c) "Let the loss lie where it falls."
    (d) "A stitch in time."

46. The common law approach to frustration was modified by the Fibrosa case when the court declared that a complete failure of consideration would result in any prepayment or deposit being returned.
    (a) True
    (b) False

47. Smith agreed to purchase a ship, the Queen Hilda, from Jones for $500 000. Unbeknownst to Jones, Smith had another contract with Brown for the resale of the Queen Hilda for $2 000 000. As Jones was having the ship prepared for delivery to Smith, one of his employees carelessly spilled some fuel oil, which was ignited by the welding torch of another of Jones' employees. In the subsequent fire the ship was destroyed. Smith was able to secure another ship of equal tonnage for only $700 000, but Brown made it clear that nothing other than the Queen Hilda would do for the purpose he had in mind and he refused to go through with the deal. Smith sued Brown. Which of the following statements sets out the likely outcome of this action?
    (a) Although the contract has been frustrated, because of the *Frustrated Contracts Act* (or other local legislation) Smith will still be required to pay for some of the expenses that Jones has incurred in preparing the ship for delivery.
    (b) Because the contract has been frustrated, Smith will lose his action.
    (c) Brown will have to pay damages for breach of contract to the extent of $200 000 (the difference in price between the two ships).
    (d) Brown will have to pay damages for breach of contract to the extent of $1 500 000 (the loss of Smith's profit as originally anticipated).
    (e) Brown will have to pay damages for breach of contract to the extent of $1 300 000 (the loss of Smith's profit with respect to the replacement ship).

48. Most common law jurisdictions have passed legislation allowing costs to be deducted from a deposit when a frustrating event occurs.
    (a) True
    (b) False

49. Examine each of the following statements with regard to breach of contract and indicate which are false.
    (a) Three types of breach are: express repudiation, incapacitating conduct and substantial performance.
    (b) Anticipatory breach refers to a situation where a promisee may be able to sue for breach of contract even though the time for performance has not yet arrived.

(c) Incapacitating conduct refers to a situation where a promisor voluntarily frustrates a contract.

(d) Whether a failure to perform a contractual obligation will constitute a fundamental breach of the contract depends on the presence of an exemption clause.

(e) A carefully drawn exemption clause may fail for any one of the following reasons: no notice, a strict-construction approach by the court or breach of a fundamental term of the contract.

50. What is the standard of measurement by which the courts determine the losses that the non-breaching party may recover when a contract is breached?

_____

51. Under what circumstances will the defendant be held liable for losses in excess of those that conform to that standard?

_____

_____

52. Jones entered into a contract with Smith whereby Jones agreed to paint a portrait of Smith's wife to be completed by her 45th birthday (6 months away at the time the agreement was made). Three months before the portrait was to be completed, Jones informed Smith that he would not be doing the portrait, as he had to leave immediately for a job in another city. Indicate which of the following accurately describes the rights of the parties in this situation?

(a) The contract has been frustrated and Jones has no obligation to Smith.

(b) The contract has been repudiated, and Smith can sue Jones right away.

(c) Smith must wait to see if Jones really fails to perform what he has agreed to do before he can sue.

(d) This is a case where the courts will award specific performance.

(e) None of the above

53. Which of the following is correct with respect to damages awarded by the court?

(a) The court will only award damages that are reduced by the amount that the victim should have mitigated.

(b) The court will only award the damages that are reasonably foreseeable to the contracting parties at the time they entered into the contract.

(c) If there is a liquidated-damages clause in the contract, the court will only order the payment of the damages specified in that clause.

(d) If a deposit has been paid, the court will calculate how much more damage has been done and award that amount.

(e) All of the above

54. Rectification means that the court will return parties to their original positions when a contract is breached.
    (a) True
    (b) False

55. Which of the following remedies may be provided for in the contract?
    (a) liquidated damages, deposits, down payments
    (b) rescission, specific performance, injunction
    (c) accounting, *quantum meruit*, laches
    (d) all of the above
    (e) none of the above

56. When two contracting parties agree to end or discharge a contract when one of the parties has already performed, what problem will they likely encounter with their agreement to discharge? How can this problem be overcome?

    _____

    _____

57. Liquidated damages include any situation where the payment of money is required in the event of a breach.
    (a) True
    (b) False

58. Which of the following are equitable remedies?
    (a) liquidated damages, deposits, down payments
    (b) rescission, specific performance, injunction
    (c) mitigation, *quantum meruit*, laches
    (d) all of the above
    (e) none of the above

59. When damages are awarded by the court, it is an attempt to put victims of breach in the position they would have been in if the contract had been properly performed.
    (a) True
    (b) False

60. Which of the following are limitations on the recoverability of damages?
    (a) Breaching party must compensate for reasonably foreseeable damages
    (b) Victims must make an effort to keep their losses as low as possible
    (c) When the breach causes equal losses to both parties
    (d) a and b
    (e) a and c

61. Which of the following describes the equitable remedy known as *quantum meruit*?
    (a) An order to go through with the deal
    (b) An order to stop breaching the agreement
    (c) An order to disclose information
    (d) An order for payment for what has been done
    (e) An order that puts parties back into the position they were in before the contract was breached

62. Identify the correct statements about the remedy of specific performance:
    (a) This remedy is discretionary and the court may grant it as it sees fit.
    (b) This remedy is regularly available when there is a breach of a contract involving an interest in land.
    (c) The plaintiff's position must be beyond reproach and the defendant must have refused to perform before this remedy will be awarded.
    (d) This remedy is the usual one awarded when the contract calls for personal performance.

63. Which of the following is not a remedy the courts may impose for breach of contract?
    (a) rescission
    (b) injunction
    (c) damages
    specific performance
    (e) laches

64. When is rescission available as a remedy in a breach of contract situation?

    _____

65. Name two forms of liquidated damages.

    (1) _____

    (2) _____

66. On what basis will a court award liquidated damages?

    _____

    _____

67. The injured party in a breach of contract case where the contract contains a liquidated-damages clause is entitled to which of the following?
    (a) All the damage that naturally and directly flows from the breach
    (b) The damages set out in the liquidated damages clause in the contract, provided that the amount set out represents an honest attempt by the parties to estimate the damages
    (c) All the loss suffered because of the breach even if the injured party took no effort to minimize his loss

68. Truck-It Ltd. bought a truck from Miles Motors Ltd. for the purpose of hauling potatoes. The proper agent of Truck-It signed a contract that included an exemption clause that excused Miles Motors Ltd. from liability arising "from any breach of condition, or warranty whether express, implied, statutory or otherwise." After only two weeks of hauling potatoes the truck was found to be utterly useless for that purpose since the weight was too much for both the engine and the walls of the truck. When Miles Motors Ltd. refused to take back the truck, Truck-It sued for breach of condition. Which of the following could, on these facts, be true?
    (a) The buyer could get around the exemption clause by arguing insufficient notice.
    (b) The buyer could be awarded damages if the exemption clause were found invalid by way of fundamental breach, or by the court's interpreting the clause narrowly.
    (c) The buyer could be awarded damages equal to all his foreseeable losses caused by the breach even if he took no steps to mitigate his losses.
    (d) The buyer would prefer the equitable remedy of an injunction rather than damages.
    (e) The buyer would receive no remedy because the contract is discharged by agreement.

69. A provision in a contract whereby a person will not be held liable for his/her own failure to perform satisfactorily is called

    _____

70. Specific performance, injunction, accounting and *quantum meruit* are what kind of court ordered remedies? _____

71. When there has been a price agreed to in a contract for services, what two circumstances must exist before the court will award a *quantum meruit* remedy?

    (1) _____

    (2) _____

72. Classic Cars. It was written in the contract that the Jaguar had new tires and a new engine. In fact the tires were recaps and the engine was an exchange engine that had not even been rebuilt. Henry discovered this fifteen days after he purchased the automobile when the engine seized up. He reread the contract and discovered a special clause stating that the car was warrantied to be free of any obvious defects. Except for those conditions or warranties expressly entered into by the parties, there were no other warranties or conditions, express or implied, and that any breach of warranty under the contract had to be brought to the attention of the seller within ten days of the sale of the vehicle, otherwise there would be no liability. Part of the deal was that Henry would trade in his 1975 Fiat Spider on the Jaguar. Because there was still some minor touch-up work to be done on the Jaguar, Henry decided to keep the Fiat until the work could be done and, in fact, had possession of it when the engine of the Jaguar seized up. Henry continued to use his Fiat for transportation.

One night when both the Fiat and Jaguar were parked in a garage there was a terrible storm that destroyed both the garage and the cars. The original deal called for $10 000 to be paid for the Jaguar in addition to the $5 000 allowed as trade-in for the Fiat. This amount was to be paid in installments of $100 per month after an initial $500 deposit had been paid which was intended to reduce the purchase price. After the destruction of the Jaguar, Henry refused to make any further payments. Conrad insisted that he not only be paid for the Jaguar, but also be compensated for the loss of the Fiat. Henry finally agreed on a compromise under pressure from Conrad and agreed to pay $8 000 in full settlement of the debt. After entering into this agreement with Conrad, Henry rethought the matter and refused to go through with the deal and countersued Conrad. What will be the court's response in these actions?

Answers to Review Questions

1. a   P. 242   D.1

2. a   P. 243   D.2

3. The contract must be essentially performed with only minor or insignificant terms left uncompleted.

    P. 243   D.1

4. a   P. 246   D.1

5. a   P. 243   D.1

6. c   P. 244-5 D.2

7. b   P. 243-5 D.2

8. d   P. 243-5 D.2

9. a   P. 243,
             246   D.1

10. d   P. 250   D.2

11. a   P. 245   D.1

12. d   P. 241   D.2

13. e   P. 246   D.2

14. conditions or warranties

    P. 246   D.1

15. a   P. 246   D.1

16. c   P. 246,
             255   D.2

17. a   P. 248   D.1

18. a   P. 248   D.1

19. a   P. 248   D.1

20. a   P. 248   D.2

21. b   P. 249   D.2

22. b   P. 250   D.1

23. b   P. 249   D.2

24. b   P. 249   D.1

25. c   P. 250   D.2

26. e   P. 249   D.2

27. The victim can treat the contractual relationship as finished and sue, or insist on performance and wait for performance to be given.

    P. 249   D.1

28. b   P. 251   D.1

29. a   P. 251   D.2

30. e   P. 251-2 D.1

31. a   P. 252   D.1

32. b   P. 252   D.1

33. a   P. 252   D.1

34. a   P. 253   D.1

35. a   P. 254   D.1

36. e   P. 253   D.2

37. b   P. 254   D.1

38. a   P. 254   D.1

39. b   P. 253-4 D.2

40. e   P. 248   D.2

41. Frustration

    P. 254   D.1

42. e   P. 255   D.2

43. a   P. 255   D.1

44. b   P. 256   D.1

45. c   P. 257   D.1

46. a   P. 257   D.1

47. c   P. 261   D.3

48. a   P. 258   D.1

49. a and d P. 245-8 D.2

50. He can only collect damages that would have been in the reasonable contemplation of the parties at the time the contract was entered into.

    P. 262   D.2

51. The breaching party must be given notice of any unusual losses that may occur.

    P. 262   D.1

52. b   P. 257   D.3

53. e   P. 262-3,
             259-60   D.2

54. b   P. 259   D.1

55. a   P. 259   D.2

56. No consideration. They must reach some sort of accord and give extra satisfaction.

    P. 252   D.2

57. b   P. 259   D.1

58. b   P. 259, 263   D.2

59. a   P. 261   D.1

60. d   P. 262-3   D.2

61. d   P. 264-5   D.2

62. a, b, c   P. 263   D.2

63. e   P. 265   D.2

64. Rescission is available where the contract is void. This is an attempt to put the parties back into their original positions.

    P. 259   D.2

65. 1. Amount specified in the contract to be paid upon breach, and

    2. Pre-paid deposit

    P. 259   D.1

66. Where there is no attempt to impose a penalty but an honest pre-estimation of damages.

    P. 259-61   D.2

67. b   P. 260   D.2

68. b   P. 246-8   D.2

69. Exculpatory/exclusionary/exemption clause.

    P. 246-7   D.2

70. Equitable remedies.

    P. 263-5   D.1

71. (1) The breach must not be caused by the person claiming *quantum meruit* and

    (2) the other person must have received some benefit for the work done.

    P. 264-5   D.2

72. The main problem here is whether Conrad is not liable for the problems with the Jaguar because of the exemption clause. Because the car is used and neither breach goes to the heart of the contract, these obligations could be covered by a properly worded exemption clause. This exemption clause does not cover the new engine and tires, however, since these were agreed to by the parties and included in the contract. These defects have to be brought to the attention of Conrad within 10 days of the sale of the car to Henry. It has been 30 days since Henry took the car and so, on the face of it, it looks as if he is out of luck. But because Henry still has the Fiat and the work to be done on the Jaguar has not been done yet it could be argued that the sale hasn't taken place yet (the title to the Jaguar has not transferred to Henry yet). In any case the parties have clearly agreed to settle this matter out of court and once they entered into the agreement to settle the dispute by Henry paying only $8 000, this was a binding contract (a settlement out of court). That then is the contract and Henry cannot later change his mind; he is bound by this new agreement. Henry must pay Conrad $8 000.

    P. 251   D.3

Chapter 9

Sales and Consumer Protection

Learning Objectives

At the end of the chapter you should be able to:

1. Describe the impact of the *Sale of Goods Act* on contractual relations.
2. Explain the conditions set by the *Sale of Goods Act* when goods are sold by description.
3. Discuss the reasons for consumer protection legislation.
4. Give some examples of unacceptable business practices.
5. List some of the federal statutes that affect consumer transactions.

Key Terms

You should be able to define the following terms.

goods	tangible items that can be bought and sold
chose in action	the right to sue another
conditional sale	the seller provides credit to the purchaser, holding title until the goods are paid for
sale	title and goods are transferred immediately
agreement to sell	goods and title transferred at some time in the future
risk	potential loss due to destruction or damage to goods
bill of lading	a receipt for goods in the care of the shipper
order bill of lading	consignee retains right to receive goods at their destination
quiet possession	goods must be usable by the purchaser
lien	charge giving the creditor the right of seizure when goods are passed on to third parties.
merchantable quality	goods ordered by description must be free of defects
seller's lien	seller who holds the goods can get a lien against defaulting purchaser
stoppage in transitu	seller retains the right to stop the shipment in event of default
collateral contract	a contract between the ultimate purchaser and the manufacturer
unconscionable transactions	merchants take advantage of disadvantaged customers

Chapter Outline

Sale of Goods

Sale of Goods Act - provincial statutes provide standardized approaches for the court to infer omitted terms in disputed contracts. Parties can contract out of the terms of the Act. The Act is a summation of common law. In order for a contract for sale to be binding all rules of contract law must be adhered to
- Restricted to the transfer of possession of goods (not land, rights or services)
- The Act does not cover goods used as security in a transaction, but does cover sales on credit
- Money must change hands in order for *Sale of Goods Act* to apply (not trade or barter unless some money is exchanged)

Statute of Frauds requires evidence in writing for transactions over a certain amount

Title and Risk

Sale - when both title and property of the goods are transferred immediately

Agreement to sell - when either title or possession is to be transferred at a future time

Specified Risk - risk follows title; therefore, the time of the transfer of title is an important factor

Methods of Transferring Title
- C.I.F. - seller assumes responsibility during shipment of goods
- F.O.B. - seller bears risk until goods are placed on carrier
- C.O.D. - seller assumes risk until delivered to purchaser and paid for

Bill of Lading - whoever holds the bill of lading is responsible for the goods until they reach their destination

Transfer of Title - rules for determining who has title stipulated in Act
- Rule 1 - title transfers immediately on specifically designated goods that require no alteration
- Rule 2 - when alteration of goods is required, seller must notify purchaser when alterations are completed in order to transfer title
- Rule 3 - when some evaluative process is required before the goods can be delivered, notice of its completion is required before title transfers

- Rule 4 - when purchaser takes goods on approval, notice of acceptance must be received before the title transfers
- Rule 5 - title to goods not yet in existence remains with seller until the goods have been unconditionally appropriated (separated out) and committed to the purchaser in such a way that it would be difficult for them to be given to some other purchaser. The assent required usually takes place when notice is given, however, such assent may be inferred from the circumstances.

Conditions and Warranties - rules governing these are included in *Sales of Goods Act*

Obligations of Seller
- Must transfer good title (i.e. must have the right to sell them)
- Give quiet possession (delivered in a useable condition)
- Free from charge or encumbrance (clear title)
- Goods sold according to description must match description, be of merchantable quality and suitable for purpose of purchase
- Reasonable price imposed when price omitted from contract
- Reasonable time and place for delivery and payment
- Sales contracts can and often do contain terms (exculpatory) which specifically override provisions of *Sale of Goods Act*

Remedies for Default

Purchaser's Default
- Unpaid seller's lien (seller has the right to retain goods until they are paid for)
- Stoppage *in transitu* - seller can retake goods in process of delivery
- Seller can sue for price when purchaser refuses to take delivery of goods if title has already transferred; otherwise only damages are available (and then only if the goods cannot be resold at same price)

Seller's Default
- Rescission for innocent misrepresentation, damages for negligent or fraudulent misrepresentation
- Purchaser can refuse to pay for goods for breach of condition or withhold enough to compensate for loss with breach of warranty
- Purchaser can sue for damages if goods have been paid for but are not delivered

Consumer Protection

Imposes controls on consumer transactions - when purchasers acquire goods for personal use

Limits effect of exemption clauses - when a product is unfit, purchaser can sue for breach of contract

Establishes liability for unsafe products; purchaser can sue in contract or tort if fault can be demonstrated

Defines unacceptable business practices - misleading statements by salesperson become part of the contract

Manufacturers and retailers have duty to warn of hazards associated with products

Identifies unconscionable transactions - when consumer is taken advantage of by seller, there is right to claim remedies available for misrepresentation

Regulates door-to-door sales - cooling off period, referral selling, money lenders, credit reporting practices

Methods of Control - consumer service bodies investigate complaints, seize records, search premises, suspend licenses, impose fines, initiate action on behalf of consumers

Role of government agencies - Department of Consumer and Corporate Affairs promotes consumer awareness, enforces legislation

Federal legislation - *Combines Investigation Act, Food and Drug Act, Hazardous Products Marketing Act*

Review Questions

1. Which of the following does not describe the *Sale of Goods Act*?
   (a) Statute embodies case law and complements normal rules of contract law
   (b) Imposes new terms and conditions on the parties to a contract
   (c) Applies to all situations where goods are bought and sold
   (d) Intended to fill the gaps in the terms of a contract
   (e) Terms in contract prevail over provisions of *Act*

2. What is the primary purpose of the *Sale of Goods Act*?

   _____

3. Identify the two essential legal elements that must be present in a sale-of-goods transaction (other than the goods themselves) for the *Sale of Goods Act* to apply to the contract.

   (1) _____

   (2) _____

4. The parties to a contract for the sale of goods are prohibited by the *Sales of Goods Act* from exempting themselves from the provisions of the *Act*.
   (a) True
   (b) False

5. All the rules of _____ law must be satisfied for the sale of goods to be held binding.

6. What is the difference between a sale and an agreement to sell?

   _____

   _____

7. Because of the *Sale of Goods Act*, contracts for the sale of goods are not required to meet all the requirements of a contract.
   (a) True
   (b) False

8. The *Sale of Goods Act* only requires that a reasonable price be paid for the goods in question.
   (a) True
   (b) False

9. *Sale of Goods Act* does not apply to services, except when it involves the installation of goods.
   (a) True
   (b) False

10. To which of the following failed contracts would the *Sale of Goods Act* not apply?
    (a) A contract for shares of Starbucks, Ltd.
    (b) A contract to have a brake hose installed in a car
    (c) A contract for a piano bought on time
    (d) A contract for a printer where the contract is not in writing
    (e) A contract for dinner at a restaurant

11. Which of the following is covered by the *Sale of Goods Act*?
    (a) services
    (a) negotiable instruments
    (b) stocks, bonds
    (c) choses in action
    (d) tangible moveable items

12. To which one or more of the following contracts would the *Sale of Goods Act* apply?
    (a) Contract for the sale and purchase of a condominium
    (b) Contract for the sale of bonds
    (c) Contract for the sale and purchase of a horse
    (d) Contract for the sale and purchase of a computer terminal
    (e) Contract to paint a portrait

13. A conditional sale anticipates that money will changes hands and so it is covered under the *Sale of Goods Act*.
    (a) True
    (b) False

14. Terms from the *Statute of Frauds* are now included in the *Sale of Goods Act*.
    (a) True
    (b) False

15. The sale of goods over which of the following amounts must be evidenced in writing in order to be enforceable?
    (a) $50.00
    (b) $100.00
    (c) $500.00
    (d) $1000.00
    (e) none of the above

16. The sale of goods over a specified value must be evidenced in writing to be legally enforceable unless some money has changed hands.
    (a) True
    (b) False

17. The sale of goods over a specified value must be evidenced in writing to be legally enforceable unless there has been part performance.
    (a) True
    (b) False

18. Which of the following is an objective of consumer protection legislation?
    (a) Imposes controls on consumer transactions
    (b) Limits effect of exemption clauses
    (c) Establishes liability
    (d) Regulates money lenders, credit reporting practices
    (e) All of the above

19. What is the significant factor when determining who bears the risk in a sale of goods transaction?

    _____

20. The precise time that possession of goods is exchanged may determine who has title and who will bear the risk of their loss.
    (a) True
    (b) False

21. The difference between a sale and an agreement to sell is that with the salepossession transfers immediately.
    (a) True
    (b) False

22. Which of the following is not an exception to the rules that risk follows title?
    (a) C.I.F. contracts
    (b) F.O.B. contracts
    (c) C.O.D. contracts
    (d) as specified in contract
    (e) none of the above

23. Timing of transfer of title determines whether seller can sue for entire price of goods or only damages when purchaser defaults.
    (a) True
    (b) False

24. Which of the following is not a rule for determining who has title to the goods?
    (a) title transfers to purchaser at the time of contract when specific goods are identified
    (b) when some repairs must be done to the goods, title remains in hands of seller until notice is given
    (c) when goods are delivered on approval, title transfers at the time of the contract
    (d) when the goods have to be weighed or measured title, transfers when that is done and notice is given.
    (e) when goods are not yet manufactured, unconditional appropriation and assent are required

25. Identify when the title (and thus the risk of loss) passes in each of the following:
    (a) When you buy a pound of peanuts from a bulk bin at the candy counter

    _____

    (b) When you buy a boat second-hand from a private owner who has agreed to scrape and paint the hull before you pick it up

    _____

    (c) When you order a coat to be made for you by your tailor

    _____

    (d) When you purchase your week's groceries at the supermarket and arrange to have the market deliver them for you

    _____

26. Parties can contract out of most terms of the *Sale of Goods Act*.
    (a) True
    (b) False

27. One of the main purposes of the *Sale of Goods Act* is to supply by implication many of the terms that have been inadvertently left out of contracts involving the purchase of goods.
    (a) True
    (b) False

28. Adam bought a car from Bill. Two months later the bank seized the car pursuant to a chattel mortgage granted to the bank by Bill.
    (a) What implied term of the contract between Adam and Bill was breached by Bill?

    _____

    (b) Is that term designated a "warranty " or a "condition" by the *Sale of Goods Act*?

    _____

(c) What is the difference between a "condition" and a "warranty"?

_____

_____

(d) Specifically, what is the significance of the distinction to a plaintiff in an action?

_____

_____

29. Terms of a sale of goods contract are called conditions or warranties.
   (a) True
   (b) False

30. Which of the following is not an option for the victim of a breach of a condition?
   (a) Sue for damages, but keep the goods.
   (b) Accept and lose the right of discharge.
   (c) Keep the goods and lose any right to complain.
   (d) Consider themselves no longer bound to the contract.
   (e) Consider the breach of condition a breach of warranty and accept it.

31. The victim of a breach of warranty is not released from obligations under the contract, but may be entitled to damages.
   (a) True
   (b) False

32. The school of business bought a TV/VCR unit from Andrew's Video. Unfortunately, because of a manufacturing defect the machine malfunctioned and hurt Diane, who sustained a serious injury caused by electrical shock. The manufacturer of the machine, Susex Ltd. sold the machine to Midmen Distributors Ltd., which in turn sold it to Andrew's Video. Which one of the following statements is false with respect to the available remedies in this situation?
   (a) Diane has an action in tort law against the manufacturer but has no action in contract.
   (b) Midmen Distributors Ltd. bears no liability here because it was just a middleman in the flow of products.
   (c) The school has an action against Andrew's for breach of contract, namely a breach of the implied condition that the TV/VCR unit be reasonably fit for its purpose.
   (d) Midmen Distributors Ltd. has an action against the manufacturers for breach of contract, namely a breach of an implied condition that the goods should be of merchantable quality.
   (e) Andrew's has an action for breach of contract against Midmen.

33. Which of the following is not a factor affecting good title?
    (a) Goods must be usable as intended.
    (b) Goods must be free of any lien or encumbrance.
    (c) Seller must convey good title.
    (d) Goods must match sample and be free of hidden defects
    (e) None of the above

34. The *Sale of Goods Act* requires that specific goods bought from a dealer be of merchantable quality. What is meant by "merchantable quality"?

    _____

35. The requirement that goods be of merchantable quality means that the goods must be free of any title claims.
    (a) True
    (b) False

36. A purchaser can default the contract if the goods don't match the advertisements for them.
    (a) True
    (b) False

37. Which of the following terms will be implied when they are not stipulated in contract?
    (a) Must pay a reasonable price
    (b) Place and time of delivery
    (c) What can be done when wrong quantity is delivered
    (d) Free from any lien or encumbrance
    (e) All of the above

38. Which of the following is not a remedy available in case of default?
    (a) Repossess the goods from the buyer
    (b) Stop delivery of goods
    (c) Sue for breach of contract and for damages
    (d) Purchasers who are injured by the product can sue for damages
    (e) Demand specific performance

39. Strict liability is imposed on both the manufacturer and the supplier of goods.
    (a) True
    (b) False

40. What would be the plaintiff's cause of action if she were injured by an exploding bottle of cola that she was taking from the shelf and placing in a shopping cart?

    _____

    _____

41. When the goods being sold are unique, the purchaser may be able to demand specific performance.
    (a) True
    (b) False

42. In the event of a sale by description, what are the buyer's two possible remedies if the goods do not correspond with the description?

    (1) _____

    (2) _____

43. Consumer transactions involve goods intended for use by the consumer and not resold.
    (a) True
    (b) False

44. In some jurisdictions the *Sale of Goods Act* imposes responsibility on sellers even when exemption clauses are in place.
    (a) True
    (b) False

45. Sam Sharp ordered a pair of custom-made jeans from his tailor for the price of $75. However, when he found that he could buy similar ones ready-made at Everready's Department Store, he called up the tailor to cancel the order. The tailor said that normally he would be willing to cancel such an order but because he had already begun to cut the cloth for Sharp's pants, he was not willing to cancel and that Sharp would have to go through with the deal. Is Sharp liable under the agreement, and if so, what will be the tailor's remedy?

    _____

    _____

46. Which of the following statements is false with respect to the consumer protection legislation in place in your jurisdiction?
    (a) An executory contract is one in which all aspects are completed at the time of formation.
    (b) A seller cannot enforce a sale of goods that involves referral selling (where the contract provides for a rebate to the buyer based on subsequent sales to other buyers referred by him to the seller).
    (c) A buyer in a door-to-door sale will have a limited period of time in which to cancel the contract.
    (d) A court may set aside any mortgage transaction that it thinks is unconscionable.
    (e) An action based on the misleading statement of a salesperson can be brought even if not included in the written contract.

47. Victims of unsafe products can sue manufacturer in tort but must establish fault.
    (a) True
    (b) False

48. What protections are available through the *Sale of Goods Act* for an "unpaid seller" who still possesses the goods?

    _____

    _____

49. People injured by a product can sue seller under contract law if the product were purchased by someone else.
    (a) True
    (b) False

50. Which of the following are features of current consumer protection legislation?
    (a) Promises the buyer satisfaction or the right to get his money back
    (b) Limits the effect of exemption clauses
    (c) Defines unacceptable business practices
    (d) Provides a cooling off period during which the buyer can cancel the deal
    (e) Regulates money-lenders and credit-reporting practices

51. Collateral contracts are ones that exist between the manufacturer and the retailer and the retailer and the purchaser.
    (a) True
    (b) False

52. Mr. Cohen bought a new microwave oven at A & C Appliances Ltd. This company, a dealer in appliances for over a decade, bought it from Distributor Inc., which bought it from the manufacturer, Hopkins Ovens Ltd. Hopkins gave an evening of instruction to new purchasers. Mr. and Mrs. Cohen and their teenage son attended. Within ten days of the purchase, the oven malfunctioned due to a manufacturing defect and both Mr. Cohen and his son were badly burned because of it. Cohen missed two days of work; his son required skin grafts on the back of his right hand. Which of the following is not correct with respect to the legal position of the parties?
    (a) Mr. Cohen has an action against both Hopkins and A & C.
    (b) The son only has an action against the manufacturer.
    (c) Mr. Cohen can sue for any damages he has suffered and he is not restricted to the cost of the oven.
    (d) Mr. Cohen can sue A & C under the *Sale of Goods Act* for breach of the condition that the goods must be of merchantable quality.
    (e) *Caveat emptor* applies and Cohen must seek redress from the manufacturer

53. If you contract for a lawnmower from a second-hand dealer of rebuilt lawnmowers, which of the following is false?
    (a) The provisions of the *Sale of Goods Act* regarding quality apply to this contract.
    (b) The *Sale of Goods Act* prohibits the seller from exempting himself from liability in the event that the machine is not fit for purpose.
    (c) If you fail to pay for it at the time specified, the seller can retain the machine until payment is received even if title had passed to you.
    (d) Unless you have agreed otherwise, the place for delivery is the seller's place of business.
    (e) There is an implied term in the contract that the seller has good title to the lawnmower (i.e., the right to sell it).

54. Recently you learned that a member of your family was the victim of an unscrupulous seller who obviously engaged in deceptive and unconscionable business practice. Which of the following is not correct with respect to the rights of the victim when faced with such practices?
    (a) If misleading advertising was involved, this can be prosecuted under the federal *Competition Act*.
    (b) A complaint can be made to the appropriate provincial consumer protection agency.
    (a) The provincial licensing agency has the power to revoke the license of the seller for such abusive practices.
    (b) The seller will be subject to punishment in the form of a fine if these allegations can be proved.
    (c) There is nothing that can be done. This is an example of operation of the principle of *caveat emptor*.

55. Which of the following would not be considered an unacceptable business practice?
    (a) door-to-door sales
    (b) false advertising
    (c) referral selling
    (d) pyramid selling schemes
    (e) abusive debt collection methods

56. Unconscionable transactions do not include which of the following kinds of selling tactics and practices.
    (a) Taking advantage of those in desperate straits
    (b) Taking advantage of the illiterate or mentally disabled
    (c) Dealing with the physical infirm
    (d) Grossly excessive pricing
    (e) Excessive interest rates

57. Consumer protection legislation does not cover which of the following?
    (a) Excessive rates of interest
    (b) Requires that the true cost of borrowing be disclosed
    (c) Prohibits misleading information in advertisements
    (d) Require moneylenders to be registered
    (e) High prices

58. Legislation requires that debt-collection agencies be registered and licensed.
    (a) True
    (b) False

59. Which of the following is not a goal of the *Competition Act*?
    (a) control mergers
    (b) prohibit abusive trade practices
    (c) restrict pricing agreements between merchants
    (d) control misleading advertisement
    (e) control prices

60. Mrs. Goode did her usual weekly grocery shopping at Hillside Super Mart. Her order included a case of Lite and Brite frozen orange juice. When she mixed the concentrate from a can and served it to her family, both her husband and their son became quite ill because the manufacturer of the product, Sun Ltd., had carelessly allowed some rotten fruit to contaminate the product in the manufacturing process. Sun Ltd. had sold the product to Interprov Distributors who in turn sold it to Hillside. Mr. Goode lost two days' wages and the son had to stay home a week from school because of their stomach pains. Mrs. Goode had no juice so she suffered no illness. Consider the following statements and determine which of them are false.
    (a) Mrs. Goode has her choice of successful actions for breach of contract against Hillside, Interprov or Sun Ltd. or any combination of them.
    (b) Mrs. Goode can only succeed in an action against Hillside for breach of contract
    (c) Mrs. Goode cannot successfully take action against anyone because she suffered no illness.
    (d) Hillside can succeed against Interprov which in turn can succeed against Sun Ltd.
    (e) Interprov cannot be held liable to anyone because it just occupied the position of intermediary.
    (f) Mrs. Goode will succeed against Hillside for breach of an implied condition of reasonable fitness for a particular purpose.
    (g) Hillside will succeed against Interprov for breach of an implied condition of reasonable fitness for a particular purpose.
    (h) Mr. Goode and the son can sue Sun Ltd. in tort.

61. Joe was a door-to-door sales representative in the business of selling portable television sets. He approached the home of Mr. and Mrs. Gull, where he talked to Mr. Gull and convinced him to buy a television plus a video recorder. Because Mr. Gull desperately wanted to watch a CFL football game that afternoon, he wanted immediate delivery. Joe explained that the only set he had was the one that he had already demonstrated. Mr. Gull agreed to take the demonstrator T.V. at once, with the video recorder to be delivered later. Mr. Gull told Joe that he was anxious to have a recorder in order to tape future games. Joe assured him that he had made the right choice and went out to his car to get the box and the cable necessary to hook up the set. As Joe was returning to the house, he watched in disbelief as a piece of metal that had separated from an airplane flying overhead crashed into the roof of Mr. Gull's house. He rushed into the house to discover that the damage was limited to the television Mr. Gull had just placed in his living room. He immediately sympathized with Mr. Gull but presented him with a bill for the set. Three days later the video recorder was delivered. When Mr. Gull tried to hook up the video recorder to another T.V. (one that he had just bought from a local television store) he found that the recorder wouldn't work. It turned out that the particular video recorder purchased from Joe could only work with the model of portable television that Joe had been selling. Mr. Gull went to the expense of going to his local electronics store and having the video recorder modified so that it could work with the television set he had bought. He then discovered that the football game signals were scrambled in such a way that they couldn't be recorded by private individuals in any case. Mr. Gull refused to pay for the television set and insisted that Joe take back the video recorder. Explain the legal positions and liability of the parties.

Answers to Review Questions

1. b   P. 273   D.2

2. To imply terms into a contract for sale that the parties haven't bothered to include.

    P. 273   D.1

3. The sale must anticipate (1) the transfer of the goods and (2) for monetary consideration.

    P. 274   D. 1

4. b   P. 273   D.1

5. Contract

    P. 273   D.1

6. A sale involves the transfer of both title and possession right away whereas an agreement to sell involves either title or possession being transferred sometime in the future.

    P. 275   D.1

7. b   P. 273   D.1

8. a   P. 273   D.1

9. a   P. 273   D.1

10. a   P. 273   D.2

11. e   P. 273   D.2

12. c, d (a involves land, b the assignment of obligations and e, personal service)

    P. 273   D.2

13. a   P. 274   D.1

14. a   P. 274   D.1

15. a (or e depending on jurisdiction)

    P. 274   D.1

16. a (depends on jurisdiction)

    P. 274   D.1

17. a (depends on jurisdiction)

    P. 274   D.1

18. e   P. 285   D.2

19. The rule is that risk follows title.

    P. 275   D.1

20. a   P. 275   D.1

21. b   P. 275   D.1

22. e   P. 275   D.2

23. a   P. 276   D.1

24. c   P. 276-8   D.2

25. (a) This is covered by Rule 5 because no specific goods have been chosen. Only when goods are separated out and unconditionally allocated with the assent of the other party does title transfer.

    (b) Rule 2. As soon as the hull has been scraped and the other person has notice of it, then the title transfers.

    (c) Agreement to sell, since the goods have not yet been made. After the goods have been manufactured and unconditionally appropriated to this particular contract, the title transfers.

    (d) Rule 1 - title transfers immediately

    P. 276-8 D.2

26. a   P. 273   D.1

27. a   P. 273   D.1

28. (a) The implied warranty that there be no liens or encumbrances against the goods.

    (b) Warranty

    (c) A condition is a major term of the contract, the breach of which allows the other party to treat the contract as ended. A warranty is a minor term of the contract and its breach entitles the victim to sue for breach of contract, but he must continue to perform his side of the contract.

    (d) The victim of the breach of a condition need not fulfill his contractual obligation.

    P. 279-280   D.2

29. a   P. 280   D.1

30. c   P. 280   D.2

31. a   P. 280   D.1

32. b   P. 279-84 D.2

33. d   P. 280   D.2

34. Merchantable quality means that, had the purchaser known of a particular defect, he still would have purchased the goods at the stated price.

    P. 281   D.2

35. b   P. 281   D.1

36. a   P. 282   D.1

37. e   P. 282-3 D.2

38. a   P. 284   D.2

39. b   P. 286   D.2

40. Since no purchase has taken place and no contractual relationship exists the victim would have to sue in tort.

    P. 286   D.2

41. a   P. 284   D.2

42. (1) refuse to take the goods

    (2) take the goods and sue for damages

    P. 280   D.1

43. a   P. 285   D.1

44. a   P. 286   D.1

45. Yes, Sharp is bound in contract. The question is whether the tailor can sue for damages or for price. Here, it's arguable that, because the cutting has taken place, the goods have been unconditionally allocated and therefore the tailor can sue for price.

    P. 283   D.2

46. (Depends on jurisdiction)

    P. 285-292   D.2

47. a   P. 286   D.1

48. The seller has an unpaid seller's lien against the goods and need not deliver them. This remedy is in addition to the regular contractual remedies available to a seller.

    P. 283   D.2

49. b   P. 286   D.1

50. b, c, d, e

    P. 285-92   D.2

51. b   P. 287   D.1

52. e   P. 286-7 D.2

53. b   P. 273-84 D.2

54. e   P. 289   D.2

55. a   P. 288-291   D.2

56. c   P. 290 -91   D.2

57. e   P. 292, 296   D.2

58. a   P. 293   D.1

59. a   P. 295-6 D.1

60. a, b, e, f, g

    P. 286   D.3

61. In this case, the first question to determine is whether the title to the T.V. set passed to the purchaser before it was destroyed. The destruction would have been frustration since it was an unforeseen outside event destroying the subject matter of the contract. If the goods still belonged to the seller it would be his/her loss, but if title had passed, the purchaser must pay. Whether title had passed would depend on the rules set out in the *Sale of Goods Act*. Here, work still had to be done (the T.V. set still had to be set up). It is arguable, however, that this has nothing to do with the T.V. set which was complete as delivered. If work still had to be done, Rule 2 would apply and title would not be passed until the work was performed and notice was given. Otherwise Rule 1 applies and the T.V. set is the purchasers at the time of its destruction. As to the video recorder, it could be argued that it was not of merchantable quality, since it would not work with any other set, but that would be difficult since it would have worked with that set. More important is the fact that the purchaser told the seller what he wanted it for and relied on the seller's skill in supplying a product that would record the football games. This, under the *Sale of Goods Act*, becomes a condition of the agreement and when the recorder could not be used in this way, it is arguable that the contract was breached by the seller and the purchaser was not obligated to pay.

    P. 273-284   D. 3

Chapter 10

Priority of Creditors

Learning Objectives

At the end of the chapter you should be able to:

1. Explain how personal property can be used to secure debt.
2. Demonstrate the effect of a conditional sales agreement.
3. Discuss how the *Personal Property Security Act* affects contractual obligations.
4. Explain how guarantees are used to ensure the repayment of a debt.
5. Describe what a lien is and how it is used.
6. Describe the characteristics of negotiable instruments.
7. List and distinguish between the various types of negotiable instruments.
8. Describe the process of negotiation.
9. Identify situations where a business person would use a letter of credit.
10. Explain the process and reasons for bankruptcy.
11. Describe how creditors are ranked to receive proceeds of bankruptcy.

Key Terms

You should be able to define the following terms:

real property	land, buildings and fixtures
personal property	tangible, moveable things, chattels or personalty
chose in action	rights or claims (intangible personal property)
chattels	tangible moveable things
pledge or pawn	pawnbroker takes possession of an item as security and holds it until repayment
bill of sale	can be used to create a chattel mortgage giving creditor title to the goods until debt is paid
secured transaction	collateral right to debt giving the creditor the right to take back the goods or intercept the debt owing used as security in the event of a default
attachment	under the PPSA where value has been given pursuant to contract and creditor now has a claim against assets used as security
perfected	registering a security or creditor takes possession of the collateral used to secure a debt

collateral	goods or property used to secure a debt
book accounts	accounts receivable that can be used as security for a loan
repossession	creditor takes possession of goods used as collateral and resells them to recover the amount owed
right to redeem	after collateral is repossessedby creditor the debtor has a right to reclaim them upon proper payment.
debenture	often used interchangeably with bond, it is an acknowledgment of debts by a corporation normally involving more than one creditor
floating charge	not fixed on any particular goods until default
bona fide purchaser for value	innocent third party who has paid full value for goods under claim by creditor
fraudulent preference	defaulting debtor pays one creditor over another guarantee
guarantor	assumes obligation to pay if the debtor doesn't
indemnity	a primary obligation to pay a debt along with the debtor
continuing guarantee	creditor can advance further funds without affecting the obligation of the guarantor to pay in the event of default
subrogation	a guarantor who pays the debt steps into the creditor's shoes
lien	a claim registered against property in order to force payment of a debt
holdback	person owing funds must retain a specified percentage to be paid later when paying out in construction contract
priority	registered lien has first claim to goods used as security over other interests
negotiable instruments	vehicles for conveniently transferring funds or advancing credit
holder in due course	an innocent third party entitled to collect on a negotiable instrument in spite of any claims of the original parties
negotiation	transferring negotiable instruments to third parties
bearer instrument	a negotiable instrument made payable to the bearer
bill of exchange	instrument where drawer directs the drawee to pay out money to the payee
drawer	person creating the negotiable instrument
drawee	person or institution ordered to pay out the amount indicated on the instrument

payee	the person designated on the instrument to receive the money to be paid out
promissory note	a promise to pay the amount stated on the instrument
endorser	person who signs the back of a cheque usually assuming the obligation to pay it if the drawee or maker defaults
insolvency	where a person is unable to pay his/her debts
bankruptcy	where an insolvent person voluntarily or involuntarily transfers assets to a trustee for distribution to creditors
receiving order	court ordering the transfer of debtor's assets to a trustee

Chapter Outline   **Notes**

Methods of Securing Debt

Secured Creditor
One who has priority over other creditors with respect to goods used as collateral security
Personal property - tangible chattels or a claim on a debt (chose in action)

Personal Property Security
Purchaser or person borrowing money has possession of goods used as security, but seller or creditor retains right to take possession of goods used as security upon default

The Traditional Approach
  (1) Conditional Sales
  - Two step transaction when goods are sold and seller provides financing
  - Possession of goods is given to purchaser
  - Seller retains title until payment completed, but upon default can regain possession of goods and resell them.
  (2) Chattel Mortgages
  - Borrower maintains possession of goods but gives the creditor title to the property through a bill of sale
  (3) Assignment of Book Accounts
  - Debtor transfers rights to intercept the accounts owed to business if he/she defaults in making payments to creditor
  - Registration required to ensure priority

Personal Property Security Act
Above types of security covered by single statute
Security **attaches** when creditor gives value under contract
Perfection gives priority over other 3rd party claimants

Accomplished by registration (filing financing statement) or by the creditor taking possession of the property used as security

One central registry with standardized procedure

When debt is paid, certificate of discharge must be produced by creditor

Remedies upon Default of Payment of Debt

- Normal contractual remedies available
- Repossession of the goods used as security is the foremost option
- Not usually necessary to get court order, but if force is required a court will order a sheriff to seize the goods
- Goods can be resold to cover the debt after an opportunity has been given to debtor to redeem goods
- if goods are sold by the creditor, the debtor is required to repay any deficit left after the resale

Other Types of Security

Floating Charges

- unique to corporations allowing them to use inventory and other assets as security without interfering with ongoing business associates with bonds and debentures

Bulk Sales

- if merchant sells significant portion of inventory and equipment (suggesting that the business is coming to an end), creditors must be notified and can require that proceeds be paid directly to them.

Guarantees

- under a guarantee a third party assumes an obligation to pay if debtor defaults (this guarantee must be evidenced in writing). An obligation to be directly responsible for a debt is an indemnity.
- Contractual requirements must be met for guarantor to be bound
- Unauthorized changes release guarantor.
- Upon payment guarantor assumes rights of creditor

Builders' Liens (in some provinces Construction or Mechanic's Liens)

- Suppliers of goods and services at a construction project where there is no direct contract with owner of the property can file a lien against the property
- Must be properly registered within specified time after project is completed

- Owner of property is required to hold back a percentage of funds owed to contractor to pay possible liens
- Lien holder has priority over subsequent creditors but requires court action to execute

Negotiable Instruments

A freely transferable substitute for cash or
Facilitates the advancement of credit
Third party acquires better rights than original parties
Bills of Exchange Act - originated in England, summarizes common law, comes under federal jurisdiction

Types of Negotiable Instruments

(1) Bill of Exchange
- an order made by the drawer to the drawee (usually a financial institution) to make payment to a payee on a certain date or on demand. (used either to transfer funds or create creditor/debtor relationship)- Payee presents instrument to drawee and if it is accepted drawee becomes primarily liable

(2) Cheque
- bill of exchange drawn on a bank and payable on demand (primarily used for exchange of funds)
- Bank's authority to pay out terminates when drawer dies or when stop-payment ordered.
- Bank becomes primarily liable when they certify the cheque.

(3) Promissory Note
- promise to pay amount set out on instrument (used as a means of advancing credit)
- can bear interest and can be paid back through installments

Negotiation

Bearer Instrument (made payable to bearer)
- negotiated through transfer to 3rd party

Order Instrument (made payable to specific person)
- must be endorsed and delivered to 3rd party

Requirements for Negotiability
- Promise to pay must be unconditional
- Must be signed and in writing
- Payable at fixed time or on demand
- Fixed sum
- whole instrument must pass

Holder in Due Course
Acquires better rights than original parties
Qualifications:
Instrument received through negotiation
Instrument complete and regular
Acquires possession before due and payable
Without knowledge of dishonour
Without knowledge of defect of title and in good faith
For value
Real defenses against holder in due course:
  - Problem with the instrument - i.e. instrument has been forged, discharged, is incomplete or where there has been a material alteration

Other Holders
When the 3rd party doesn't qualify as a holder in due course they are in no better position than and assignee of contractual rights and where there are problems with the original transaction such as fraud, breach of contract and the like that can be used as a defense.

Endorsers

Negotiation of order instrument involves delivery and endorsement
Endorser is liable if instrument is refused by drawer

Consumer Bills and Notes

Cheques, bills of exchange and promissory notes used for the advancement of credit in consumer transactions (services and sales for non-commercial purposes)
  - The advantage of being a holder in due course is lost

Letters of Credit

Facilitates credit transactions and transfer of funds in international transactions

Bankruptcy

Bankruptcy - a debtor transfers assets to a trustee who distributes them among creditors
  - Can be either voluntary or forced through a receiving order
  - Consumer and commercial proposals provide an alternative to bankruptcy for insolvent debtors and protection against creditors while they try to reorganize their affairs.

- Creditors often given right to force the insolvent into "receivership" without going through the bankruptcy process
- Discharge restores bankrupt to debt free status.

Review Questions

1. What is a secured creditor?

   _____

2. "Choses in action" is another term for tangibles.
   (a) True
   (b) False

3. What kind of security is involved when the borrower has possession of the goods until there is a default in payment?

   _____

4. List three common methods of securing transactions.

   (1) _____

   (2) _____

   (3) _____

5. Most of these common law principles related to secured transactions have been incorporated into legislation.
   (a) True
   (b) False

6. A purchaser is obligated to conditional seller for performance of the contract.
   (a) True
   (b) False

7. When a mortgage is taken on personal property in a PPSA jurisdiction, the borrower temporarily transfers title to lender.
   (a) True
   (b) False

8. In a chattel mortgage transaction the creditor gains possession of the goods.
   (a) True
   (b) False

9. Which of the following securities is not covered by the *Personal Property Security Act*?
   (a) pledges
   (b) assignment of accounts receivable (book debts)
   (c) guarantees
   (d) conditional sale contracts
   (e) chattel mortgages

10. Repossession is available upon default when the creditor has a bill of sale.
    (a) True
    (b) False

11. In which one of the following situations is a chose in action given as security by a debtor to a creditor?
    (a) Singer pawns his electric guitar.
    (b) Driver buys a new truck under a conditional sale contract.
    (c) Weaver gives Average Finance Ltd. a chattel mortgage on her sports car as collateral for a loan.
    (d) Farmer borrows $50,000 from bank pursuant and has Jones sign a personal guarantee.
    (e) Collins assigns his accounts receivable to the bank that lent him $25 000.

12. What is the effect of failing to register a secured transaction document between the original parties?

    _____

13. What is the primary significance of the *Personal Property Security Act* ?

    _____

    _____

14. Which of the following statements is not true of the *Personal Property Security Act*?
    (a) Single statute enacted in most jurisdictions
    (b) Replaces most other personal property security legislation
    (c) Permits creation of more types of security interest
    (d) Creates unpaid seller's liens
    (e) Gives right to debtor to redeem seized property

15. Which of the following is not part of the process of creating a secured relationship under the *Personal Property Security Act*?
    (a) Parties enter contractual agreement.
    (b) Secured interest is attached to collateral.
    (c) Secured interest is perfected.
    (d) Creditor may obtain possession of the collateral.
    (e) Debtor registers transaction.

16. Which of the following is false with regard to secured transactions in a non-PPSA jurisdiction?
    (a) In a secured transaction, a creditor is attempting to secure repayment of a debt.
    (b) In a conditional sale contract, the conditional seller keeps the title until the conditional buyer makes all his payments.
    (c) In both the conditional sale situation and the chattel mortgage situation, the creditor has title but the buyer has possession of the asset held as security.
    (d) The assignment of debts cannot be given as security for a debt because it is an intangible property.
    (e) A pledge can be security for a debt but the borrower transfers possession of an item to the lender (but not the title).

17. Which of the following statements is false, concerning the remedies available in the event that the debtor does not pay the secured creditor:
    (a) If the creditor repossesses the collateral, sells it and the proceeds do not cover the debt, the debtor may still be required to pay the balance.
    (b) If there is no objection within a specified time period of notice, the creditor may take the collateral in full satisfaction.
    (c) Where the collateral has been seized and sold and there are surplus proceeds after all debts have been retired, the debtor is entitled to that surplus.
    (d) Normally if the creditor seizes the collateral, he must give other interested parties a specific period of notice before sale.
    (e) In the event of default, the creditor must give the debtor and other interested parties a specified period of notice before seizing the security.

18. James, a recent business graduate, has a consulting business with a good record of monthly billings of about $4 000 per month. He rents his office and furniture and has very little in the way of physical assets. James rents an apartment, has no car and spends most of his income on travel. If he were to come to you, a bank manager, and ask for a loan of $15 000 for the purpose of increasing his working capital, which of the following securities would you most likely request?
    (a) conditional sale contract
    (b) chattel mortgage
    (c) Section 178 security under the *Bank Act*
    (d) assignment of accounts receivable
    (e) mechanic's lien

19. Which of the following rights available to the secured creditor upon default are not included under the *Personal Property Security Act*?
    (a) Legislation provides means to enforce rights to collateral property
    (b) Secured party can retake possession of good
    (c) May retain goods in satisfaction of amount owed
    (d) Sell them after giving appropriate notice to debtor
    (e) Instead of repossession, sue for the entire amount owing

20. Rules governing fraudulent preferences and transfers are designed to protect

    _____.

21. Although the contract creating a conditional sale or a chattel mortgage may give the secured party all sorts of rights in the event that the debtor defaults, the relevant statutes provide a number of restrictions on such default rights. Which one of the following is not such a restriction?
    (a) While the creditor may seize the goods if he is not paid, he or she may only do so with a court order.
    (b) Where the debtor has willfully, recklessly or negligently allowed the goods to deteriorate to the extent that the security is materially impaired, the creditor may be able to both seize and sue for the deficiency if the resale value of the goods is less than the balance of the debt.
    (c) Even though the contract creating the debt may contain an acceleration clause that makes the entire balance due and owing upon default of the debtor, the creditor will have to wait a period of time before he or she can claim the entire amount.
    (d) A private person who becomes a debtor in these transactions is prohibited from waiving the "seize or sue" restriction even if he could get a better deal from the creditor by doing so.
    (e) Even though the debtor may have lost the right to redeem the goods because he or she has failed to pay his debt within 20 days after seizure, the debtor is still entitled to any surplus value of the goods beyond the balance of the debt and the creditor's cost of repossession.

22. Banks can still use mortgages and assignment of debt to secure transactions under the *Bank Act*.
    (a) True
    (b) False

23. Which one of the following cannot be used as security?
    (a) debentures (used by corporations to acknowledge debt)
    (b) floating charges (secures debenture against general property of the corporation)
    (c) bulk sales (merchant sells most of business inventory not in the ordinary course of business)
    (d) chattel mortgage (debtor puts up goods to secure loan)
    (e) assignment of book accounts (merchants conditionally assigns accounts receivable)

24. A conditional seller can seize chattels from a defaulting conditional buyer, sell the goods and sue the conditional buyer for any deficiency.
    (a) True
    (b) False

25. What is the difference between a guarantee and an indemnity?

    _____

    _____

    _____

26. Which of the following statements is not true with respect to guarantees?
    (a) The creditor can turn to a third party the guarantor, to be paid.
    (b) It is a secondary obligation that arises only in the event of a default.
    (c) Must give guarantor fair return for guarantee
    (d) Must be evidenced in writing.
    (e) Must meet all the requirements of a contract.

27. Repossession and resale is the principal remedy for default in a secured transaction.
    (a) True
    (b) False

28. What requirement must a secured creditor fulfill before he can resell seized security assets?

    _____

    _____

29. The creditor has significant duties toward a guarantor excluding which of the following?
    (a) Ensure that the guarantor understands the nature of the agreement
    (b) Encouraging guarantor to get independent legal advice
    (c) To do nothing to weaken the position of the guarantor
    (d) To sue the debtor first before seeking payment from guarantor?
    (e) Not to change significant terms of the agreement

30. A guarantor assumes the rights of a creditor if he has to pay.
    (a) True
    (b) False

31. Which of the following statements about the position of a guarantor is not true?
    (a) A guarantor is a primary debtor along with the debtor.
    (b) The guarantor must consent to any changes in the agreement between the debtor and creditor.
    (c) Upon default and payment by the guarantor, he becomes creditor.
    (d) Upon default and payment by guarantor, he has the right to claim any other security.
    (e) He can use any defenses against creditor that the debtor had except infancy.

32. Builders' liens create security for the supplier of goods and services against the property for which they have been supplied.
    (a) True
    (b) False

33. What is the purpose and effect of the *Builders/Construction Lien Act*?
    (a) It guarantees that the sub-trades are paid all that they are owed.
    (b) It protects the homeowner against poor workmanship and defects.
    (c) It over comes the privity of contract problem between sub-trades and homeowner.
    (d) It protects the contractor from action by homeowner.
    (e) It protects the sub-trades from action by homeowner.

34. To whom are builders' construction liens available?

    _____

    _____

35. What is the obligation placed by the *Builders/Construction Lien Act* on the owner of real property for work done or materials supplied that were incorporated into his land?

    _____

    _____

36. Failure to register a builders' lien within the time specified in the legislation will invalidate the lien.
    (a) True
    (b) False

37. What is the result of the owner's failure to comply with this legal requirement?

    _____

    _____

38. Legislation and the regulations associated with them stipulate the nature and process of registering liens.
    (a) True
    (b) False

39. Which of the following is a definition for a holdback?
    (a) The sum the contractor is obligated to pay his/her employees.
    (b) A portion of the contract fee that an owner must holdback to satisfy potential liens
    (c) The amount a supplier charges to compensate for the possibility of not getting paid.
    (d) The unpaid contracted amount owed to the contractor
    (e) The unpaid portion of the amount earned by the subcontractor or supplier

40. A holdback is the limit of the liability for the owner without notice of claims.
    (a) True
    (b) False

41. If a lien claimant files a lien on time, which of the following is false?
    (a) The claimant can be assured of payment in full.
    (b) The claimant will have the lien registered as a charge against the owner's property.
    (c) The claimant will have the right to commence an action within one year to prove his lien.
    (d) The claimant would still have his contractual right to sue.
    (e) The claimant would still have the right to sue on the trust provisions in the *Builders' Lien Act.*

42. An owner may pay a disputed amount to the court in order to free him/herself of a builders' lien.
    (a) True
    (b) False

43. R & S Electric Supplies Limited sold machinery and tools to Ed, an electrical contractor, who used them to help install wiring in an apartment under construction. Suspicious of Ed's ability to pay, R & S registered a lien against the property on which the apartment building was being built. Ed failed to pay and R & S took an action to enforce the lien. Will R & S succeed in its claim? Explain.

_____

_____

44. When you first stopped by the bank to inquire about a loan, the loans officer was busy, but you heard him asking another interested party, "What will you give me as security?" You left to think about that. Which of the following is false with regard to secured transactions?
    (a) The bank could take a debenture from a company as security.
    (b) The bank could take a car or other tangible personal property as security.
    (c) The bank could take an assignment of accounts receivable even though no tangible property is involved.
    (d) The bank could not take future crops.
    (e) The bank could take a guaranty.

45. The *Bills of Exchange Act* is a federal statute.
    (a) True
    (b) False

46. A cheque is a bill of exchange drawn on a bank and payable on demand.
    (a) True
    (b) False

47. Three types of negotiable instruments are:
    (a) bills of exchange, promissory notes and debit cards
    (b) cheques, credit cards and promissory notes
    (c) debit cards, cheques and bills of exchange
    (d) bills of exchange, promissory notes and cheques
    (e) credit cards, cheques and bills of exchange

48. A bank has an obligation to the payee to honour a cheque when the drawer has sufficient funds to cover it.
    (a) True
    (b) False

49. A cheque is an order instrument made payable to a specific person.
    (a) True
    (b) False

50. A certified cheque does not have the same validity as an accepted bill of exchange.
    (a) True
    (b) False

51. Which of the following describes promissory notes:
    (a) Promises to pay the amount stated
    (b) Promises to pay at some future time
    (c) Can be used for granting credit

(d) May bear interest and be paid by installment

(e) All of the above

52. How must a cheque (a negotiable instrument) drawn by Bob, payable to Gail and signed only on the back of the cheque by Gail be negotiated? _____

53. Johal did work for Dadwal who agreed to pay him in advance by cheque. Dadwal prepared a cheque for Johal. In which of the following situations would Dadwal have to honour the cheque to Gill after it had been transferred to her by Johal?

(a) Where Gill was Johal's girlfriend and had been given the note as a gift. Johal had not yet started the job.

(b) Where Gill knew that Johal had taken the completed cheque from Dadwal's desk while Dadwal was out to lunch

(c) Where Gill and Johal had worked together in a scheme to cheat Dadwal

(d) Where Gill, operating a finance company and not knowing Johal but recognizing Dadwal's signature and knowing his good reputation, gave Johal $400 for the $500 cheque.

(e) Where Johal had changed the $500 to read $5000 by adding a zero and rubbing out the word hundred and writing thousand over it. The alteration was clearly visible on the cheque.

54. A bearer instrument is negotiated by just delivering it to the holder.

(a) True

(b) False

55. What are the six requirements of negotiability?

(1) _____

(2) _____

(3) _____

(4) _____

(5) _____

(6) _____

56. Which of the following is not a way to negotiate a negotiable instrument?

(a) By merely delivering to a third party a bearer instrument (i.e., one made payable to bearer)

(b) By endorsing an order instrument (e.g., one made payable to you and by delivering it to the third person)

(c) By signing a bill of exchange as an "acceptor"

(d) By endorsing a bearer instrument and delivering it to a third party

(e) Through certification by a bank

57. What are the primary advantages of being a holder in due course?

_____

_____

58. A holder in due course must meet which of the following requirements.
    (a) Receive instrument through negotiation
    (b) Must have been acquired before it was due and payable
    (c) Must have no knowledge of any defect
    (d) Must acquire instrument in good faith
    (e) All of the above

59. Which of the following is false with regard to a "holder in due course"?
    (a) A holder in due course is always a remote holder in the sense that he is never an immediate party.
    (b) A holder in due course is in a better position to be paid by the drawer or maker of the instrument than is an immediate holder because there are fewer defenses against his claim for payment.
    (c) A person cannot be a holder in due course if he or she knew the instrument had been obtained by the payee by fraud.
    (d) A person cannot be a holder in due course if he/she acquired the instrument in bad faith (e.g., he tricked the person into giving him the cheque).
    (e) A holder in due course is the same as the "acceptor."

60. Endorsers are liable if the instrument is refused by drawer.
    (a) True
    (b) False

61. The holder in due course of a note stamped "Consumer Purchase" does not get the same rights as a normal holder in due course
    (a) True
    (b) False

62. Identify the two main purposes of the *Bankruptcy Act*.

    (1) _____

    (2) _____

63. What are the two procedures provided for in the act for becoming bankrupt?

    (1) _____

    (2) _____

64. When a debtor voluntarily puts his/her property in the hands of a trustee in bankruptcy, it is referred to as:
    (a) receiving order
    (b) an act of bankruptcy
    (c) assignment
    (d) insolvency claim
    (e) fraudulent transfer

65. Which of the following would not be considered an act of bankruptcy?
    (a) Voluntary assignment of assets to a trustee in bankruptcy
    (b) Fraudulent transfers of money or assets
    (c) Preference given to one creditor over another
    (d) Leaving the jurisdiction
    (e) Having more debts than assets

66. Creditors may reject a debtor's restructuring proposal and force him/her into bankruptcy.
    (a) True
    (b) False

67. The consumer proposal provides protection against unsecured creditors.
    (a) True
    (b) False

68. A person who knows that he/she is going into bankruptcy can transfer assets to family members to avoid them becoming distributed to creditors.
    (a) True
    (b) False

69. For eight months, Mr. Lean has been unable to meet his financial obligations as they came due. He is now $7 000 in debt to the people and companies that have supplied goods for his hardware business. His creditors could successfully take which three of the following actions?
    (a) Sue him for breach of contract.
    (b) Place him in bankruptcy.
    (c) Obtain judgment and garnishee funds owed to Lean by others.
    (d) Put a builder's lien on his property.
    (e) Sue him on the trust provisions of the *Builders' Lien Act*.
    (f) Picket his store.

70. Mr. Redd bought a new car from Clyde's Cars under a conditional sale agreement, paying $1000 down with the remainder of $12 000 to be paid in instalments over the next four years. Clyde registered this agreement, but in the process put down the wrong serial number for the car. Clyde sold the agreement to Brown' Finance Company. Redd, with the approval of Clyde but without the knowledge of Brown,

resold the car to Green for $12 000 but chose to continue paying his debt to Clyde in monthly installments which went to Brown's Finance Co. after he was served notice that he was to pay them. The car proved to be defective and Green refused to pay Redd. Redd in turn refused to pay Brown. Brown found out that Green had the car and repossessed it, immediately reselling it to a friend of the family for $4 000. There was now a deficit of $7 000, since $2 000 had been paid off by Redd.

Green sued both Brown's Finance Company and Redd. Redd in turn sued Clyde. Brown's Finance Company sued Redd. As part of the original deal between Redd and Clyde, Clyde had insisted that in addition to the conditional sale agreement, Redd provide a guarantor to the loan so Redd had his friend Black guarantee the loan. The car had been resold to Green without the permission of Black. Clyde sued Black and Black in turn sued Redd. Explain the rights and obligations of all the parties.

Answers to Review Questions

1. A secured creditor is one who has priority over other general creditors. Usually this priority is attached to a specific item or good.

    P. 303   D.1

2. b   P. 303   D.1

3. Personal property security (chattel mortgage or a conditional sale)

    P. 303   D.1

4. (1) chattel mortgage

    (2) conditional sale

    (3) pledge

    (4) assignment of book accounts

    P. 304-5 D.1

5. a   P. 306   D.1

6. a   P. 304   D.1

7. b   P. 308   D.1

8. b   P. 305   D.1

9. c   P. 308   D.2

10. a   P. 311   D.2

11. e   P. 303   D.1

12. It has no effect between the original parties. It only affects the rights of an outsider or third party who eventually acquires possession.

    P. 306   D.2

13. There is one statute and one process for all forms of personal property security.

    P. 306-7 D.1

14. d   P. 308,
        311   D.2

15. e   P. 308   D.2

16. d   P. 303-4 D.2

17. e   P. 311-2 D.2

18. d   P. 305   D.2

19. e   P. 311   D.2

20. the creditors

    P. 314-5 D.1

21. a (will vary provincially)

    P. 311   D.2

22. a   P. 313   D.1

23. c   P. 304,
         314   D.2

24. a (watch for provincial variations)

    P. 311   D.1

25. A guarantee is a contingent liability, i.e. the guarantor only has an obligation to pay if the debtor fails to pay. An indemnity is a commitment to assume the primary obligation along with the debtor so that an indemnifier can be required to pay whenever payment is demanded from the debtor.

    P. 315   D. 2

26. c   P. 316   D.1

27. a   P. 311   D.1

28. He must hold the goods for a specific period of time to allow the purchaser to repay the amount owed. Then he can sell the goods in adherence to the legislation (e.g., auction if required).

    P. 311   D.2

29. d   P. 316   D.2

30. a   P. 318   D.1

31. a   P. 315   D.2

32. a   P. 318-9 D.1

33. c   P. 319   D.2

34. Suppliers of goods and services including contractors, sub-contractors, wage earners, suppliers of material and in some provinces equipment used on the project.

    P. 319   D.1

35. The owner of the property must hold back a certain amount of funds from the contract with the general contractor so that it will be available to pay the lien claimants if they are unable to collect from the contractor. If the owner fails to comply, he can be required to pay the amount of the holdback to the lien claimants even if he hasn't withheld the funds.

    P. 319   D.2

36. a   P. 319   D.1

37. The owner of the property must hold back a certain amount of funds from the contract with the general contractor so that it will be available to pay the lien claimants if they are unable to collect from the contractor. If the owner fails to comply, he can be required to pay the amount of the holdback to the lien claimants even if he hasn't withheld the funds.

       P. 319   D.2

38. a   P. 319   D.1

39. b   P. 319   D.2

40. a   P. 319   D.1

41. a (watch for provincial variations)

       P. 319   D.1

42. a   P. 319   D.1

43. This can vary from one jurisdiction to another but it is unlikely that R & S will succeed because the materials supplied weren't incorporated into the property.

       P. 318-9   D.2

44. d   P. 313-5   D.2

45. a   P. 322   D.1

46. a (by delivery alone)

       P. 325   D.1

47. a   P. 324   D.1

48. b   P. 325   D.1

49. a   P. 325   D.1

50. b   P. 325-6   D.1

51. e   P. 326   D.2

52. as a bearer instrument

       P. 328   D.1

53. d   P. 322-3   D.2

54. a   P. 328   D.1

55. (1) must be unconditional

(2) must be in writing and signed

(3) must be payable at some fixed time or on demand

(4) must be made out for a fixed amount of money

(5) must have been delivered to the payee for the first time

(6) whole instrument must pass

       P. 327   D.2

56. c   P. 328   D.2

57. The holder in due course actually acquires better rights on the instrument than the person he obtained it from. Only real defenses can be used against him by the maker or drawer of the instrument.

       P. 322   D.2

58. e   P. 322-3   D.2

59. e   P. 322-3   D.2

60. a   P. 328   D.1

61. a   P. 327   D.1

62. (1) To protect the creditors by insuring that they get as much as possible.

(2) To rehabilitate the debtor and allow them to start over again free of debts and incumbrances.

       P. 330   D.1

63. Voluntary bankruptcy by making an assignment. Involuntarily by a creditor getting a receiving order.

       P. 330   D.2

64. c   P. 330   D.2

65. e   P. 330   D.2

66. a   P. 331   D.1

67. a   P. 331   D.1

68. b   P. 332   D.1

69. a, b, c   P. 329-30   D.2

70. In this case it must be remembered that the car was defective (assume this is a breach of the original contract of sale) and that the registration of the original secured transaction was incorrect (wrong serial number). Brown is an assignee of Clyde's rights and is in no better position than Clyde. Since the registration was incorrect, Clyde had no right to repossess the car and neither would Brown. Green then will be successful in an action against Brown (or the family friend) to get the car back. But Green wants more than this. He wants

compensation for the defects in the car. Green therefore sues Redd and, assuming that the defect is a breach of the contract of sale, he will be successful in getting damages against Redd. Redd then sues Clyde for what those defects cost him and again assuming the defects were in breach of the sale agreement between Redd and Clyde, Redd will be successful against Clyde in recovering what he has had to pay to Green plus his costs. Brown in turn sued Redd, but Redd has a good defense. Since the car was defective he would have a good defense against the person who sold it to him—Clyde. And since Clyde has assigned

his rights to Brown, Brown can be in no better position than Clyde was. Any defense that Redd could raise against Clyde, he can raise against Brown. The position of the guarantor (Black) is also interesting. Clyde (the creditor) has an obligation to protect Black's position and in two ways he has failed to do this. Clyde allowed the car to be sold, thus taking away an important security that would have been available to Black if he paid off the debt, and he registered the wrong serial number. Because of these factors, Clyde and Brown would not be able to seek any kind of recourse against Black the guarantor.

Chapter 11

Employment

Learning Objectives

At the end of this chapter you should be able to:

1. Distinguish between relationships of employment, independent contractors and agency.
2. Summarize the rights of employees upon termination.
3. Explain legislative provisions that protect employee health and welfare.
4. Describe how the rights and obligations of the parties in an employment relationship can be modified through collective bargaining.
5. State under what circumstances employers will be liable for the acts of their employees.
6. Explain how legislation limits and modifies the use of strikes and lockouts.

Key Terms

The following terms are highlighted in the text:

control test	defines employment in terms of authority and service
organization test	whether or not service-provider is part of employee's organization
employee	a person working for another who is told what to do and how to do it
independent contractor	a person working for himself who contracts to provide specific services to another
agent	a person entering contracts on behalf of a principal
pay in lieu of notice	an amount paid to a dismissed employee rather than notice to terminate
reasonable notice	must be calculated in terms of position and time served
just cause	valid reason to dismiss an employee without notice
constructive dismissal	demoting an employee may be the same as dismissal
wrongful dismissal	dismissal without reasonable cause or notice
recognition disputes	disputes arising between unions and employers while union is being organized

interest dispute	disagreement about the terms to be included in a new collective agreement
rights dispute	disagreement about the meaning of a term in the current collective agreement
jurisdictional dispute	dispute as to which union has the right to represent a group of employees
bargaining agent	a bodied certified to act on behalf of a group of employees
bargaining unit	group of employees who have been certified
employer organizations	bargaining agents representing groups of employers
ratification	majority agrees with terms of collective bargain
union shop	new employees must join the union
closed shop	only workers who are already members of the union can be hired
check-off provision	employees agree to have employer deduct dues
lockout	employer prevents employees from working
strike	employees withdraw services
work to rule	employees perform no more than is minimally required
picketing	job action during a legal strike when employees circulate at the periphery of the jobsite to persuade others not to do business with struck employer

Chapter Outline

Notes

Tests for Employment

(1) *Control* - degree of control exercised by the person paying for the service. Employer controls employee; independent contractor works for himself
(2) *Organization* - a person is an employee when considered part of the "organization" of the employer
An employee can also be an agent (a person who enters into legal relationships with others on behalf of a principal)

Master/Servant Relationships

Employer must provide wages, safe workplace, compensation for reasonable expenses
Employee must be competent and careful, follow instructions, be honest, and punctual

Contract law applies - restrictive covenants must be reasonable - breach may give rise to compensation for injured party or injunction]

Termination - reasonable notice required of both employer and employee except for just-cause dismissal or where employee required to work in unreasonably dangerous or illegal situations

Vicarious Liability- an employer can be held liable for the tort of an employee performed during course of employment

Legislation

Designed to protect employees by setting standards for minimum wages, hours of work, termination, child labour, discrimination, and regulating such things as workers' compensation, health and safety, and employment insurance.

Human rights legislation prohibit most forms of discrimination, and workplace harassment and allow for gender based pay equity.

Collective Bargaining

Unions and collective bargaining resisted in England and United States until the passage of the U.S. *Wagner Act*, which formed basis of Canadian labour legislation and the *Canada Labour Code*

Provincial legislation covers areas of provincial jurisdiction

Types of Disputes

(1) **Recognition dispute** - a disagreement between the union and employer related to the process by which a union attempts to become certified

(2) **Jurisdictional dispute** - conflict between unions as to which one should be the bargaining agent for a particular employee

(3) **Interest dispute** - concerns the terms that ought to be in the collective agreement

(4) **Rights dispute** - concerns the interpretation of terms in a current agreement

Organization of employees - a group of employees (representing a majority of the work force) wanting to be unionized must apply to labour relations board for certification

Bargaining agent - must be only one for a given unit of employees

Rules of conduct govern organization and recognition of labour unions

Legislation governs unfair labour practices (e.g. threats or coercion by either party)

Bargaining

Once a union has been certified either party can give notice to commence negotiations. Must bargain in good faith. The object of the bargaining process is the collective agreement. The agreement must be ratified by both employer and employees

Conciliation - third party intervention to assist parties in reaching an agreement

Arbitration - collective agreement must be for at least one year, must set out a method for resolving disputes (e.g. binding arbitration - a substitute for court action)

There can be no strikes when contract is in force

Contract can provide that all new employees join the union

Strikes and Lockouts

Job action occurring when agreement has expired and parties cannot agree to terms to be included in a new agreement (legal only during an interest dispute). Parties must bargain in good faith before taking job action

Strike - the withdrawal of services by employees.

Lockout - action taken by employer to prevent employees from working

Picketing - strikers standing near or marching around a place of business trying to persuade people to refrain from doing business there.

Severely restricted - permissible only when lawful strike or lockout is in progress, must be peaceful and involve merely the communication of accurate information

Number of picketers or location may be limited by the court

Tradition of union solidarity makes picketing effective

Secondary picketing - extended to businesses with which employer has business dealings or to other locations where employer does business (permitted in some provinces)

Customers have no legal obligation to honour picket lines

Right to job action controlled for public sector employees

Structure of Unions

Democratic organizations with elected officers

Subject to human rights legislation

Regulated by labour relations boards

Review Questions

1. The control test for employment attempts to determine how much control the employee has over working conditions.
   (a) True
   (b) False

2. Which of the following describes the control test in employment relationships?
   (a) The degree of control the employee has over his work environment
   (b) The control exercised by the employer in determining when the job will be done (the work schedule)
   (c) The amount of skill the person brings to the job
   (d) How the person is paid
   (e) Whether the employer is paying taxes for the employee

3. The organization test is based on the involvement of the employee in the employer's organization.
   (a) True
   (b) False

4. Which of the following questions would not be asked when applying the organization test?
   (a) Is the person doing the work on a salary?
   (b) Is person an essential part of employer's organization?
   (c) Has the person been given a set date for termination?
   (d) Does the person have a responsibility to the organization?
   (e) Could the organization continue to exist with the services of this person?

5. Which of the following does not describe the agent/principal relationship?
   (a) An agent enters into legal relationships with others on behalf of a principal.
   (b) An agent may be an employee or an independent contractor.
   (c) An agent owes a fiduciary duty to the principal.
   (d) An agent cannot profit from knowledge gained in the service of a principal.
   (e) An agent must reveal the identity of his principal.

6. Liability can be determined by nature of the employment relationship.
   (a) True
   (b) False

7. General provisions of contract law apply to employment relationships.
   (a) True
   (b) False

8. Contractual provisions may exceed the standards set in employment statutes.
   (a) True
   (b) False

9. What are the primary responsibilities of an employer?

   _____

10. What are the primary responsibilities of an employee?

   _____

11. Robson agreed to hire Jeff for a six-month period, but the other terms of the contract were not so easily agreed upon. In fact, they had four meetings about the terms before they reached an agreement. A day later, when Jeff received the contract for his signature, he noticed that it did not provide for some of the things he felt they had agreed upon, namely that he would have access to their laser printer on the weekends for his own use, and secondly, a non-disclosure clause (i.e., a clause prohibiting him from telling trade secrets). It did include other matters discussed: a non-competition clause; ownership clause; termination clauses; non-waiver clause; whole-contract clause, and a severance clause. Despite the surprises, he signed it and returned it to Robson's offices. Which of the following is true?
    (a) Because the contract has a clause stating that the written document is the "whole contract," Jeff would have a difficult and maybe impossible task in proving he is entitled to use the printer on the weekends.
    (b) Because the contract omitted a non-disclosure clause Jeff has no obligations to keep confidential the firm's trade secrets.
    (c) No matter how unreasonable the terms of the non-competition clause might be, Jeff will be bound to them because he signed the contract.
    (d) Despite the provisions in the contract about terminating the contract, Jeff is entitled to "reasonable" notice.
    (e) None of the above

12. Which of the following is an employer not required to provide under the employment statutes?
    (a) Safe working conditions
    (b) A workplace free of harassment and discrimination
    (c) Maternity pay
    (d) A minimum wage
    (e) Termination notice

13. Reasonable notice of termination is required of both employer and employee.
    (a) True
    (b) False

14. If there are no provisions in the employment contract concerning termination of employment, which of the following is an example of wrongful dismissal according to the common law rules?
    (a) Employee Smith is dismissed for incompetence and is given no notice or pay in lieu of notice.
    (b) Employee Smith is dismissed because the employer doesn't like his personality and is given reasonable notice.
    (c) Employee Smith is dismissed because of an economic slump in that industry and is given neither notice nor pay in lieu of notice.
    (d) Employee Smith is dismissed because he continually disobeys reasonable instructions.
    (e) Employee Smith is dismissed with reasonable notice because the boss wants to replace him with his son.

15. When an employer decides to dismiss an employee, how much notice is required at common law?

    _____

16. List three situations where an employer can dismiss an employee without any notice.

    (1) _____

    (2) _____

    (3) _____

17. Two computer students were talking about their experiences last week. Both were offered jobs. Len was told that "we really need some help in here to get this business in order. How about coming to work here on Monday June 3? We'll put you on the payroll and pay you $3,000 a month to start out." Len agreed. The other student, Joe, was given a three-page employment contract that included a non-competition clause ownership clause, whole-contract clause, non-waiver clause, severance clause and a termination clause. Joe noticed it did not contain a non-disclosure clause nor did it contain their promise to pay him $2,000 for moving expenses. Joe hasn't yet signed the contract. Which of the following is false with regard to these contracts?
    (a) Although it wasn't mentioned, Len owes his employer reasonable notice if he ever wants to leave that job.
    (b) Although it wasn't mentioned, both owe their employers competence, honesty, obedience and punctuality if they accept the offers.
    (c) If Joe signs the contract as it is, with the whole-contract clause (the written agreement contains the whole contract), he would have a difficult and maybe impossible task in proving he is entitled to money for moving expenses.
    (d) No matter how unreasonable the terms of the non-competition clause, if Joe signs the contract he will be bound by it.
    (e) Although the written contract omitted a non-disclosure clause, if Joe signs, he still has an obligation to keep confidential what the firm has indicated are its trade secrets.

18. Employer is required to give reasonable notice or pay in lieu of notice of termination.
    (a) True
    (b) False

19. Where there is no contract or collective agreement, an employer may dismiss an employee for any reason unless it violates human rights legislation.
    (a) True
    (b) False

20. Mr. Wood owned a small manufacturing company that specialized in building kitchen cabinets. He employed 7 workers. They were not unionized. His supervisor, Tom Loyal, had worked for him for 14 years on a monthly salary. Because of an economic slowdown in the building industry and because of his age (he was now 52), it would be difficult for Loyal to find work. Nevertheless, Wood dismissed Loyal because could no do longer do the work due to a recurring and prolonged illness. Under the rules developed in the common law, Mr. Wood owes Loyal:
    (a) Reasonable notice or pay in lieu of notice
    (b) No notice if there is no other job he could do
    (c) Six months notice or pay in lieu of notice
    (d) Nine months notice or pay in lieu of notice
    (e) A disabled employee cannot be dismissed

21. Legislation sets minimum standard for the length of notice required.
    (a) True
    (b) False

22. If an employer in a non-unionized business dismisses an employee without just cause, which of the following is false?
    (a) The amount of notice to be given the employee is "reasonable notice."
    (b) The amount of notice could be set out in the employment contract and that amount would override the amount set by the common law unless it was less than the minimum amount set out in the Employment Standards Act.
    (c) No notice need be given at all if the employer pays the employee an amount of money equivalent to the amount of money the employee would have earned during the notice periods (i.e., money in lieu of notice).
    (d) If the employee sues for wrongful dismissal, he/she will win even if the owner has evidence of "just cause" at trial time, because on the date of firing the owner did not have just cause.
    (e) The Employment Standards Act sets a minimum notice that must be given unless there is just cause.

23. Tom worked for The Huge Company as chief personnel officer, a non-union position. He had worked for this company for eight years. Gregory, the vice president, in the process of reorganizing the company, demoted Tom to a non-

supervisory position. Tom refused to take on the new assignment. The company responded by terminating his employment, "effective immediately." Tom sued for wrongful dismissal.

(a) The company would win the wrongful dismissal case because they did not dismiss Tom; he, in fact, disobeyed by not taking the new assignment.

(b) The company would win the wrongful dismissal case because an employer can always dismiss an employee who is not protected by a collective agreement.

(c) Tom would win the wrongful dismissal case because demotion is a type of dismissal, and he did not receive notice or pay in lieu of notice

(d) Tom would win because he cannot be dismissed without cause, no matter how much notice is given.

(e) The company would win because his failure to take the new position amounts to just cause for dismissal.

24. Just cause dismissal requires no notice.
(a) True
(b) False

25. Paul had worked for Canadian Cash Register for nine years as a programmer when the company suffered a serious financial setback. It faced reduced sales and was being sued by customers who found that the machines bought from the company could not handle credit cards with a year 2000 expiration date. The owner of the company told Paul it could no longer afford so many programmers and, as a university graduate with some accounting background, he would be moved into bookkeeping and two bookkeepers would be laid off. He also told Paul his wage would be cut by 25%. When Paul came to work the next day, he told the owner that he wouldn't accept the bookkeeping job. The owner became very angry and said, "If you don't like it, then leave right now! I don't have to put up with your insubordination one minute!" Paul left and then sued the owner for unlawful dismissal. The owner argued that he had "just cause" because of financial problems and disobedience. Based on the above facts, identify the false statement.

(a) Financial problems are not just cause for dismissal.

(b) The owner could fire Paul without notice or pay in lieu of notice because Paul refused his order to do the bookkeeping.

(c) Paul would win the unlawful dismissal action because the owner "dismissed" him by unilaterally changing Paul's job without Paul's consent.

(d) The owner can dismiss Paul for any reason not contrary to the human rights legislation, as long as he gives proper notice or pay in lieu of notice.

(e) If Paul were wrongfully dismissed, he would still have to mitigate his losses and there is case law that may include his taking the bookkeeping job as long as it is not demeaning to do so.

26. An employee discharged without adequate notice can sue for wrongful dismissal.
(a) True
(b) False

27. State the principle of vicarious liability as it applies to the employer/employee relationship.

_____

28. An employee can leave without notice when required to work in dangerous conditions or work involves immoral or illegal activities.
    (a) True
    (b) False

29. Joan worked as an employee for Royal Greeting Cards for ten years and had worked her way up to the position of a designer at a salary of $2 000 per month. Joan's job was to design Christmas cards and one day her boss informed her that the company was going to devote all its efforts to producing and marketing a special form of friendship card, and that they would discontinue their line of Christmas cards. Joan was informed that if she wanted to stay with the company she would have to take a job in the production department pasting up other artists' designs in preparation for silk screening. This job would be at the same rate of pay she had been getting as a designer. Over the years Joan had acquired quite a reputation as a designer in the industry and she informed her boss that she was not interested in doing anything else but design work. She was then told that she would be paid until the end of the month but would not have a job after that time.

   A term of Joan's employment contract prohibited her from working for any other greeting card manufacturer anywhere for a period of five years after leaving the employment of Royal. Joan ignored this provision and immediately went to work for one of Royal's competitors, Cheery Cards. Joan sued for wrongful dismissal. As Royal prepared its case, it was discovered that during the last three years of her employment, Joan had been moonlighting (working part-time) and using her design skills with another company that produced Christmas novelties. After due inspection, it became clear that many of the products sold by that company bore a startling resemblance to the designs Joan had produced for Royal. Royal in turn sued Joan. Explain the legal positions and legal obligations of each of the parties.

_____

_____

_____

30. Which of the following is not protected under statutes designed to protect employees by setting minimum standards for
    (a) advancement
    (b) wages
    (c) hours of work
    (d) child labour
    (e) termination

31. What are the main concerns of employee legislation?

    _____

32. Which of the following are provided for in the *Employment Standards Act*?
    (a) Licensing of farm-labour contractors
    (b) Minimum notice for dismissal without cause
    (c) Strike notice
    (d) Employment agency registration
    (e) Employment insurance

33. Which of the following does the human rights tribunals not have the power to do?
    (a) hear complaints
    (b) investigate
    (c) levy fines
    (d) order compensation to be paid to the victim
    (e) impose jail terms

34. In addition to the common law rules governing employment, our legislators have passed laws to improve the position of employees. Which of the following is false with regard to this legislation?
    (a) Employment Standards Acts set out some minimum standards with regard to such matters as wages, hours of work, termination, etc.
    (b) The Workers' Compensation Act requires businesses covered by the act to contribute to a fund that is used to pay for job-related injury.
    (c) When a worker is injured on the job and would have a claim under the Workers' Compensation Act, he has the option of claiming under the act or directly suing the person at fault.
    (d) Businesses covered by the Workers' Compensation Act are assessed on the basis of the risks associated with that industry.
    (e) Employment insurance is regulated by a federal statute.

35. Workers' Compensation is a type of insurance policy.
    (a) True
    (b) False

36. Employees give up their right to sue the employer and fellow employees when they are covered by workers' compensation plans.
    (a) True
    (b) False

37. Employment insurance is a plan designed to:
    (a) Compensate seasonal workers
    (b) Employers and workers pay into a fund
    (c) Provide benefits to qualified unemployed

(d) Decisions may be appealed to Board

(e) All of the above

38. Labour relations legislation in Canada is modeled after the legislation passed in Great Britain.

(a) True

(b) False

39. The *Wagner Act* is:

(a) The inspiration for Canadian legislation

(b) Federal legislation

(c) Canadian Labour Relations Code

(d) Act from Great Britain adopted in Canada

(e) Federal health and safety legislation

40. Which of the following is not covered under labour relations statutes?

(a) recognition disputes

(b) interest dispute

(c) conduct dispute

(d) rights dispute

(e) jurisdictional dispute

41. A difference in opinion between an employer and a union over the interpretation of terms in their existing contract is called:

(a) an interest dispute

(b) a rights dispute

(c) certification

(d) a jurisdictional dispute

(e) a conciliation procedure

42. The only kind of disagreement between union and employer that can lead to a lawful strike is called

(a) an interest dispute

(b) a rights dispute

(c) certification

(d) a jurisdictional dispute

(e) a conciliation procedure

43. Which of the following is an "interest dispute?"

(a) A disagreement over the meaning or interpretation of a provision that has been included in a collective agreement

(b) A dispute between the union and the employer as to what terms should be included in a collective agreement

(c) A dispute between two unions as to which union should represent a particular group of employees

(d) A dispute as to whether the union ought be certified or not

(e) A dispute concerning the desertification of a union

44. Eastside Nurseries, an old established family business, has 12 workers who have decided to unionize. Enough of the workers have joined the union to allow it to be certified as the collective bargaining agent for that bargaining unit. The owner of the business refuses to deal with the bargaining agent and insists on dealing personally with each worker as to the terms of his contract of employment. This dispute is known as which of the following?
    (a) a jurisdictional dispute
    (b) a recognition dispute
    (c) an interest dispute
    (d) a rights dispute
    (e) a conduct dispute

45. What procedures can be used to resolve the dispute in question 44?

   _____

   _____

46. In which of the following disputes do the workers have the right to strike?
    (a) A dispute between the workers and the management because management will not recognize the union as the bargaining agent
    (b) A disagreement over the meaning or interpretation of a provision that has been included in a collective agreement
    (c) A dispute between the union and the employer as to what terms should be included in a new collective agreement
    (d) A dispute between two unions as to which union should represent a particular group of employees
    (e) A dispute where the employees are the victims of discrimination and the employer refuses to do anything about it

47. Labour relations is primarily a federal jurisdiction.
    (a) True
    (b) False

48. Outline the process by which a group of employees organizes to form a union.

   _____

   _____

49. What is the objective of the bargaining process between the union and the employer?

   _____

50. Which of the following is not considered an unfair labour practice during the certification process?
    (a) coercion
    (b) conciliation
    (c) intimidation
    (d) threat of dismissal
    (e) failure to bargain in good faith.

51. When an employer engages in unfair labour practices, that alone may provide for automatic certification of a union.
    (a) True
    (b) False

52. Which of the following is not an element in reaching a collective agreement?
    (a) Parties must bargain in good faith
    (b) Management must agree to the union's terms
    (c) Either party can give notice to commence bargaining
    (d) Parties must make every reasonable effort to reach an agreement
    (e) Agreement must be ratified by both employees and employers

53. Labour legislation sets out a method for organizing employees into a bargaining unit.
    (a) True
    (b) False

54. A certified union is a bargaining agent for a group of employees.
    (a) True
    (b) False

55. Even when there is a union, individual employees can try to work out a deal for themselves with their employer.
    (a) True
    (b) False

56. Conciliation or mediation may be mandated by legislation and the decision is binding on the parties.

    (a) True
    (b) False

57. Arbitration is a method for settling disputes and grievances arising out of the agreement.
    (a) True
    (b) False

58. The process of dispute settlement is set out in the union agreement and both parties are required to follow it.
    (a) True
    (b) False

59. The process by which a particular union achieves the status of bargaining agent for a group of employees is called:
    (a) binding arbitration
    (b) certification.
    (c) conciliation
    (d) job action
    (e) collective bargaining

60. Which of the following is not a form of job action?
    (a) strike
    (b) lockout
    (c) work to rule
    (d) certification
    (e) picketing

61. It is unlawful for a strike or lockout to take place while a collective agreement is in force. Only after it has expired and before the next one comes into effect can this type of job action take place.
    (a) True
    (b) False

62. Which of the following statements is accurate with respect to picketing in your jurisdiction?
    (a) An employee can only picket the location where he/she actually works.
    (b) The public cannot lawfully cross a legal picket line.
    (c) Employees of other employers cannot legally cross a lawful picket line.
    (d) Picketing is illegal .
    (e) Employees can picket wherever the employer does business.

63. A strike is the withdrawal of services by employees.

    (a) True
    (b) False

64. A lockout is action by a negotiator to encourage disputing parties to come to the bargaining table.
    (a) True
    (b) False

65. Which of the following would amount to working to rule?
    (a) Employees do no more than minimally required by agreement.
    (b) Employees attempt to influence the public by putting adds in the newspaper.
    (c) Blacklisting the employer's product.
    (d) Striking
    (e) Picketing

66. Right to job action is limited by legislation.
    (a) True
    (b) False

67. Which of the following statements is not true with regard to public sector employees?
    (a) Special legislation covers public sector employees.
    (b) May be required to participate in compulsory arbitration.
    (c) Government retains the right to impose a settlement.
    (d) People involved in essential services may have their right to strike limited.
    (e) Public sector employees have no right to bargain collectively.

68. People rendering essential services often have their right to job action restricted.
    (a) True
    (b) False

69. George operates a heavy machinery manufacturing company employing 100 people. One of his employees was approached by members of the Iron Workers' Union to organize George's work force. When George heard of this (after approximately 40% of the work force had already been organized), George fired Sam, the employee responsible for the organization. George held a meeting of his employees at which time he informed them that if they did succeed in organizing a union and having it certified, he would close down the plant and move his company to Mexico. At this stage several of the people who had already signed up approached Sam and told him that they didn't want to be members of the union. When the other workers heard that Sam had been fired and about the comments of George, several of them immediately went out on strike and with reinforcements from the Iron Workers' Union formed a mass picket line across the entranceway to the plant. George hired the services of a private security agency to ensure that the rest of his workers and some substitute workers hired to take the place of the strikers (whom he had also fired) got through the picket line. The ensuing confrontation was violent and some of the picketers were seriously injured. At this stage George had acquired signatures from 90% of the present work force on a petition stating that they wanted nothing to do with a union and the Iron Workers' Union in particular. Summarize the legal position of the parties and the courses of action that may be available to either side to resolve the confrontation.

Answers to Review Questions

1. b   P. 343   D.1
2. a   P. 343   D.2
3. a   P. 344   D.1
4. c   P. 344   D.2
5. e   P. 343, 345; 386-8 (next chapter) D.2
6. a   P. 352   D.1
7. a   P. 346   D.1
8. a   P. 354   D.1
9. pay wages, provide safe workplace and good working conditions, pay specific wage or salary (usually)

   P. 345   D.1

10. possess skills claimed, be competent and careful, follow reasonable instructions, treat employer's property carefully, be honest, loyal, and courteous, be punctual and work for the contracted time, act in best interests of employer

    P. 346   D.1

11. a   P. 346-7   D.2
12. c   P. 345   D.2
13. a   P. 347   D.1
14. c   P. 351   D.1
15. reasonable amount of notice unless there is just cause.

    P. 347   D.1

16. consistent absenteeism (but note duty to accommodate), dishonesty, incompetence, misuse of information, disclosing confidential information

    P. 348   D.1

17. d   P. 346   D.2
18. a   P. 347   D.1
19. a   P. 347   D.1
20. b   P. 347   D.2
21. a   P. 348   D.1
22. d   P. 348   D.2
23. c   P. 351   D.2
24. a   P. 348   D.1

25. b   P. 348   D.2
26. a   P. 347   D.1
27. Vicarious liability holds an employer responsible for the torts committed by his employees if they are committed during the course of employment.

    P. 352-3   D.2

28. a   P. 350   D.2
29. When Joan was reassigned, this was probably an example of constructive dismissal. She has the right to continue doing her job and if the employer chooses to reassign her they must have her agreement to do so. When she refused she was within her rights and the employer is then obligated to give her reasonable notice. Here, payment until the end of the month would not be enough. Because the company had breached their contract with Joan she would not be bound by any provision prohibiting her from working for a competitor and also the period of time (5 years) was likely unreasonable and so the clause would be void in any case. Her main problem will be the fact that she worked for another company during this period. This was not another greeting card manufacturer and so she would not be in violation of the non-competition clause even if it was valid, but she has been using the design developed for her employer. She has, in effect, taken the property of the employer (the designs) and given it to someone else. That would violate her fiduciary duty to her employer and be just cause for dismissal. This would be just cause and support the dismissal even though it was not known by the employer until after Joan left her job.

    P. 346-8, 351   D.3

30. a   P. 353-60   D.2
31. employment standards, wages, hours of work, termination, human rights, child labour, workers' compensation, health and safety, employment insurance

    P. 353-60   D.1

32. b   P. 354   D.2

33. d   P. 356   D.2

34. c   P. 359   D.2

35. a   P. 358   D.1

36. a   P. 359   D.1

37. e   P. 360   D.2

38. b   P. 362   D.1

39. a   P. 362   D.2

40. c   P. 362   D.2

41. b   P. 362   D.2

42. a   P. 362, 369   D.2

43. b   P. 362   D.1

44. b   P. 362   D.2

45. government supervised certification vote

     P. 363   D.2

46. c   P. 369   D.2

47. b   P. 362   D.1

48. Union approaches employees or employees themselves get together; enough have to sign up to apply for certification vote (varies from province to province). If over 50% (usually) vote for the union it is certified. In some jurisdictions if over a certain percentage are signed up, certification is automatic without a vote.

     P. 363   D.2

49. Collective agreement covering terms and conditions of employment.

     P. 366   D.2

50. b   P. 367   D.2

51. a   P. 365   D.1

52. b   P. 366-7   D.2

53. a   P. 365   D.2

54. a   P. 364   D.1

55. b   P. 364   D.1

56. b   P. 367-8   D.1

57. a   P. 367   D.1

58. a   P. 367   D.1

59. b   p. 363   D.1

60. d   P. 363, 369-70   D.1

61. a   P. 369   D.1

62. a or e depending on the jurisdiction

     P. 369-71   D.2

63. a   P. 369   D.1

64. b   P. 369   D.1

65. a   P. 369   D.2

66. a   P. 369   D.1

67. e   P. 371   D.2

68. a   P. 371-2   D.1

69. When George fired Sam for union activities, this was not only a violation of the provincial labour statute in place but also a crime under the criminal code of Canada. When George threatened to move the plant to Mexico if the union was certified, this was probably an unfair labour practice by George (depending on the jurisdiction). (This is more than simply expressing an opinion as protected under the freedom of expression provision of the charter.) The mass strike and picketing was also illegal and George could get an injunction to have it stopped. The infliction of injuries by either party would be both a crime and the people hurt could sue for the tort of battery. Even though 90% of the employees now don't want the union, this would be considered the result of the intimidation by George and in many jurisdictions the labour relations board would have the power to order certification of the union without a vote.

     P. 365   D.3

Chapter 12

Agency

Learning Objectives

At the end of the chapter you should be able to:

1. Define how an agency relationship can come into existence.
2. Explain the rights and obligations between principals and agents, principals and third parties, and agents and third parties.
3. Describe specifically the difference between estoppel and promissory estoppel and the concept of apparent authority.
4. Define the unique responsibilities and rights of specialized agents.

Key Terms

The following terms are highlighted in the text:

agent	represents and acts on behalf of a principal in dealings with third parties
agency	the service an agent performs on behalf of a principal
agency agreement contract	creates an agency relationship between principal and agent
power of attorney	an agency agreement in writing and under seal
express authority	the authority of the agent as actually stated by the principal
implied authority	the authority of the agent as implied by the principal
actual authority	authority given to agent expressly or by implication
apparent authority	conduct of principal suggests to third party that agent has authority to act
estoppel	principal leads third party to believe the agent has authority to act on his/her behalf
reasonable person test	standard to determine the existence of apparent authority
ratification	principal confirms a contract entered into by his agent
agency by necessity	consent to act as an agent is implied when there is an urgent reason
duty of care	agent must function in a reasonable manner when acting for principal

delegation	agent normally cannot turn his responsibilities over to someone else
accounting	agent must pay over money or property collected on behalf of principal
fiduciary duty	agent must act in the best interests of the principal
utmost good faith	another term for fiduciary duty
undisclosed principal	when the agent doesn't make it clear they are working for a principal they can be held liable for the contract
repudiation	third party can refuse to go through with contract if the identity of the undisclosed principal is important

Chapter Outline

Notes

Agency Relationship

An agent represents and acts for a principal in dealings with third parties

Relationship usually created through contract (agency agreement); thus, contract rules apply

A defect in the agency agreement usually won't affect the contract made by an agent between the principal and third party

Consent essential requirement for an agency relationship to exist

Authority - contracts made by an agent on behalf of a principal are binding if authority is present:

- *Actual* - expressed in contract (verbally or in writing) or implied by conduct
- *Implied* – from the circumstances
- *Apparent* (estoppel) - the principal makes it appear or leads someone to believe that the agent has authority to act on his behalf and the third party relies on that representation

Ratification of agent's contracts - if agent has acted beyond actual or apparent authority, the contract is binding if principal approves it.

Third party can set time limit for ratification

Inadvertent ratification possible - principal accepts a benefit under the agreement

Agency by necessity rarely used today

Duties of Parties

Agent

Must act within authority granted

Perform as required
Use reasonable care
Not delegate responsibility
Account for monies
Act in best interests of principal (fiduciary duty)

Principal

Honour terms of contract
Pay reasonable amount for services
Undisclosed Principals - third party can sue agent or principal
  or repudiate if the personality of the undisclosed principal
  is important
Only identified principals can ratify

Third Party Rights and Remedies

Where agent does not have authority claimed, third party can
  sue agent for breach of warranty of authority or for fraud or
  negligence where appropriate.

Vicarious Liability of Principals

Limited to employees acting as agents except when agent
  makes a fraudulent misrepresentation. Principal is directly
  liable if he gives false information to agent

Termination of Agency

Usually terminated through agreement or by frustration, death,
  insanity, bankruptcy

Specialized Agency Relationships

Travel agents, real estate agents, insurance agents, etc.
General agency principles apply

Review Questions

1. Agency relationships are subject to all the rules of contract.
   (a) True
   (b) False

2. A defect in the agency agreement will adversely affect a contract between the principal and the third party.
   (a) True
   (b) False

3. Agents represent and act for a principal in dealings with third parties.
   (a) True
   (b) False

4. What is the essential requirement for an agency relationship to exist?

   _____

5. A person under the age of majority cannot function as an agent.
   (a) True
   (b) False

6. How old must a person be before he/she can act as an agent?

   _____

7. Which of the following is not an agent in the eyes of the law?
   (a) The cashier at Home Depot
   (b) A photographer for The Times who, along with taking photos, sometimes writes the accompanying articles.
   (c) The paperboy who collects for The Sun and takes subscriptions
   (d) A janitor at a college who also orders supplies
   (e) An accountant preparing and submitting your taxes.

8. A purchasing agent bought goods for his principal, unaware that the principal had gone insane the night before. Explain the rights of the third party.

   _____

   _____

9. What are the two methods by which authority can be given to an agent?

    (1) _____

    (2) _____

10. Which of the following would not give authority to the agent to bind the principal?
    (a) expressed authority
    (b) implied authority
    (c) estoppel
    (d) res judicata
    (e) ratification

11. Identify three ways by which an agent-principal relationship may come into existence.

    (1) _____

    (2) _____

    (3) _____

12. What can a principal do if an agent acts beyond his/her authority
    (a) if the principal is happy with the agreement?

    _____

    (b) if he/she is not happy with the agreement?

    _____

13. What are the agent's duties to a principal?

    (a) _____

    (b) _____

    (c) _____

    (d) _____

    (e) _____

14. What is meant by the term "fiduciary duty"?

    _____

    _____

15. The agent owes a fiduciary duty to the third party.
    (a) True
    (b) False

16. Identify the false statement concerning the law of principal and agent:
    (a) Agency is usually created by way of a contract although it is not necessary to have a contract to have agency.
    (b) The principal and his/her agent owe each other the same duties.
    (c) An agent who puts him-/herself in a position where his/her interests conflict with those of his principal is in breach of his/her duties even though no actual harm comes to his/her principal.
    (d) An agent may bind his/her principal into a contract with a third party even though the agent has no actual authority to do so.
    (e) In certain circumstances, an agent may be liable to the third party while the principal will bear no such liability.

17. What recourses are available to a third party if the principal is undisclosed?

    _____

    _____

18. If Matt is an agent for Art, which of the following is false?
    (a) Matt owes a fiduciary duty to Art.
    (b) Art could be bound by a contract that was entered into on his behalf by a sub-agent contacted by Matt.
    (c) Matt could act as an agent for Hawkins even if he were not paid to do so.
    (d) Even when Matt is acting as an agent he need not put the interest of Art above his own.
    (e) Matt must use reasonable care, skill and diligence in his service to Art.

19. The agent acts as a go-between between principal and third party
    (a) True
    (b) False

20. Apparent authority is determined by the representations of the principals.
    (a) True
    (b) False

21. In an agreement to create an agency relationship, which of the following statements does not apply?
    (a) Principles of contract law apply.
    (b) All the elements of a contract must be present.
    (c) Should set out nature and extent of authority to act.
    (d) Agency contracts must be in writing.
    (e) In some types of agency relationships, licensing requirements must be satisfied.

22. Power of attorney is an agency contract under seal.
    (a) True
    (b) False

23. The presence of apparent authority can be determined by the job title an agent has.
    (a) True
    (b) False

24. An agency agreement should set out the limits of an agent's authority.
    (a) True
    (b) False

25. Even ambiguous references may be interpreted as express authority.
    (a) True
    (b) False

26. The board of directors of Hale Ltd. wants to borrow $45,000 from Bopp Bank. If the company sends an agent to negotiate and sign a debenture on behalf of the company, which of the following is false?
    (a) The agency relationship is usually created by way of a contract, but it is not necessary.
    (b) An employee of the bank could act as an agent for the bank for this transaction.
    (c) If the agent for the bank enters a contract on behalf of the bank that is necessarily incidental to his carrying out his express obligation regarding the debenture, the bank would be bound by that contract too.
    (d) The bank is responsible for any fraudulent misrepresentation made by its agent, even if the agent is not an employee.
    (e) If the person sent says he is an agent, and appears to be one because of statements made by the bank management, and he exceeds his express authority, he is personally bound by the contract.

27. Implied authority can be conveyed by actions of the agent.
    (a) True
    (b) False

28. An agent who exceeds actual authority may be liable for injury their conduct causes principal.
    (a) True
    (b) False

29. An agent with no express, implied or apparent authority to do so identified himself as an agent for his principal and on behalf of his principal bought a computer. On these facts, which of the following is true?

(a) The principal would have to pay for the computer because the agent was an agent for that principal.

(b) Even though the agent has exceeded his authority he has no liability to the seller of the computer.

(c) By exceeding his authority, the agent has become the buyer of the computer himself.

(d) The principal could ratify the agreement and it would be seen as binding from the time of the ratification.

(e) In these circumstances the principal would have no right to ratify the agreement because the agent didn't tell the third party that the contract would have to be ratified.

30. A principal who merely acts in a way to make a third party believe that an agent has authority to act will not be bound.
(a) True
(b) False

31. Extremely pleased with the work of a team of students who had written a report as to what hardware and software the business needed to increase its chances of economic survival, the owner hired one of the team, Lee, to act as its agent in purchasing the system. The owner both visited and wrote to Super Systems Ltd. to advise them Lee would be acting as his agent for the purpose of buying computer hardware and software. The owner then told Lee that Super Systems Ltd. understood he was the owner's agent, but told him, "Don't buy a new printer; ours is fine." Lee examined the wares of Super Systems Ltd. but in the end bought some software from London Drugs as an agent of the owner. On these facts which of the following is true?
(a) Lee needs to be hired as an employee to carry out this agency function.
(b) If Lee exceeds his express authority and buys a new printer at Super Systems Ltd. the owner would have to pay for it anyway.
(c) When Gordon bought software from London Drugs as an agent of the owner, the owner would have to pay for it anyway because Lee said he was his agent. The owner has had no previous dealings with London Drugs.
(d) London Drugs could sue Lee for breach of contract; Lee has bought himself some software and he has to pay for it.
(e) In determining whether or not Lee could bind the owner in a contract, the law poses this question: Did the acts and words of Lee lead the seller into thinking that Lee was an agent for the owner?

32. What test is used to determine apparent authority?
(a) res ipsa loquitur
(b) promissory estoppel
(c) reasonable foreseeability
(d) ratification
(e) none of the above

33. A manufacturer sent an agent to buy materials, giving him instructions and forms of contract to use when buying, and authorizing him to sign the contract forms on behalf of the manufacturer. The agent bought materials from Reed, completing a contract form. The manufacturer declined to accept the materials, stating that the agent's instructions were that he was to stipulate in the contract form that it was not to be binding on the manufacturer until he approved samples. The agent did not inform Reed of that fact. Reed sued the manufacturer for the price. Could he succeed? Explain.

_____

_____

34. In certain cases, a third party can hold a principal to a contract even though the agent acted outside the authorization given him by his principal and even though his principal elected not to ratify the contract made by the agent. The third party can enforce the contract because:
   (a) Of the reasonable agent theory
   (b) Of agency by express agreement
   (c) The principal did not register the agency agreement
   (d) The agent's apparent authority
   (e) *Res ipsa loquitur*

35. In the above situation, what should the principal do once he performs the contract with the third party?

_____

36. John Agent entered into a contract with Sam Third Party to buy 50 stoves, payment to be made two weeks after John Agent picked up the stoves from Sam Third Party's warehouse. The stoves were picked up but 8 weeks later, Sam still had not been paid. Sam found out that John Agent had been authorized to buy 50 stoves for Gord Principal. For some reason, John had not made it clear to Joe that he was acting as an agent, nor had he indicated that he was buying the goods for himself. Under the circumstances, which of the following is true?
   (a) Third Party can successfully sue only Gord Principal.
   (b) Third Party can successfully sue only John Agent.
   (c) Third Party can successfully sue both Principal and Agent.
   (d) Third Party can elect to recover from either Principal or Agent but not both.
   (e) None of the above statements is correct.

37. Which of the following is incorrect with respect to the law of agency?
   (a) When a principal ratifies a contract that was negotiated by his agent in excess of that agent's authority, the contract is effective from the date that contract was made.

(b) An agent normally must perform his duties personally because the principal chose him for his particular judgment and skill.

(c) When a principal does not ratify a contract that his agent had no authority to make, the party who thought he was entering into that contract can sue the agent for breach of warranty of authority.

(d) When an employee disobeys specific instructions and enters a transaction he has not been authorized to make, the employer can be sure they are not bound by the agreement.

(e) The agent owes a fiduciary duty to the principal, not the third party.

38. A principal can ratify a contract even if the agent acted beyond both actual and apparent authority.
   (a) True
   (b) False

39. Which of the following is not true with respect to ratification?
   (a) The agent must have made it clear he was acting as an agent and indicated the identity of the principal.
   (b) The principal must have been able to enter into the contract himself at the time it was ratified.
   (c) The principal must have had capacity when the agent made the contract.
   (d) The agent must have made it clear that the contract was "subject to ratification"
   (e) The principal can ratify inadvertently.

40. Which of the following is not a necessary condition of ratification?
   (a) Agent must have been acting for a specific principal.
   (b) Principal must have been capable of entering into the contract.
   (c) A principal can ratify a contract even if the agent acted beyond the authority granted.
   (d) The agent must have disclosed that they had no authority.
   (e) A principal can ratify merely by accepting a benefit from the contract.

41. Which of the following is not included among the duties of an agent?
   (a) An agent must act within limits of contract.
   (b) Must perform functions set out in agreement.
   (c) Must not go against specific instruction.
   (d) Can delegate responsibility unless stipulated in contract.
   (e) Must account for funds.

42. If an agent goes beyond the authority granted he/she may be:
   (a) Sued for breach by principal
   (b) Liable for acting beyond authority
   (c) Sued by third party
   (d) Fired
   (e) All of the above

43. Mr. Oburg hired Sung as the manager of his used car lot. Sandoval brought in a car and made arrangements for Sung to sell it on consignment. Which of the following is correct with respect to the law of agency?
    (a) If Sandoval has acted within his apparent authority, he cannot be fired for this action.
    (b) If Sung gave a friend a particularly good deal on a used car this could be a violation of Sung's fiduciary duty to Oburg.
    (c) If Sung had been specifically told that he was not to take any cars to sell on consignment, there would be no contract between Oburg and Sandoval.
    (d) If Sung had no authority express, implied or apparent, in this situation, Sandoval is out of luck and has no recourse against anyone.
    (e) If Sung sold a used car to Brown and it was defective, Brown could sue either Jones or Sung.

44. Which of the following is not a component of an agent's fiduciary duty?
    (a) Duty to act only in the best interests of the principal
    (b) Cannot take personal advantage of opportunity because of position
    (c) Duty to disclose information that would benefit principal
    (d) Duty to bear loss
    (e) Must not compete with principal and turn over all benefits

45. Moffat needed to find land for his new plant. He hired Johal, who worked for Sure Fire Realty Ltd., to find the land. He found an appropriate site owned by Brown. Which of the following is incorrect with respect to this legal relationship?
    (a) Even though the eventual transaction will be between Brown and Moffat, Johal is still acting as an agent of Moffat.
    (b) If, in addition to his commission from Moffat, Johal takes a commission from Brown without telling Moffat, this will be in violation of his fiduciary duty to Moffat.
    (c) If Johal makes a deal with Brown to give up half of his commission to get the deal to go through without telling Moffat, this would not be in violation of his fiduciary duty to Moffat since it doesn't cause Moffat any loss.
    (d) If Johal discloses to Moffat that he is giving up a portion of his commission to get the deal to work, there is no violation of the fiduciary duty.
    (e) If Johal fraudulently misrepresents information to Moffat, Moffat can sue Johal and Sure Fire. Although Johal is an agent of Moffat, he is an employee of Sure Fire.

46. Which of the following does not illustrate a breach of duty owed by the agent to the principal?
    (a) Without telling his employer, a purchasing agent for a large department store accepts a trip to Reno as a prize awarded by one of their suppliers.
    (b) An agent for the vendor who wants at least $200,000 for his house sells the property for $196,000 but does not tell the vendor that he, the agent, is also getting a commission from the purchaser.

    (c) A travel agent working for a large company in charge of a separate community office uses the computer and photocopier to carry on her Amway business in her spare time.

    (d) A real estate agent who has listed the property for the vendor buys the property himself without telling the vendor all of the details, but the deal was more than fair because the agent paid 5% more than the fair market value at the time of contract.

    (e) A project developer working for a large mining company is approached by a prospector and offered a claim that he feels has considerable potential. He informs the employer of the opportunity and they reject it. After full and frank disclosure he buys it himself and later sells it at a handsome profit.

47. Which of the following is not a duty of a principal?
    (a) Principal must honour terms of contract.
    (b) Pay a reasonable amount for services.
    (c) Reimburse for reasonable work related expenses.
    (d) Give agent lawful assignments.
    (e) Supervise all contracts entered into on his behalf by agent.

48. Ambiguities concerning authority will be interpreted in favour of broader agent's authority even when the contract is to borrow money.
    (a) True
    (b) False

49. Agent cannot be held liable to a third party when acting for an undisclosed principal.
    (a) True
    (b) False

50. How does the principle of vicarious liability affect principal/agent relationships?

_____

51. Third party is usually bound to contract even when principal is undisclosed, except where the identity of principal is important.
    (a) True
    (b) False

52. Only identified principals can ratify a contract.
    (a) True
    (b) False

53. A principal can only ratify contracts where the agent has clearly indicated to the third party that he was acting beyond his authority.
    (a) True
    (b) False

54. When an agent has informed the third party that he is acting beyond his authority, such a contract cannot be ratified by the principal.
    (a) True
    (b) False

55. A principal can ratify a contract without intending to.
    (a) True
    (b) False

56. Which of the following remedies are available to an injured third party when he/she entered a contract through an agent.
    (a) When agent goes beyond authority a third party can sue the agent.
    (b) Breach of warranty of authority.
    (c) Intentional deception on part of agent may lead to the award of damages.
    (d) Tort remedies may be available for fraud or negligence.
    (e) All of the above

57. When the agent is an employee, the principal may be vicariously liable for agent's tortious conduct.
    (a) True
    (b) False

58. Liability for an agent's torts will not be imposed on a principal in which of the following situations?
    (a) A stockbroker on his way to the stock exchange to sell shares on behalf of his client, Lee, negligently ran over a pedestrian.
    (b) A real estate salesperson fraudulently lied about the zoning of a house he was selling for his client, Lee.
    (c) A cashier at the grocery store carelessly dropped a can of tomatoes on the toe of Lee as she checked out his groceries at the register.
    (d) A vacuum cleaner salesman selling door-to-door, who was working for Ace Vacuum Cleaners, fraudulently misrepresented the nature of the contractual obligations his customer, Lee, entered into.
    (e) Lee, an independent agent of Smith and Co. Ltd. acting outside his actual but within his apparent authority, intentionally misled a customer about the quality of the abrasives he was selling.

59. Because of modern communication agency by necessity is not common today.
    (a) True
    (b) False

60. Where fraud is involved a principal may be liable even when the agent is not an employee.
    (a) True
    (b) False

61. Which of the following is not true with regard to the termination of an agency agreement.
    (a) Term may be set out in contract or by agreement.
    (b) Principal may give notice to withdraw authority from agent.
    (c) If agent's duties become illegal, principle of frustration may terminate agent's authority.
    (d) Death, insanity or bankruptcy of principal will terminate agency relationship.
    (e) When a principle tells his agent he no longer has authority, he can be sure that he will no longer be bound by contracts entered into by that agent.

62. What principles of agency law protect consumers when they have been taken advantage of by agents?
    (a) ratification
    (b) breach of authority
    (c) breach of fiduciary duty
    (d) vicarious liability of principal
    (e) agency by necessity

63. How is an agency agreement terminated?

    _____

    _____

64. Franklin is the owner and manager of Franklin's Fine Cars Ltd. and he hired Brown as a management trainee. The first night on the job, Brown was told to look after the shop while Franklin and the other sales representatives were at a meeting. He was told to sweep the floors and clean the windows, but if anybody came by to look at cars, he was merely to take their names and phone numbers and ask them to come back the next day. He was specifically told to have no dealings with the customers and not to talk to them about the vehicles. While Brown was cleaning up, Mr. and Mrs. Rhodes dropped by to have a look at a new station wagon for their family. Brown could not restrain his enthusiasm and talked to the customers in great detail about the wonderful qualities of the cars. He finally convinced them that one particular model, the most expensive one in the showroom, was ideal for them. He allowed the Rhodes to take the car out for a test drive. Brown went with them and Mr. Rhodes, because he was unfamiliar with the vehicle, pressed the gas pedal too hard and spun the car out in the middle of the street, smashing into Mr. Green's car, which was coming in the opposite direction. Mr. Green was seriously injured and both cars were damaged beyond repair. Fortunately, Mr. and Mrs. Rhodes and Brown were uninjured and went back to the showroom. They were all a little shaken, but at that time, Mr. Rhodes decided he would like to buy a car like the one he had been driving. Brown wrote up the appropriate documents, signing his signature for authorization and stating that it would take about two weeks to replace the one that had been destroyed.

When Franklin returned to the store, Brown enthusiastically told him about the car he had sold to the Rhodes and then hesitantly told him about the car that had been destroyed. Franklin was extremely angry, declared that he would not go through with the deal and fired Brown. The next day Rhodes came in with a $250 deposit for the car he had purchased the night before. He showed another sales representative the papers that had been signed by Brown. The sales representative examined the papers, took the deposit and handled the sale in the normal way. It wasn't until the following week that Franklin discovered the deposit had been taken on the Rhodeses' order. Explain the legal position of each of the parties.

Answers to Review Questions

1. a   P. 378 D.1

2. b   P. 378-9 D.1

3. a   P. 378 D.1

4. consent

    P. 379 D.1

5. b   P. 378-9 D.1

6. Old enough to understand what he/she is doing.

    P. 379 D.1

7. b   P. 378 D.1

8. The authority of the agent was determined by the insanity and therefore there is no agreement.

    P. 379 D.2

9. actual or apparent

    P. 379-380 D.2

10. d P. 379-383 D.2

11. In writing, verbal, implied from conduct, apparent authority

    P. 379-380 D.2

12. (a) ratify

   (b) disavow or repudiate

    P. 382 D.2

13. The agent must act within authority granted, perform as required in the contract, use reasonable care, not delegate the responsibility unless agreed, account for any monies and act in the best interest of the principal.

    P. 384-8 D.2

14. This is an utmost good faith relationship, an obligation to act in the best interest of the principal. (e.g. not to compete, or take advantage of information coming through agency position).

    P. 386-8 D.2

15. b P. 387 D. 2

   He could sue the agent

16. b P. 378-391 D.1

17. When dealing with an undisclosed principal, the third party has the legal option of either suing the principal or suing the agent as if he were the principal. The choice has to be made. Once the third party learns of the existence of the principal and once the choice is made the third party is bound by it.

    P. 389-391 D.2

18. b (in some industries, where sub-agents are used, there is a right for an agent to delegate his authority and therefore such a contract would be binding) , d.

    P. 385 D.2

19. a P. 377 D.1

20. a P. 379 D.1

21. d P. 378 D.2

22. a P. 378 D.1

23. a P. 379-381 D.1

24. a P. 379 D.1

25. a P. 378 D.1

26. e P. 378-380 D.2

27. a P. 379-380 D.1

28. a P. 379 D.1

29. d P. 382 D.2

30. b P. 379-380 D.1

31. b P. 379 D.2

32. e P. 379-380 D.2

33. Yes, he would succeed. This is an example of apparent authority

    P. 379-381 D.2

34. d P. 379-381 D.2

35. He could sue the agent.

    P. 379   D.2

36. d   P. 389   D.2

37. d   P. 379   D.2

38. a   P. 382   D.1

39. d   P. 382-3   D.2

40. d   P. 382-3   D.2

41. d   P. 384-8   D.2

42. e   P. 379-381, 384   D.2

43. b   P. 385-8   D.2

44. d   P. 385-8   D.1

45. c   P. 385-8   D.2

46. e   P. 384-8   D.1

47. e   P. 388-9   D.2

48. b   P. 388   D.1

49. b   P. 389   D.1

50. Vicarious liability is only available where employment relationship can be demonstrated, so if the agent is acting as an independent agent there is no vicarious liability. The exception is when an agent fraudulently or negligently misrepresents something on behalf of the principal; then the principal is liable.

    P. 392-4   D.2

51. a   P. 390   D.1

52. a   P. 391   D.1

53. b   P. 382-3   D.1

54. a   P. 382-3   D.1

55. a   P. 383   D.1

56. e   P. 391-2   D.2

57. a   P. 392   D.1

58. a   P. 392-4   D.2

59. a   P. 383   D.1

60. a   P. 392   D.1

61. e   P. 394-5   D.2

62. d   P. 392   D.2

63. agreement, notice, withdrawal of authority by principal, at the end of a specified time, frustration, death, insanity, bankruptcy of principal

    P. 394-5   D.2

64. Because Franklin left Brown in charge, he has been held out to have the authority to act as he did. This then is an example of apparent authority and the contract to sell the car to the Rhodeses is binding on Franklin. Even if there had been no authority the act of the other agent taking the money as a deposit would have ratified the deal. Franklin however would have the right to fire Brown for his incompetence and disobedience. Green would be able to sue Mr. Rhodes but not Franklin or Brown. Franklin would only be liable to Green if there was a statute in place making the owner of such a vehicle vicariously liable for the conduct of its driver.

    P. 379-384, 392-4

Chapter 13

Sole Proprietorship and Partnership

Learning Objectives

At the end of the chapter you should be able to:

1. Identify the different methods of carrying on business and the advantages and disadvantages of each.
2. Explain the nature of a sole proprietorship and the responsibilities associated with it.
3. Differentiate between intentional and inadvertent partnerships.
4. Summarize the rights and obligations of partners to each other and to third parties.
5. Define a limited partnership and explain how limited partners are different from ordinary partners.

Key Terms

The following terms are highlighted in the text:

sole proprietorship	an individual carrying on business alone
partnership	ownership and responsibilities of a business shared by two or more people
corporation	a business organization that is a separate legal entity from the owners
non-profit society	separate legal entity with different rules for incorporation
holding corporation	owns shares in other corporations
joint venture	several corporations join together to accomplish a major project
unlimited liability	business owner or partners are liable for all debts incurred by the business to the extent of their personal resources
vicarious liability	employer is liable for the injuries caused by employees during the course of their employment
professional associations	the governing bodies of professionals such as the law society or medical association
partnership	two or more people carrying on business together with a view towards profit
inadvertence	two people working together may be held liable for one another's actions even if they did not have a partnership agreement

estoppel	an indication by someone to another that he is a partner in a partnership will prevent him from later denying it
agents	partners are agents of one another
joint liability	all partners must be sued together. If one is left out you cannot sue them later
several liability	each partner can be sued separately
fiduciary	a duty to act in the best interests of other partners
limited partnership	partners liable only to the extent of their investment

Chapter Outline

Notes

Types of Business Organization

Sole Proprietorship
Partnership
Society
Corporation

Sole Proprietorship
An individual carrying on business alone
- Government Regulations - registration, licenses, tax records
- Relatively free from outside interference
- Personally responsible for all business decisions, financing, debts and liabilities
- Unlimited Liability - personal assets at risk for liabilities incurred by the business
- Vicariously liable for employees' actions

Partnership
Groups of people carrying on business in common for profit
- Governed by contract law and the *Partnership Act*
What constitutes a partnership?
Where the purpose is for profits to be *shared* in an *ongoing* business relationship
Created by:
- inadvertence - implied from conduct
- agreement - either verbal or written (the contents of the private agreement between partners does not affect third parties dealing with the partnership)
Partner as agent - every partner is considered an agent of every other partner (apparent authority and estoppel)

Unlimited liability - all partners are liable for wrongful acts in relation to the business of other partners (vicarious liability)

Profits and losses - shared equally or proportionally by agreement

All personal assets at risk - third party can collect from any partner regardless of agreement

Partners are jointly liable for all debts and obligations of the partnership

In any action against the business all partners must be included

Registration

Most provinces require registration of certain types of partnerships and there are legal advantages for doing so

Rights and obligations of partners

Fiduciary duty (each must act in the best interest of the other)

Accountability for monies earned or paid out

- Must not start up any business in competition with partnership
- Be reimbursed for all business expenses
- Participate in management
- Not entitled to salaries
- Unanimous agreement for major changes

Advantages of Partnership

- Unanimous consent a protection
- Less costly than incorporation
- Ease of dissolution - through notice, death, bankruptcy, insolvency, agreement, request to court
- Disadvantages can be alleviated by carrying adequate insurance.

Limited Partnerships

Liability limited to amount invested

Requires registration

Limited partners cannot participate in management

Review Questions

1. Unlimited liability means that all business and personal assets are at risk for liabilities associated with business.
   (a) True
   (b) False

2. Which of the following is not a method of carrying on business?
   (a) sole proprietorship
   (b) partnership
   (c) corporation
   (d) non-profit society
   (e) partnership of corporations

3. A sole proprietor is relieved from the responsibility of vicarious liability.
   (a) True
   (b) False

4. A sole proprietorship is an individual carrying on business alone.
   (a) True
   (b) False

5. Which of the following is not a concern of a sole proprietor?
   (a) government regulations
   (b) avoid restricted/illegal activities
   (c) meet zoning bylaws
   (d) comply with workers compensation, employment insurance and income tax regulations
   (e) annual reports

6. A sole proprietor is not vicariously liable for the torts of employees.
   (a) True
   (b) False

7. Partnership is a group of people carrying on business together for the purpose of making a profit.
   (a) True
   (b) False

8. The following are statements about the legal relationship of partnership. Identify the true statement.
   (a) "Partnership" is defined in the *Partnership Act* as "two or more persons sharing profits from business."
   (b) Once a person retires from a partnership he or she is automatically freed from any liability as a partner.

(c) People who invest in a partnership business are just like shareholders in a limited company in that they cannot be made liable for more than they have invested in the firm.

(d) Each partner bears a fiduciary duty toward every other partner in the firm and to the firm itself.

(e) A partnership only comes into existence by way of the express intention of the partners to be associated in such a relationship.

9. Partnership is governed by federal statute.
   (a) True
   (b) False

10. Why is agency law important to partnerships?

   _____

   _____

11. Which of the following statements is false?
    (a) Isolated transactions carried on jointly do not by themselves establish parties as partners.
    (b) Sharing of profits of a jointly carried on business alone is sufficient evidence of partnership.
    (c) Sharing of gross receipts does not create a partnership.
    (d) Paying back a loan out of the profits of a business is not sufficient evidence of partnership.
    (e) Giving employees a bonus based on profitability will make them partners.

12. Which of the following circumstances will create a partnership?
    (a) Owning property in common
    (b) Sharing gross returns from business activity
    (c) A spouse inherits a dead partner's share
    (d) Employees profit sharing
    (e) Sharing net returns form a business

13. You can become a partner without knowing it.
    (a) True
    (b) False

14. Bercov and Barre are friends and are both violin-makers. Which of the following is incorrect with respect to their legal responsibility (read each separately)?
    (a) Even if they are not connected in business in any way, if Bercov introduces Barre as his partner Barre may be liable to the people with whom Bercov does business.

(b) If they do any activities together, such as interchange parts (Bercov carves the necks and Barre bends the ribs) or supply each other wood, they may be considered partners.

(c) They can be partners even if they haven't entered into a formal partnership agreement.

(d) If they specialize in different instruments and send customers to each other they will be considered partners if they have an arrangement to give each other 15% of the price of each sale.

(e) If Barre has a serious business and Bercov is just an amateur, they can still be partners if Bercov spends time working with Barre and helping him in his shop.

15. The finding of a partnership has serious financial liability implications for partners.
    (a) True
    (b) False

16. Which of the following is/are true with regard to partnership?
    (a) No partnership can be formed unless the parties intend to create a partnership.
    (b) Sharing gross receipts is sufficient evidence of the existence of a partnership.
    (c) A limited partnership is an arrangement in which a partner may limit his liability to his capital contribution.
    (d) A general partner is not an agent of the firm and the other partners.
    (e) Giving employees a bonus based on profits will make them partners.

17. Kaatz accuses Sandhu of being a partner with Brown. Kaatz is owed a considerable amount of money by Brown and is seeking to collect it from Sandhu. Which of the following is not one of the factors the court will look at to determine if a partnership exists?
    (a) Sandhu and Brown carry on business together.
    (b) Sandhu and Brown share net returns from a business.
    (c) Sandhu and Brown own a rented apartment together and share the rent.
    (d) Sandhu and Brown have entered into a partnership agreement.
    (e) Sandhu and brown refer to each other as partners.

18. What dangers are present when people work together without a specific partnership agreement?

    _____

19. Many of the obligations of partners to outsiders set out in the *Partnership Act* can be modified by contract.
    (a) True
    (b) False

20. Atkins and Sung owned an apartment building together and shared the rent. This creates a partnership.
    (a) True
    (b) False

21. What term best describes the duty owed by partners to each other?

    _____

22. What is the legal hazard faced by a lender to a business who stipulates that the borrower's repayment shall be made by means of paying a share of the profits of the business?

    _____

23. Wright and Pei opened up an accounting business together. They shared office space, secretarial and bookkeeping services as well as the office equipment. They also owned the building together. However, they retained their separate clients. If Wright cheats his clients, Pei is not responsible.
    (a) True
    (b) False

24. Mangitt was an accountant working for an accounting partnership in a small town. In the evening on his own time, he provided some accounting services for his friends for a reduced fee. This is a violation of his fiduciary duty.
    (a) True
    (b) False

25. Pietro, Paulo and Maria run a market survey business, which they have never bothered to incorporate. They also do contract work with advertising firms on behalf of these firms' clients if asked to do so. All three were very good at conducting market surveys. They agreed informally that, of the remaining duties, Paulo and Maria would work to attract clients and Pietro would take care of the bookkeeping. On these facts, which of the following is false?
    (a) Pietro, Paulo and Maria are partners, even if they had no such intention.
    (b) Pietro, Paulo and Maria are partners, even though they did not sign a partnership agreement.
    (c) Pietro, Paulo and Maria, with no agreement to the contrary, will have to share the profits and losses equally.
    (d) None of them is entitled to a wage for acting in the business.
    (e) None of them can be secure about their position because the other two could make major changes in the business (e.g., bringing in another person by majority vote).

26. Mr. Chapman approached Mr. Liang on the street and said that he heard that Liang was partner of Mr. Godard, that Godard owed him (Chapman) $30,000 under a contract and that if Liang didn't pay up, he (Chapman) would sue him and Godard. Liang denied he was a partner. Chapman cited the following facts, all of which he could prove. Which of these facts is the strongest evidence of the existence of a partnership?
    (a) That Liang and Godard co-own an apartment building (real property)
    (b) That Liang and Godard share the profits from a business
    (c) That Liang and Godard share gross returns from a business
    (d) That Liang and Godard work together for a non-profit charity
    (e) That Godard had entered into an agreement with Liang to repay a debt by paying him a percentage of his business profits although Jordan didn't participate in that business in any way

27. A verbal partnership agreement must contain all the elements of a contract.
    (a) True
    (b) False

28. Partners are agents of each other.
    (a) True
    (b) False

29. Dennis Sam and George were partners in an accounting business, and Dennis and Sam decided to bring in another partner, Ray. This they can do without George's approval since they have the majority vote.
    (a) True
    (b) False

30. Many of the obligations of partners to each other set out in the *Partnership Act* can be modified by contract.
    (a) True
    (b) False

31. How can someone retiring from a partnership be sure that he or she will not be liable for partnership debts contracted for after the date of retirement?

    _____

    _____

32. Agency law applies to partners and the most significant impact this has is:
    (a) Contracts made by a partner are binding on all the partners
    (b) Vicarious liability (all partners are liable for the tortious conduct of a partner or an employee)
    (c) Personal assets may be used to satisfy claims against partnership

(d) Third party can collect from any partner

(e) All of the above

33. Which of the following is incorrect with respect to the vicarious liability of partners?

(a) Partners are vicariously liable for the wrongful conduct of employees of the partnership performed within the scope of their duties.

(b) Partners are liable for any wrongful conduct done by their partners.

(c) The liability of partners for the torts of their partners is limited to activities associated with the partnership business.

(d) Partners can't limit their share of the liability for the partnership to outsiders even by clearly so stating in their partnership agreement.

(e) Although an outsider can collect the whole amount of a judgement for tort from any partner, that partner can then seek to collect a portion from the other partners.

34. Generally speaking, a partner is personally responsible together with the other partners for the debts and liabilities of the partnership.

(a) True

(b) False

35. General partners are not agents for each other for the purpose of the business of the partnership.

(a) True

(b) False

36. Each partner is vicariously liable for the torts committed by the other partners.

(a) True

(b) False

37. If a section of the *Partnership Act* reads "Any difference as to ordinary matters connected with the partnership business may be decided by a majority of the partners, but no change may be made in the nature of the partnership business without the consent of all existing partners," what difficulty would it cause in the event of a dispute among the partners?

_____

_____

38. With regard to general partnerships, which of the following statements is false?

(a) Each partner is an agent for the other partners.

(b) Every partner has unlimited liability for the debts of the partnership.

(c) The *Partnership Act* provides some terms that will be implied into a partnership relationship if the partners failed to discuss the terms of their arrangement.

(d) A partnership is the relationship that exists between persons carrying on business in common with a view to making a profit.

(e) A partnership is formed only when those wishing to form a partnership have an express agreement to form a partnership.

39. The unlimited liability of partners means that they can only lose their investment in the business.
    (a) True
    (b) False

40. What is the consequence of a limited partner taking an active part in the management of the partnership?

    _____

    _____

41. Failure to register a partnership may increase liability.
    (a) True
    (b) False

42. Fiduciary duty in a partnership does not require which of the following?
    (a) Partners must act in the best interests of their clients.
    (b) Partners must account for all profits.
    (c) Partners must not use partnership property for personal benefit.
    (d) Partners cannot compete with partnership.
    (e) Disclose all information and not use it for personal gain.

43. Which of the following is not a characteristic of a partnership arrangement?
    (a) Partners share profits equally
    (b) Expenses are reimbursed by partnership.
    (c) All partners have right to participate in management.
    (d) A right to salary or wage.
    (e) Major changes must have unanimous agreement.

44. Mangitt was an accountant working for an accounting partnership in a small town. In the evening on his own time, he provided some accounting services for his friends for a reduced fee. This is a violation of his fiduciary duty.
    (a) True
    (b) False

45. Partners have no right to assign their partnership status without consent of all partners
    (a) True
    (b) False

46. When one partner dies and the partnership dissolves, the heir to that dead partner can demand a distribution of the assets.
    (a) True
    (b) False

47. Which of the following would not mean the dissolution of a partnership?
    (a) Notice of intention to dissolve can bring partnership to an end
    (b) The death of a partner
    (c) Insolvency of one of the partners
    (d) Agreement
    (e) The court if business is deemed illegal, etc.

48. Which of the following is incorrect with respect to the law of partnership?
    (a) Chang owns a bookstore as the sole proprietor. He is also a partner in a hotel which borrowed $100,000 from the bank. If the debt is not paid by the partnership, the bank can look to the assets of the bookstore to pay off the debt.
    (b) Jones, Chang and Kozack are in partnership together. Unless stated otherwise in their partnership agreement, if one of them dies, the entire partnership is terminated.
    (c) If you are not associated with another in any business way and you allow him to introduce you as a partner, you may be liable to those with whom he does business.
    (d) Corporations can be in partnership with each other.
    (e) If a partner dies and there is nothing in the partnership agreement to the contrary, the heir of that partner automatically steps into his shows and assumes his position as partner.

49. Public notice must be given of dissolution to escape further liability.
    (a) True
    (b) False

50. Partnership liabilities to third parties can be modified by contract.
    (a) True
    (b) False

51. Alex was a computer student at college where she met Laura, a student studying art and design. After graduation they worked together to create some graphic designs, which they began to sell. Much to their delight and surprise the demand for their work increased. They asked an old classmate of Alex, Jim, to join them in their business; he had the skills to do the necessary bookkeeping and also the personality to do needed marketing. All went well until an employee they had hired negligently failed to make a delivery, which caused their client to lose $8,000. The employee, Hank, was 100% at fault. In a meeting of Alex, Laura and Jim, Jim was so furious he wanted Hank fired. The ensuing argument so upset Laura that she left with $2000 a

client had entrusted to the business for safekeeping. She didn't come back; she seemed to disappear. On these facts, which of the following is false?
(a) Alex, Laura and Jim are general partners even though they never put their minds to the type of business organization they have formed.
(b) Alex, Laura and Jim are responsible to the full extent of their personal fortunes if the funds of the business are not sufficient to pay the business' debts.
(c) Because Hank was 100% at fault in causing a loss to their client, Hank is solely liable, not Alex, Laura or Jim.
(d) Alex and Jim could be successfully sued for Laura's misappropriation of the client's $2000.
(e) When Jim ordered supplies for the business, he was acting as an agent for the business and for Alex and Laura.

52. Which of the following does not apply to limited partnerships?
(a) Limited partners are liable only to the extent of their investment.
(b) Limited partners must follow provisions set out in the Act to avoid risk of being considered a general partner.
(c) Limited partners must share management decisions.
(d) Limited partners must register as limited partner.
(e) Limited partners must not allow their name to be included in firm name.

53. It is possible to create partnerships in which a partner has limited liability.
(a) True
(b) False

54. Sam, Dennis and George are considering starting an accounting business together. In their jurisdiction they can't incorporate and if they want to work together they must do so in a partnership. They are meeting to consider the implications of this and make the following observations. Indicate which is correct.
(a) They can still have the advantages of limited liability by all registering as limited partners.
(b) Any that are limited partners have all of the advantages of participating in the partnership but with no liability.
(c) Even a limited partner can lose what he has invested.
(d) The advantage of limited partners is that they can lose nothing, whereas general partners can also lose what they have invested.
(e) Even limited partners must concur with any major decisions.

55. Nicole and Alice had been friends in grade school. They met again at a party at college. Nicole had just graduated with a business degree and Alice from computing. The more they talked about their plans the more they recognized common interests. Both wanted to be involved with structuring new businesses. They met over the next month determining the expertise of each and how they would structure and operate their own business. It was clear they needed more operating capital than either had. Nicole invited her brother, a manager of a manufacturing plant to join them in their

discussion of setting up their business. His experience, contacts and reputation could help them not only to establish their business, but also to run it on a day-to-day basis. With these facts in mind, which of the following is false?

(a) There need be only one general partner in a partnership.

(b) If the brother would agree to be a limited partner, his contribution must be in money or property, not services.

(c) If the brother agreed to be a limited partner, he must follow the statutory provisions governing limited partners, otherwise he could be deemed a general partner.

(d) If the brother agreed to be a limited partner, his proper position would be as a part-time co-manager, so that his experience could facilitate the operation of the business.

(e) If a limited partnership is formed, papers must be filed at the appropriate registry.

56. Sam, Dennis and George are considering starting an accounting business together. In their jurisdiction they can't incorporate and if they want to work together they must do so in a partnership. They have decided not to enter into a formal partnership agreement and to just be bound by the provision of the *Partnership Act*. They are discussing the implications of this decision and make the following observations. Indicate which is correct.

(a) At least they know that they don't have to worry about getting locked in; any two can out vote the other in important matters related to the partnership, since all partners have an equal say.

(b) Any earnings will be paid out in the same proportion to their investment. Sam put in $5,000, Dennis $10,000 and George put in $20,000.

(c) At least they know that they don't have to worry about getting locked in. If they decide to end the partnership, any one of them can serve notice on the others to that effect and the partnership will be dissolved.

(d) They also know that each working partner will be entitled to a salary from the partnership.

(e) They have the reassurance of knowing that if any individual works harder, that person will be rewarded since they will take out of the partnership earnings whatever they bill their individual clients minus their share of the operating expenses.

57. Sam, Dennis and George decided to go into an accounting partnership together. Green, a client, lost $60 000 because of Sam's negligence and is suing for that amount. Which of the following is correct with respect to their liability?

(a) If they have included a term in the formal partnership agreement that they made to the effect that each partner would be responsible for no more than 1/3 of partnership liabilities, Green will only be able to collect $20 000 from Dennis.

(b) Even though there is a partnership agreement to the effect that each partner will be responsible for no more than 1/3 of the liabilities of the partnership, Dennis could be sued for the entire amount and could lose his house.

(c) Without a partnership agreement, each partner can lose only what they have invested.

    (d) If Dennis is registered as a limited partner and has been careful to take an equal share of the management responsibilities of the partnership, his liability will be limited to 1/3 of the claims against the partnership

    (e) If the partnership agreement specifically limits the authority of each partner to enter into contracts of no more than $10 000 without the approval of the others, and Sam enters into a contract of $15 000 (for 3 computers, a scanner, printer, photocopier and fax machine), that contract will not be binding on the other partners.

58. The advantage of being a limited partner is that they can't lose anything if things go wrong for the partnership.
    (a) True
    (b) False

59. When a partner dies and the partnership agreement provides that the partnership will not dissolve, the heir of that partner automatically takes over his share and becomes the new partner.
    (a) True
    (b) False

60. Which of the following is incorrect with respect to the dissolution of a partnership?
    (a) Where there are 3 or more partners the partnership will automatically dissolve upon the bankruptcy of one of the partner unless it states otherwise in the partnership agreement.
    (b) The partnership will dissolve by one partner giving notice to that effect to the others unless it says otherwise in the partnership agreement.
    (c) Where there are 3 or more partners the partnership will dissolve upon the death of one of the partners, but just with respect to that one partner unless it states otherwise in the partnership agreement.
    (d) The partnership can be dissolved by court order no matter what it says in the partnership agreement.
    (e) The partnership may dissolve at the end of a specified time if it says so in the partnership agreement.

61. Three students, Tom, Dick and Harry, needed a way to earn some money while going through university. They were all knowledgeable about computers and had some contacts in the industry and decided to get together to put on a computer show at the university to display new equipment and programs. They rented a hall and made arrangements with local merchants to display their equipment and agreed to give them a commission on any sales that were generated from the show. The first attempt was quite successful and they were optimistic about the prospects. They entered into an agreement with each other that stated if they put on any other activities such as this they would share the profits equally and that any liabilities or debts that were incurred would also be shared equally between the parties. They put on one other computer show three months later, which was also a success. Then

Tom, through his contacts in his home town, discovered that a major manufacturer of computer hardware (IPM) wanted to sponsor an international computer fair in the area. Tom jumped at the opportunity and in his name and on his own behalf entered into a contract with the IPM to promote the activity in the city and at the university. He made arrangements to get auditorium and convention space in the city reserved for the three days designated for the fair. As part of the deal, Tom had to guarantee a gate receipt of at least $100 000, but also acquired all of the souvenir and program rights for the fair. This he sold to a local promoter for a set fee of $10 000, which was paid well in advance of the fair. Tom never talked to his other two friends Dick and Harry and never got their consent for the activity. In fact he tried to keep it a secret from them.

As the designated time for the fair arrived, a tremendous problem developed. It turned out that the city's national hockey team, for the first time in their history, managed to place in the Stanley Cup playoffs. There were seven games in all and the schedule for the last three games corresponded to the same nights as the computer fair. In fact the series was very close and it had to go to the last game to be decided. Only 100 people in total showed up for the computer fair. At $10 per ticket this was terribly disappointing for Tom and, to make matters worse, on the day when most of the people showed up at the fair, a motorcycle gang who had a small grudge to settle against Tom, crashed in, beat up several of the patrons, damaged thousands of dollars of equipment and caused considerable damage to the facilities as well. The university had insisted that Tom arrange for adequate security just in case such an event were to take place. Tom had ignored this requirement. Tom and Dick were just poor students and had very little money, but Harry had been very successful developing computer games before he came to the university and had considerable assets including a large house and several valuable cars. Explain the legal position of the parties. Would your answer be any different if the three students together arranged and put on the fair, but Harry had registered as a limited partner, investing $10 000 in the enterprise?

Answers to Review Questions

1. a   P. 404   D.1
2. d   P. 403   D.1
3. b   P. 404   D.1
4. a   P. 403   D.1
5. e   P. 404   D.2
6. b   P. 404   D.1
7. a   P. 404   D.1
8. d   P. 411   D.2
9. b   P. 405   D.1
10. Each partner is both an agent and a principal to every other partner. This is the basis for liability of each partner for the conduct of the other partners.

    P. 409   D.2
11. e   P. 406   D.1
12. e   P. 406   D.2
13. a   P. 407   D.1
14. d   P. 406-8   D.2
15. a   P. 407   D.1
16. c   P. 417   D.2
17. c   P. 405-8   D.2
18. The general provisions of the *Partnership Act* apply and they may be appropriate in the individual situation. In other words, certain activities may be interpreted as constituting a partnership whether or not it was.

    P. 406-8   D.2
19. b   P. 408   D.1
20. b   P. 406   D.1
21. fiduciary duty

    P. 411   D.1
22. There is the danger that this will be viewed as the creation of a partnership, but if it's done properly, the *Partnership Act* specifically excludes this kind of arrangement.

    P. 406   D.2
23. b   P. 409   D.1

24. a   P. 412   D.1
25. e   P. 413   D.2
26. b   P. 405-8 D.2
27. a   P. 408   D.1
28. a   P. 409   D.1
29. b   P. 413   D.1
30. a   P. 407-8 D.1
31. Agreement to that effect and notice served on all potential third parties (i.e., all customers of the business) and he or she must make certain that his/her name is no longer associated with the firm.

    P. 410   D.2
32. e   P. 409   D.1
33. b   P. 409, 411   D.2
34. a   P. 410   D.1
35. b   P. 409   D.1
36. a   P. 409   D.1
37. If there were a major dispute the business would grind to a halt. Nothing can be done without unanimous agreement .

    P. 413   D.2
38. e   P. 406   D.2
39. b   P. 410   D.1
40. The limited partner loses that status and becomes a full partner.

    P. 417   D.1
41. a   P. 411   D.1
42. a   P. 411-2 D.2
43. d   P. 413   D.2
44. a   P. 411-2 D.1
45. a   P. 413   D.1
46. a   P. 415   D.1
47. c   P. 415   D.2
48. e (also b in many jurisdictions)

    P. 415   D.2
49. a   P. 415   D.1

50.	b	P. 416	D.1
51.	c	P. 409	D.2
52.	c	P. 417	D.2
53.	a	P. 417	D.1
54.	c	P. 417	D.2
55.	d	P. 417	D.2
56.	c	P. 416	D.2
57.	b	P. 410	D.2
58.	b	P. 417	D.1
59.	b	P. 415	D.1
60.	c (a in B.C.)		
		P. 415	D.2

61. The primary question is whether Tom, Dick and Harry are partners in this disastrous adventure. The fact is that they have put two of these fairs on already and so they are carrying on a business together with a view to profits and so people dealing with them in this venture would be entitled to assume they were in partnership and seek redress from any one or all of the three. IPM would be able to sue them for damages caused by failure to have $100 000 in gate receipts. The local promoter may or may not be able to seek redress depending on what the terms of his agreement. If that contract for the souvenir and program rights has no liability for Tom then the $10 000 he received would be available to his creditors to pay for their losses. If there was a partnership involved and it looks as if there is, Dick and Harry would have been entitled to a n equal share of this money, if there is any left. It is apparent, however, that it will all be taken up to pay for the debts. It would also seem that Tom was negligent in not providing proper security and so he (and his partners on the basis of vicarious liability) would be responsible for the damage caused to the facilities and equipment and also for any injuries suffered by the patrons especially because he had been warned of the likelihood of this happening. If a partnership is found between Tom, Dick and Harry, Harry stands to lose all he has. Partners in these situations are all liable for the entire loss and if the creditors cannot collect from one partner who has no assets they can collect from the partner who has, in this case Harry. Had Harry's role been limited to that of a limited partner and all the requirements for such a limited partnership had been fulfilled, such as registration and refraining from participation, then Harry's liability would have been limited to the $10 000 that he had invested. That is all he could have lost.

P. 406,
409,
416-7   D.3

Chapter 14

Corporations

Learning Objectives

At the end of the chapter you should be able to:

1. Outline the method of incorporation in three different jurisdictions.
2. Discuss what is meant by the myth of separate legal entity.
3. List and describe the various ways corporations obtain funding.
4. Summarize the rights and obligations of shareholders, directors, other officers and outsiders to the corporation.
5. Discuss the advantages and disadvantages of incorporating a company.

Key Terms

The following terms are highlighted in the text:

deeds of settlement	early means of setting up a company
registration	a legislated requirement for incorporating a company in some jurisdictions in Canada
letters patent	granted by government when company set up in some jurisdictions in Canada
articles of incorporation	a method of incorporating based on U.S. approach used in some jurisdictions in Canada
memorandum of association	constitution of a corporation in registration jurisdiction
articles of association	sets out the procedures for governing a corporation in registration jurisdiction
separate legal entity	a corporation exists separately from the people who created it
limited liability	a corporation shields owners, directors and managers from liability
share	the means of acquiring funds from a large number of sources to run a company
par value	a share with a stated value at issuance (most shares are no-par-value which allows the market to set the value of the share)
preferred shares	give the shareholder preference when dividends are declared and other benefits

bonds or debentures	a share interest in the indebtedness of a corporation
closely-held corporations	a corporation in which there are relatively few shareholders
broadly-held corporations	a corporation that is publicly traded on the stock market
fiduciary duty	directors owe a duty to act in the best interest of the corporation
liability	the corporation can hold directors responsible for failure to live up to duties
derivative action	(sometimes called representative action) the right of shareholders to sue the directors on behalf of an injured company
insider knowledge	directors managers and large shareholders cannot profit by improperly using confidential knowledge about the company
due diligence	doing everything reasonable to avoid the problem leading to legal liability
securities commission	provincial agency serves as watchdog on stock market
prospectus	public document disclosing relevant information about a company
auditor	unbiased outside accountant who ensures financial statements for a corporation are properly done
annual general meeting	a meeting where shareholders vote for directors and on other important resolutions
common shares	allow for one vote at shareholders meeting
preferred shareholders	normally can only vote for directors when dividends have not been paid
oppression action	shareholders bring an action against the directors who have offended the rights of the minority shareholders
dissent	when major changes adversely affect a shareholder, they can force the company to buy back the shares at a fair price
shareholder agreement	protects the rights of shareholders in relations with the company
dividends	payments to shareholders out of company profits

Chapter Outline

Incorporation

The most common method of setting up a business that
requires large-scale financing by shareholders who have a
limited role in the organization

The corporation has a separate legal identity from the people
who make it up

Three methods of incorporation used in Canada:

(1) *Registration* - developed from the parliamentary power
to incorporate through special acts
- Based on contractual relationship between parties
- System used in British Columbia and Nova Scotia

Requires registration of memorandum and Articles of
Association
- Memorandum similar to a constitution
- Sets out name, purpose of company and authorized share
capital.
- Articles of association set out rules for day-to-day
operation of corporation

(2) *Letters Patent* - developed from practice of monarch
granting royal charters
- Granted by government agency upon application and
meeting certain qualifications (government has power to
refuse right to incorporate)
- System used in Quebec and Prince Edward Island
- Letters patent corresponds to royal charter and becomes
constitution of new company.
- Bylaws that govern day-to-day operation of company
must be filed

(3) *Articles of Incorporation* - follows a system used in the
U.S. based on filing of Articles of Incorporation and the
granting of certificate of incorporation (government does
not have power to refuse right to incorporate)
- Used in most provinces
- Articles of incorporation are like a constitution
controlling the activities of parties
- System uses bylaws to govern operation but there is no
requirement to file them

Separate Legal Entity

An incorporated company is a legal entity (person) separate and apart from the individuals who make it up

Shares bestow the right to control but not ownership (unless company is being wound up)

Shareholders liability limited to amount invested

Capacity was a problem in registration jurisdictions, but now they have "all the powers of a natural person" unless there is notice of limited capacity

Agency

Corporations must act through agents; therefore, agency law important

Funding

Major reason for incorporation is to provide capital from a large number of sources

Two primary methods:

(1) *Shares* - give holder an interest in the company but not ownership

Types of shares:

(a) par value (face value) - original price set by company

(b) non-par-value - the price of share reflects actual worth of the business (most common practice)

Types of shareholders:

(a) preferred - has right to collect a specified dividend when they are declared and to vote if they are not paid

(b) common - receives dividends only when declared and after preferred shareholders have been paid

Various rights and restrictions can be placed on shares by company issuing them

(2) *Borrowing*

(a) loan from single large investor (bank)

(b) bonds (debentures) establish creditor/debtor relationship

- can involve many small investors

- bondholder has loaned money to company and has right to payment but has no right to participate in management of company unless there is a default

Closely-Held and Broadly-Held Corporations

Closely-held - private corporations with relatively few shareholders; freer of government control

Broadly-held - large, public corporations; require more directors and more public access to records

Duties of Corporate Officers

Directors - elected by shareholders (in some jurisdictions must be a shareholder)
- Responsible to company, owes duty not to be negligent
- Fiduciary duty (must act in good faith)
- Duty owed to corporation not shareholders
- Shareholders may be able to sue directors on behalf of the company

Managers - fiduciary duty (same general duties as directors)

Shareholders rights and remedies:
- May see records, receive annual reports, right to vote for directors and on major changes, organize proxy voting
- Pre-emptive rights (shareholders may have right to be offered any new shares first)
- If directors abuse their power with respect to a shareholder, that shareholder can seek a court order for relief from oppression
- Dissent - a right requiring corporation to buy back shares

Advantages of Incorporation

- Liability of shareholder limited to investment
- Tax advantages
- No disruption when shareholder dies or shares are sold
- Few obligations placed on shareholders
- Separate management

Disadvantages

- Weak position of minority shareholders
- Expensive to incorporate and maintain required records

Termination of Corporation

- Failure to file annual reports
- By agreement
- By court order
- Bankruptcy

Review Questions

1. The process of incorporation developed to overcome which of the following problems associated with sole proprietorship and partnership?
   (a) Personal liability
   (b) Need for large amounts of capital
   (c) Major decisions needing unanimous consent
   (d) Flexibility in decision-making
   (e) All of the above

2. Providing access to large amounts of capital equipment is the main reason for incorporating a company.
   (a) True
   (b) False

3. Shareholders have a limited role in the management of a corporation.
   (a) True
   (b) False

4. There are three methods of incorporating a company in use in Canada today. What is the method used in your jurisdiction?

   _____

5. Registration of corporations is based on the practices developed in the U.S.
   (a) True
   (b) False

6. Special companies such as the CBC and the CPR were created by:
   (a) royal patents
   (b) letters patent
   (c) registration
   (d) acts of parliament
   (e) articles of incorporation

7. Registration is a form of incorporation that requires the company to register with a government body.
   (a) True
   (b) False

8. Registration is the method of incorporation used throughout Canada.
   (a) True
   (b) False

9. There are three recognized methods for incorporating a company, and the effect of each system is distinct.
    (a) True
    (b) False

10. The letters patent method of incorporation is based on the *Royal Charter* approach.
    (a) True
    (b) False

11. The letters patent method results in a charter of incorporation granted by the Crown.
    (a) True
    (b) False

12. The letters patent method is used in which of the following provinces?
    (a) Ontario and British Columbia
    (b) Maritime provinces
    (c) Quebec and P.E.I.
    (d) Alberta, Saskatchewan and Manitoba
    (e) Quebec and the Territories

13. The letters patent method of incorporation is the method most jurisdictions are moving toward.
    (a) True
    (b) False

14. Letters patent is based on which of the following concepts:
    (a) Contractual relationship between the members
    (b) Common sense
    (c) Act of parliament
    (d) Granting of *Royal Charter*
    (e) All of the above

15. The articles of incorporation method has been adopted by the federal government.
    (a) True
    (b) False

16. Which of the following is incorrect with respect to the letters patent method of incorporation?
    (a) Applicant petitions Corporations Society
    (b) Crown grants a letters patent
    (c) Certificate of corporation issued
    (d) Not based on contract, therefore, capacity not limited
    (e) a and c

17. Which of the following is incorrect with respect to the articles of incorporation method of incorporation?
    (a) Has features of both registration and letters patent systems
    (b) Not based on contractual relationship
    (c) Government body has no discretion to refuse requests
    (d) Based on *Royal Charter*
    (e) None of the above

18. Which of the following statements are true with regard to incorporating a company in your province?
    (a) The Provincial Registrar of Companies will issue a certificate of incorporation if you fulfill the requirements of the *Canada Business Corporation Act*.
    (c) The *Charter* document to be submitted to the Registrar of Companies is called the "Memorandum."
    (d) The incorporating document that must be filed is a letters patent.
    (e) The documents that must be filed to incorporate are articles of incorporation.
    (f) You would need another "subscriber" since it takes two or more natural persons to form a company.

19. Which of the following is an example of an incorporated body?
    (a) cities
    (b) public institutions (e.g., hospitals)
    (c) universities
    (d) non-profit societies
    (e) All of the above

20. Which of the following is not a characteristic of incorporation?
    (a) Creates a distinct legal entity separate from the people who make it up.
    (b) Isolates shareholders from business activity
    (c) Limits liability of shareholders and directors
    (d) Provides flexibility for investors to buy and sell shares
    (e) Gives minority shareholder veto power.

21. All methods of incorporation now provide for corporations to have all the legal capacity of a natural person.
    (a) True
    (b) False

22. What benefits are gained by a company having a separate legal existence from the managers and shareholders?

    (1) _____

    (2) _____

    (3) _____

23. How does agency law apply to corporations?

    _____

    _____

24. All activities of a corporation are carried out by agents.
    (a) True
    (b) False

25. An agent's actual or apparent authority must be detailed in publicly-filed documents and the agent must act within that authority for the company to be bound.
    (a) True
    (b) False

26. All employees owe a fiduciary duty to the corporation.
    (a) True
    (b) False

27. In which of the following relationships is a fiduciary duty owed?
    (a) An agent to a principal
    (b) The director of a company to the shareholders
    (c) The director of a company to the company
    (d) The officers of a company to the shareholders
    (e) All of the above

28. What are the major sources of funding for corporations?

    (1) _____

    (2) _____

29. Which of the following is not an example of debt financing (borrowing) available to a corporation?
    (a) shares
    (b) bonds
    (c) debentures
    (d) security
    (e) bank loan

30. Selling shares can be a means of providing capital from a large number of sources.
    (a) True
    (b) False

31. Another name for a share is
    (a) a loan
    (b) a negotiable instrument
    (c) a stock
    (d) a debenture
    (e) a bond

32. A bond is a written acknowledgement of an obligation or debt.
    (a) True
    (b) False

33. A bondholder is a participant in the corporation, not a creditor.
    (a) True
    (b) False

34. The company is in debt to the bondholder for the amount of the bond, but the company is not in debt to the shareholder for the price paid for the share.
    (a) True
    (b) False

35. A restriction on the transfer and sale of shares is usually imposed where the company is closely held.
    (a) True
    (b) False

36. A major source of funding for corporations is loans.
    (a) True
    (b) False

37. A debenture is usually secured by a specific asset.
    (a) True
    (b) False

38. The payment of debts always takes priority over payment of dividends.
    (a) True
    (b) False

39. A closely-held corporation is distinguished by the fact that shares are not sold openly on the stock market.
    (a) True
    (b) False

40. A broadly-held corporation is a more highly structured and regulated company.
    (a) True
    (b) False

41. A closely-held company is required to file additional reports.
    (a) True
    (b) False

42. Directors or managers of a corporation do not owe which of the following duties?
    (a) A duty to be careful to the company
    (b) A fiduciary duty to the company
    (c) A duty to act in the best interests of the shareholders
    (d) A duty to act in the best interest of the company
    (e) Not to take advantage of any opportunities that would violate fiduciary duty

43. Kent incorporated a provincial company, Dynamite Data, Ltd., which worked with small businesses in developing graphs and charts from their data which they might have to present to bankers, partners, shareholders, etc. Kent lent the company $25,000 by way of a shareholder's loan and took as security computers, plotters and printers under a chattel mortgage document. The company had no other assets. A company employee, delivering some graphs to a customer, got into an argument with the customer, who was complaining that the graph was in red and not in the "hot pink" as requested. It ended with the employee punching the customer who fell onto a microscopic camera. The damage to the nose and camera: $80,000. Which of the following is correct with respect to the legal position of the parties?
    (a) Kent will have first claim on the computers and printers etc.
    (b) Kent will lose his $25,000.
    (c) The employee is responsible for his own wrongful conduct and the customer has no recourse against Dynamite Data, Ltd. or Kent.
    (d) Because Kent is a shareholder, the injured customer will have first claim against the assets of Dynamite Data, Ltd.
    (e) a and b

44. What recourse does a shareholder have against directors who abuse their power?

    _____

    _____

45. Shareholders are agents of the company and thus can bind the company to contracts with third parties so long as they are acting in their capacity as shareholders.
    (a) True
    (b) False

46. A derivative or representative action is the right that shareholders have to sue the directors on behalf of a company.
    (a) True
    (b) False

47. Which of the following is false with respect to the position of a minority shareholder in a closely held company with only four other shareholders?
    (a) They can be locked in and outvoted.
    (b) They have the right to bring a representative action if the directors do something not in the best interests of the company.
    (c) They should enter into a shareholders' agreement to protect their position.
    (d) They often can't sell their shares without the approval of the directors.
    (e) This is an incorporated partnership and any major decision must be approved by all of the shareholders.

48. If a company had been wronged by negligent and fraudulent acts of one of its directors and consequently suffered a $25 000 loss and the board of directors would not take any action on behalf of the company against the wrongdoer, which of the following is true?
    (a) The shareholders could force the directors to start the action on the basis of their "pre-emptive rights."
    (b) If the company failed to commence an action through its authorized agents (e.g., its directors), no action could be taken because a company is merely a legal concept and must act through its authorized agents.
    (c) The shareholder could proceed under the "dissent" procedure and force the company to pay them a fair market value for their shares.
    (d) A shareholder could, with leave of the court, commence an action on behalf of the company.
    (e) The shareholder can directly sue the directors for negligence and fraud.

49. Directors may be personally liable if they do which of the following:
    (a) Fail to give proper notice of shareholder meetings
    (b) Fail to adhere to the restrictions on company power
    (c) Use insider knowledge to their own advantage
    (d) Allow dividends to be paid out to shareholders when the company is insolvent
    (e) All of the above

50. Directors or managers may be held personally liable for which of the following:
    (a) Unpaid wages
    (b) Dividends paid when company insolvent
    (c) Unpaid taxes
    (d) Damage to the environment
    (e) All of the above

51. Which of the following is an example of breach of fiduciary duty?
    (a) The directors of the company, contrary to the request of the shareholder, refused to declare dividends.
    (b) The officers of the company failed to disclose at a meeting of the directors their interest in a proposed contract.
    (c) A director of a company, as director, learned of a good deal and took advantage of it for himself before the company had the opportunity to do so.
    (d) A promoter of a company sold property to the company for three times what he paid for it after he made full disclosure of his interest to an independent board of directors that voted for the purchase.
    (e) A shareholder started a business that competed directly with the business.

52. Officers and senior executives are responsible for day-to-day management of the company and owe which of the following duties to the company?
    (a) Fiduciary duty
    (b) Duties of care and competence
    (c) Duties similar to those of directors
    (d) Duty of full disclosure
    (e) All of the above

53. If a promoter wants to sell property to the company at a profit what must he do to avoid having to give the profit up to the company?

    _____

    _____

54. Shareholders owe similar duties to the corporation as do director and senior executives.
    (a) True
    (b) False

55. An agent owes a fiduciary duty to his principal; a director owes a fiduciary duty to the company; partners owe a fiduciary duty to the firm and to the other partners. Which of the following is not true with regard to one's fiduciary duty?
    (a) An agent would be in breach of his fiduciary duty if he let his interest conflict with his duty.
    (b) A fiduciary is in a position of trust and owes a duty to act in the best interests of the person to whom the duty is owed.
    (c) A fiduciary is responsible for any losses suffered by the person to whom the duty is owed.
    (d) A partner secretly competing with his own firm would be in breach of his fiduciary duty.
    (e) An agent failing to disclose to his principal all information relating to the principal's business transaction would be in breach of his fiduciary duty.

56. If directors of a company, in their capacity as directors, learned of a business opportunity intended for the company and intercepted it for their own benefit, what liability would they face?

_____

_____

57. Is there any way in which the directors in the previous question could have taken that opportunity without liability to the company?

_____

_____

_____

58. Which of the following is false with regard to the duties of the directors of the company?
    (a) The directors have an obligation to manage the company.
    (b) The directors have an obligation to act honestly and in the best interests of the company.
    (c) The directors owe a fiduciary duty to the company, not the shareholders directly.
    (d) The standard of care owed by the directors to the company is merely not to do anything intentionally to harm the company.
    (e) A director cannot avoid all liability by putting an exemption clause in the shareholder's agreement.

59. Mr. Ace of ABC Ltd., a non-reporting company, is one of three shareholders. After several years of considerable success, the company hit hard times. The other shareholders, Mr. Bane and Mr. Curr, voted Mr. Ace out as a director and voted not to renew his employment contract. Upset by these events, Mr. Ace just wanted to sell his interest and leave the company. The other two shareholders, however, refused to buy his shares. Furthermore, when he attempted to sell his shares to his brother, who was interested in the company, they refused to register the brother as a member. Which of the following is true?
    (a) Mr. Ace could "dissent" under the dissent procedure in your province's *Company Act* and thereby force the company to pay him a fair market value for his shares.
    (b) Mr. Ace could sue the company for breach of its fiduciary duty.
    (c) The court would "lift the corporate veil" because Mr. Bane and Mr. Curr were hiding behind the company to commit a fraud.
    (d) Mr. Ace could sell his shares to whomever he chose and the remaining shareholders must register the new owner.
    (e) Mr. Ace could have avoided such a dilemma through provisions of a shareholders' agreement.

60. Which of the following is not a right of a shareholder?
    (a) Access to all records and financial reports
    (b) Receive notice of annual general meetings
    (c) Right to elect directors
    (d) To be free from oppression
    (e) Derivative (representative) action

61. What are the main advantages of incorporation?

    (1) _____

    (2) _____

    (3) _____

    (4) _____

    (5) _____

    (6) _____

62. Which of the following is not a disadvantage of incorporation?
    (a) It is costly.
    (b) It is difficult to make major changes without changing incorporation documents.
    (c) Shareholders owe fiduciary duty to the corporation.
    (d) Weak position of minority shareholders.
    (e) Shareholders don't own assets.

63. Joan Gau incorporated a company in your province called Quick Courier Ltd. as a city delivery service. Gau lent the company $12 000 and took from the company, as security for the loan a chattel mortgage covering three motorcycles and one new truck owned by the company. Ted Speede, one of the employees of the company, while making a delivery for the company, negligently crashed a company motorcycle through an office window of a building owned by Mr. A. Turney and caused $7 000 worth of damage to the building. Turney sued Ted Speede for negligence and Joan Gau as vicariously liable for the tortious act of her employee.

    Answer the following questions with respect to the above facts.

Part A

(a) _____ (T/F) Gau will be liable to A. Turney for the damage if no money is recovered from Ted Speede.

Part B

Which of the following would be true if Gau bought those motorcycles for the company a day before the Certificate of Incorporation was issued?

(a) The company would be bound by the contract unless the other party actually knew that fact.
(b) The company would not be bound by the contract unless it ratified the contract after the issuance of the Certificate of Incorporation.
(c) The company would not be bound by the contract even if it tried to ratify it.
(d) None of the above

Part C

What would be the legal effect of the contract if the company had bought three motorcycles, after incorporation, directly contrary to the restrictions contained in the company's charter document?
(a) The company would not be bound because the company had no authority to make such a purchase; therefore, the contract is *ultra vires* and of no effect.
(b) The company is bound but only if the director later ratified the contract.
(c) The company is bound even if the province's *Company Act* states that no company should do what it is restricted from doing in its memorandum.
(d) The courts would "lift the corporate veil."

Part D

If Quick Courier Ltd. went bankrupt, which creditor stands in a better position to be paid?
(i) A person who loaned the company $3 000 without security
(ii) Joan Gau

64. A, B, C, D and E are all of the shareholders of a limited liability company specializing in high technology research and development. Each owns 20% of the issued shares of the company and each has a total of $20 000 invested in the company for their shareholdings.

   A, B, and C are the directors of the company, with A and B performing all of the managerial functions. C is a director merely for appearances, since he was a high-profile figure in the industry before retiring. D and E have refrained from becoming directors or officers because they are part of management in competing companies. A and B see major opportunities for the company, which would require a great deal of financing to acquire needed machinery. They have approached the company's banks, but the proposals they have received for bank financing require personal guarantees from all the shareholders in addition to other security.

   A and B have limited personal resources and can get very little cash from their personal banks to invest in the company. They are willing to guarantee. C does not wish to be involved with active management anymore, nor is he willing to commit any further personal resources, including any guarantees. He is happy with the current level of the company's business, and with the director's fee he gets yearly for his services. D is not willing to invest more capital or guarantee, but is willing to give the company an opportunity of large proportions that he knows is to be offered to another corporation in which he is a director. He can divert this job to the company without the other corporation finding out. In return he wants more shares in the company.

E has large personal resources and also controls and has majority (51%) ownership of XYZ Research Corporation, a limited company that could lease or sell the needed equipment to the company. He is aware of all of the above information concerning the company. He is very interested in the company even though it could possibly compete with XYZ Research Corporation, and is motivated solely by his own potential personal gain. He is also a director of the above-mentioned corporation in which D is a director, and D has offered him cash or shares in the company if E keeps quiet about the "opportunity" D wants to direct to the company.

(a) What options would A and B have to get the needed equipment for the company? Which of the options is in your opinion the best for the company?

(b) You are E's personal lawyer. Advise him fully concerning the relevant issues.

(c) What issues would arise if A and B:

(i) left the company to start up their own operation as partners?

(ii) left the company to work for the corporation which D controlled, to follow-up the same opportunities that the company had?

Answers to Review Questions

1. e   P. 423   D.2

2. b   P. 423   D.1

3. a   P. 423   D.1

4. (varies with jurisdiction)

        P. 423   D.1

5. b   P. 424   D.1

6. d   P. 423   D.2

7. a   P. 424   D.1

8. b   P. 424   D.1

9. a   P. 423   D.1

10. a   P. 424   D.1

11. a   P. 424   D.1

12. c   P. 425   D.1

13. b   P. 425   D.1

14. d   P. 424   D.1

15. a   P. 425   D.1

16. e   P. 424-5 D.2

17. d   P. 425   D.2

18. (varies with jurisdiction)

        P. 424-5 D.2

19. e   P. 425   D.2

20. e   P. 423-7 D.2

21. a   P. 427   D.1

22. (1) limited liability

     (2) does not die

     (3) free transferability of shares

        P. 427,
        445   D.2

23. The corporation acts through agents

        P. 428   D.2

24. a   P. 428   D.1

25. b   P. 428   D.1

26. b   P. 431   D.1

27. a, c P. 433   D.2

28. (1) equity funding (shares)

     (2) loans, bonds, debentures

        P. 428-431 D.1

29. a   P. 428-431 D.2

30. a   P. 428   D.1

31. c   P. 428   D.2

32. a   P. 430   D.1

33. b   P. 430   D.1

34. a   P. 430   D.1

35. a   P. 431   D.1

36. a   P. 430   D.1

37. b   P. 430   D.1

38. a   P. 430   D.1

39. a   P. 431   D.1

40. a   P. 431   D.1

41. b   P. 431   D.1

42. c   P. 433   D.2

43. e   P. 428   D.2

44. Depending on the nature of the abuse, the shareholders may be able to sue for oppression, sue on behalf of the company using a derivative or representative action, or file a dissent.

        P. 433, 441-2 D.2

45. b   P. 439-441 D.2

46. a   P. 441   D.1

47. e   P. 441   D.2

48. d (may vary with jurisdiction)

        P. 441   D.2

49. e   P. 434   D.2

50. e   P. 434   D.2

51. b, c P. 433   D.2

52. e   P. 436   D.2

53. He must disclose his interest in the commodity being sold; he must declare that he is making a profit on it to the other directors; let them make the decision, not

participate in the decision-making process himself.

54. b P. 439 D.2

55. c P. 433, 436-7 D.3

56. They would have to account for any profits because this is a violation of their fiduciary duty to the company.

  P. 433 D.2

57. If they declared their interest to the company, made sure they didn't participate in the decision as to whether to take it or not, disclosed the interest and then if the company rejected it, they would probably be free to make their decision.

  P. 433 D.3

58. d P. 431-5, 443 D.2

59. e P. 427, 431, 433, 442-3, 445 D.3

60. a P. 439-441 D.2

61. (1) limited liability

(2) tax advantages

(3) no disruption when shareholder dies

(4) few obligations placed on shareholders

(5) separate management

(6) ease of transfer of shares

  P. 444-7 D.2

62. c P. 447-8 D.2

63. The statement in Part A is false. In Part B, b or c is correct, depending on the jurisdiction. In Part C, c indicates the legal effect. In Part D, Joan Gau would be in the better position.

  P.443-440

64. (a): If A and B cannot persuade C, D and E to guarantee a loan for the new machinery, they will have to come up with another alternative. They could form a partnership or a separate corporation and purchase the machinery themselves, then lease or sell it to this corporation. Still, they would have difficulties arranging the financing unless they could persuade the bank to accept only their personal guarantees as enough. Since E is in a position to supply the equipment needed, arrangements could be made directly with the suppliers for the financing, and either lease the equipment or purchase it on a conditional sales agreement. Because C, D and E are not interested in the business or themselves incurring more debt, A and B would have to go into this new project in such a way that since they will bear a greater risk, they will get a greater profit. They could form a separate company and have that company acquire the equipment leasing it then to the first. The lease rate would reflect the greater commitment and risk faced by A and B. Alternatively, they could be given more shares in the original company. If they have to invest more in the company or personally assume more of the debt, they could be given preferred shares to cover their additional involvement or risk. Of these options perhaps the simplest would be for them to arrange to acquire the equipment directly from XYZ on terms if E is willing to arrange that. They could then form their own company to hold this equipment, sign a personal guarantee to XYZ Co. to secure the debt and to lease that equipment out to the original company at a favourable rate to compensate them personally for their added risk.

(b): E is in a conflict position with both XYZ Co. and this company and has to act in the best interests of both (assuming he is also a director or officer of XYZ Co.). When he supplies the equipment to this company he must be careful to disclose his interest and avoid voting. When he deals with XYZ Co. he must do the same. He is also a director in the company that D is a director of and has knowledge that D will divert a business opportunity from that company to this one. He must disclose this as well and if he fails to, especially if he profits by it as well, he is in breach of his duty to that company.

(c): In both of these cases they are taking away a corporate opportunity from their company that would not be in the best interests of the corporation. This would violate their fiduciary duty to the company as directors even if they have the votes to control the vote. In fact, in these circumstances they should refrain from voting. (Note that there are many different approaches that could be used on this question.)

P. 431-440

Chapter 15

Personal and Real Property

Learning Objectives

At the end of the chapter you should be able to:

1. Distinguish between real and various forms of personal property.
2. Identify and describe the various kinds of interests a person may have in land.
3. Explain the duties in a bailment
4. Outline the rights and responsibilities of landlords and tenants.
5. Describe the process by which a person assumes, redeems or forecloses on a mortgage.

Key Terms

The following terms are highlighted in the text.

chattels	tangible, moveable personal property that can be measured and weighed
chose in action	intangible personal property, a claim or the right to sue
intellectual property	personal property in the form of ideas and creative work
copyright	gives author control over the use and reproduction of the expression of creative work
patent	gives inventor the right to profit from inventions
trademarks	protect the name or logo of a business
real property	land and anything attached to it
fixture	a thing permanently attached to land or building
bailment	when one persons takes temporary possession of chattels owned by another
bailor	the owner giving up possession of property in a bailment
bailee	person acquiring possession of property in a bailment
quantum meruit	reasonable price paid for requested services
estate in land	and interest in land (all land is owned by the Crown)
fee simple	highest interest in land, equivalent to ownership
life estate	an interest in land ending at death.

reversionary interest	upon death of life tenant ownership reverts to original owner
remainderman	third party with the right to the fee simple after the death of a life tenant
dower rights	protect the rights of spouse, have been modified or abolished in most jurisdictions
homestead rights	give spouse a claim to a substantial portion of family property upon divorce
easement	the right of a person other than the owner to use a portion of private property
right of way	type of easement that allows the crossing of another's land
dominant property	property that has the advantage of an easement
servient property	the property subject to an easement
licenses	permission to use another's land that can be revoked
easement acquired by prescription	free use of land without interference over a number of years gives a right to the use of that land
adverse possession	a right to actual possession can be acquired by non-contested use of the land
profit à prendre	contracts to take resources off the land
restrictive covenant	seller imposes restrictions on what the purchaser can use the land for
building scheme	restrictions placed on all the properties in a large development
tenancy in common	two people with undivided half interest in land
joint tenancy	shared ownership with right of survivorship
option agreement	consideration given to hold an offer open to sell land
agreement for sale	purchase of land by installments
mortgage	title of property is held by the money-lender as security
deed of conveyance	document transferring an interest in property
registration system	a means of registering and tracking property deeds
land titles system	registration system that certifies title to property.
certificate of title	conclusive evidence of the owner of property
cooperative	members own shares in a residential building
leasehold estate	tenant has exclusive possession until a specific date
license	a non-exclusive right to use property
periodic tenancy	automatically renewing tenancy with no specific termination date

vacant possession	owner has obligation to provide premises that are empty and ready for occupancy
quiet enjoyment	landlord must ensure that nothing interferes with tenant's use of the property
tenancy at sufferance	tenant who fails to leave after lease has expired must compensate landlord
frustration	where leased premises become unusable by an unforeseen event the lease is terminated
abatement	a court order to reduce the rent to be paid to compensate for breach of lease by landlord
forfeiture	when lease is breached the landlord may terminate the lease and require the tenant to vacate the property.
distress	landlord can seize and sell property left by tenant to pay rent owing
equity of redemption	mortgagor retains an interest in land even after default
order nisi	an order establishing the time limit within which the mortgagor can redeem his interest
order absolute	final order of foreclosure ending the right to redeem
suing on the covenant	creditor can sue for breach of contract
foreclosure	court process ending the mortgagor's right to redeem

Chapter Outline

Notes

Property

The nature of the interest a person has in an item
Ownership - the highest form of property rights also known as
    possession of title
Personal Property - moveable property
    (a) tangible property or chattels are measurable and
    moveable items
    (b) chose in action
    - intangible property
    - a claim or right to sue
When a chattel is affixed to real property it becomes part of
    that real property
Bailment occurs when possession of chattels is acquired by
    someone else. Bailee has a duty to care for the goods.
    Standard of care determined by whether bailment is

gratuitous or for value (by contract) and whether it is for the benefit of the bailee or bailor

Legal Interests in Land

Real Property - land and anything that is affixed to or constructed on the land

Interest in Land

Fee Simple - "ownership" - the right to use or transfer land subject to local restrictions

Life Estate - property cannot be willed to heirs
- reverts back to original owner or other designated party upon life tenant's death

Leasehold Estates - the right to use property granted for a definite period of time (landlord/tenant relationship)

Lesser Interests in Land
- Easement - the right to use a portion of another's land (right of way)
- License – arrangement with owner to use land - Hotel
- In some provinces where the landowner tolerates people using his land over a long period they may acquire right to it by prescription or adverse possession
- *Profit à prendre* - contract to make use of some aspect of the land for personal profit (e.g. cutting the trees)
- Restrictive covenant - restrictions on how the land may be used that is binding on all holders

Tenancy

In common - two people share an estate in the same piece of land with each owning a half that can be sold or willed independent of the other

Joint tenancy - where two people share ownership of the whole property and upon the death of one, ownership of the whole reverts to the other – called survivorship.

Other interests in land
- Option agreement - by giving some consideration to hold the offer open a prospective buyer has the right to purchase the property at a given price
- Agreement for sale - bestows right to possess and eventually acquire property in the purchaser, but title remains with the seller as security for amount still owing
- Mortgage - title to property is transferred to moneylender as security for loan

Transfer and Registration of Interest in Land

In registration system land registry is a depository for documents that affect the title of property - parties must determine the legal effect of those documents

Land Titles System - in use many jurisdictions the certificate of title determines rights of parties. Onus is on parties to register their interest

- Condominium Interests - establishes individual ownership of designated area and common ownership of some parts of building and land
- Cooperative Interests - collective or shared ownership of whole building. Governed by bylaws of the cooperative

Landlord/Tenant Relationship

Leasehold estates - limited to a specific time
- Tenant has right to exclusive possession
- Lease (contract) specifies obligations (registration and writing required for leases for longer than three years)
- Leasehold interests run with land

Types of tenancies
- Term lease - exclusive possession for specified duration (can be sub-leased) Periodic tenancy (i.e. month-to-month)
- no specific time when tenant will terminate
- Tenancy at will (e.g. when purchaser takes possession before title transfers)
- Tenancy at sufferance - when tenant fails to vacate after receiving notice
- Legislation - varies with provinces and some provisions can be modified by contract

Landlord's obligations
(a) To give tenant vacant possession when lease period begins
(b) To assure quiet enjoyment and not interfere with tenant's use of property
(c) No general obligation to repair premises unless unfit for purpose intended

Landlord's remedies in event of breach of lease:
(a) Sue for payment of rent due and compensation for cost of repairs
(b) Injunction if there is a failure to honour lease obligations
(c) Evict tenant
(d) Seize property left by tenant (distress)

Tenant's rights and obligations:
(a) Pay the rent (this obligation independent of landlord's duties)

      (b) Keep premises in good repair (not responsible for normal wear and tear where property used in manner intended)

      (c) Upon leaving, remove fixtures that have been attached by tenant providing no damage

Tenant's remedies in event of breach of lease:

      (a) Sue for compensation of any injury suffered because of breach

      (b) Injunction to stop landlord's interfering activity

      (c) Treat lease agreement as discharged and vacate

Residential Tenancies

Special legislation (e.g. *Residential Tenancies Act*) covers: rentalsmen, rent controls, notice of rent increases, quality of facilities, security deposits

Real Property (Mortgages)

Mortgages - the borrower of money temporarily transfers title in property to creditor as security for loan

Equity of Redemption - the right to redeem after defaulting on repayment of loan

Foreclosure - *1st stage* - mortgagee obtains court order establishing time limit within which mortgagor must redeem. *2nd stage* - an order ending the right of mortgagor to redeem that allows property to be resold

Second mortgages - transfers equity of redemption
- Increased risk because of 1st mortgagor's power to foreclose

Obligations of Mortgagor
- Must carry adequate insurance
- Must pay property taxes and keep buildings in good repair
- Must make all payments

Rights of Mortgagee
- Right to sue for breach of contract if mortgagor fails to repay (cannot then foreclose since the two actions are inconsistent)
- Term in mortgage contract usually gives mortgagee the right to sell
- Upon default mortgagee can get order to take possession until property is redeemed
- Judicial sale - an application to the court that the property be sold under court's supervision to recover mortgagee's money
- Creditor can still sue for deficit

Review Questions

1. Property is simply defined as some physical object.
   (a) True
   (b) False

2. What is the primary distinction between personal and real property?

   _____

3. Which of the following is not considered personal property in legal terms?
   (a) land
   (b) anything permanently attached to land
   (c) moveable items
   (d) chattels
   (e) a and b above

4. When a chattel has been affixed to real property to enhance a commercial tenant's business, the tenant has the right to remove it when he vacates the premises.
   (a) True
   (b) False

5. The owner loses his/her claim to an item that has been found by another.
   (a) True
   (b) False

6. Which of the following is an example of the "finders keepers" rule?
   (a) The item was found on private property
   (b) The item was found by an employee of the original owner
   (c) the item was found on the private property of the owner
   (d) the item was never lost
   (e) the item has no traceable owner

7. If you turn a valuable watch that you have found over to the police, they gain prior title to the watch.
   (a) True
   (b) False

8. The rule when dealing with fungibles is that the exact goods need not be returned by the bailee.
   (a) True
   (b) False

9. Bailment for value means that only one of the parties is benefiting from the bailment.
    (a) True
    (b) False

10. Which of the following is an example of a gratuitous bailment for the benefit of the bailor?
    (a) Where Joe rents a video.
    (b) Where Joe loans his friend a shovel to do garden work.
    (c) Where Joe gives his plant to a friend to look after while Joe is on vacation.
    (d) Where Joe parks his car at a car lot.
    (e) Where Joe rents a car for the weekend

11. Identify two general classes of bailments.

    _____

    _____

12. Which of the following is incorrect with respect to bailment?
    (a) The duty imposed on a bailee for value may be determined by the terms of the contract.
    (b) There is no duty on a gratuitous bailee because there is no contract.
    (c) Innkeepers and common carriers at common law are in the position of insurers.
    (d) When there is an involuntary bailment, the bailee does not have as great a duty in relation to the goods as is the case where there is a gratuitous bailment for the benefit of the bailee.
    (e) A finder of a chattel has a claim against that chattel that is good against all but someone with a prior claim.

13. What is the difference between real property and chattels?

    _____

    _____

14. Included in the title to property is all the space above and below the land.
    (a) True
    (b) False

15. The right to the area above an individual's property is limited to the area the landowner can permanently use or occupy.
    (a) True
    (b) False

16. The right to the area under the land is subject to the Crown's sub-surface rights.
    (a) True
    (b) False

17. Which of the following does not constitute a legal interest in land?
    (a) Fee simple
    (b) Family estate
    (c) Life estate
    (d) Leasehold estate
    (e) Freehold estate

18. Which is the greatest interest a person can have in land?
    (a) estate in fee simple
    (b) life estate
    (c) leasehold estate
    (d) homestead estate
    (e) prescription

19. A leasehold estate is the right to use or hold property for a fixed amount of time.
    (a) True
    (b) False

20. The interest in land that is recognized as ownership is called

    _____.

21. Leasehold estates govern what important relationship?

    _____

22. Fee simple is ownership or the right to use land subject only to government restrictions.
    (a) True
    (b) False

23. No form of land ownership precludes a government from expropriating it.
    (a) True
    (b) False

24. When a property owner wants to insure that a member of his family has secure use of his property until the time of their death, he would create which of the following means of owning property?
    (a) Family estate
    (b) Life estate
    (c) Leasehold estate
    (d) Freehold estate
    (e) None of the above

25. Dower rights or homestead rights were designed to protect which of the following?
    (a) estate taxes owed to the government upon the death of property owner
    (b) the interests of brothers and sisters of property owner
    (c) the interests of children of property owner
    (d) the interests of the spouse of property owner
    (e) all of the above

26. A husband and wife own Lot A as joint tenants and Lot B as tenants-in-common. The husband's will reads: "I leave Lot A to my son John and Lot B to my daughter Mary." Who takes what when the husband dies?
    (a) The son, John, gets Lot A and daughter Mary gets Lot B just as their father wished and designated in his will.
    (b) John will get Lot A but Mary will not get Lot B because it was co-owned with the mother as tenants-in-common so the mother takes Lot B as the other tenant-in-common.
    (c) Mary will get all of Lot B but John will not get Lot A because it was co-owned with the mother in joint-tenancy so the mother takes Lot A as the surviving joint tenant.
    (d) Mary will get her father's interest in Lot B but John will get no interest in Lot A.

27. Freehold estates and leasehold estates are different terms of the same rights to property.
    (a) True
    (b) False

28. Indicate which of the following statements regarding the nature of the landlord-tenant relationship is accurate:
    (a) A leasehold is one kind of interest less than an estate.
    (b) A characteristic shared by leaseholds and life estates is that they both grant to the holder the right of exclusive possession.
    (c) Like other interests in land, all leases must be in written form to be enforceable.
    (d) The term of a lease must be either for a definite period of time or one that can be calculated with certainty.
    (e) All written leases must be registered.
    (f) In some circumstances an oral lease is valid and enforceable.

29. Last weekend Robert bought a house in Caledonia. He asked his friend to explain the meaning of the title of the transfer document: "transfer of estate in fee simple." Which of the following statements by his friend is false?
    (a) In relation to that property, you would have the greatest bundle of rights you can have, but not ownership of the land, because technically only the Crown owns the land.
    (b) Your fee simple interest is divisible; e.g. you can grant a life estate, based on the span of another's life, and the remainder could revert back to you or heirs.

(c) The essence of the estate, the fee simple as well as a life estate, is the right to possess the land without restriction as to what you can do with it.

(d) The fee simple interest is subject only to the superior rights of the Crown, such as the right to expropriate.

(e) None of the above

30. A periodic tenancy in a leasehold estate is renewed automatically.
(a) True
(b) False

31. Leasehold estate means that upon the death of a life tenant property reverts back to original owner.
(a) True
(b) False

32. Which of the following is not considered a lesser interest in land?
(a) Easement
(b) Right of way
(c) License
(d) Fee simple
(e) none of the above

33. An easement is the right to use a portion of another's land for a particular purpose.
(a) True
(b) False

34. A right of way, otherwise known as easement, gives someone exclusive right to use a portion of the property that belongs to another.
(a) True
(b) False

35. Which of the following would not be covered by a public easement?
(a) Roads
(b) Sewer pipes
(c) Hydro lines
(d) Public access to the beach
(e) Overhanging billboard

36. In some provinces a person may assume that he has a license to use another's land if over a period of time no one has interfered with his doing so.
(a) True
(b) False

37. In some provinces when a person crosses land over a period of time without interference that can become a right of way.
(a) True
(b) False

38. License to use another's property is granted by municipal authority.
(a) True
(b) False

39. A building scheme that provides for only the building of semi-detached houses in a particular area is a type of restrictive covenant.
(a) True
(b) False

40. In some jurisdictions a squatter can acquire the right to land if he occupies it for sometime without objection from the owner.
(a) True
(b) False

41. Tenancy in common occurs when two people share an undivided interest in property with each owning a portion.
(a) True
(b) False

42. A joint tenancy is when two or more people own a piece of real property together.
(a) True
(b) False

43. Which of the following would not sever a joint tenancy?
(a) The sale by one joint tenant of his interest to his uncle.
(b) The sale of one joint tenant of his interest to himself.
(c) The joint tenants agreeing between or among themselves to terminate the joint tenancy.
(d) One joint tenant commences a partition action
(e) Both b and d

44. Legislation to regulate condominium ownership had to resolve what particular problem?

____

____

45. What rights does a leasehold estate give to a tenant?

____

____

46. With respect to commercial tenancies only, which of the following describes legal responsibilities or duties accurately?
    (a) An obligation to mitigate losses by rerenting promptly when a tenant abandons the premises.
    (b) A tenant's obligation to return the premises at the end of the term of the lease in the same condition in which he or she received them.
    (c) An implied obligation on the tenant to repair reasonable wear and tear.
    (d) The landlord's implied obligation to provide premises that are reasonably fit for occupancy.
    (e) The landlord's implied obligation to allow the tenant to sublet or assign his interest in the leasehold.
    (f) The landlord's implied obligation not to interfere with the tenant's "quiet enjoyment" of the premises.

47. Which of the following statements concerning the remedies in the event of breach of the covenants in a commercial lease is/are accurate?
    (a) When the tenant proposes or begins to use the premises in a manner prohibited by the lease, the landlord's only remedy is to evict him and then sue for damages.
    (b) While a landlord may be able to obtain an injunction in some circumstances, this remedy is not available to the tenant.
    (c) The failure to provide the tenant with quiet enjoyment may excuse the tenant's obligations and allow him to terminate the lease.
    (d) When the landlord refuses to allow the tenant to take possession of the premises, the tenant is not entitled to an order for specific performance and must be satisfied with a claim for damages.
    (e) A breach of covenant amounts to frustration of the contract and therefore, both parties are excused from any further obligations.

48. Joint tenancy is when two people own the entire property and can will it to their individual heirs.
    (a) True
    (b) False

49. A tenancy in common allows one of the parties to will his or her share of the property to his or her heirs.
    (a) True
    (b) False

50. In a residential tenancy situation, which one of the following terms is not automatically made part of the agreement by the residential tenancy legislation in effect in your jurisdiction?
    (a) A prohibition against the landlord's receiving consideration for giving his consent to a sublease or assignment.
    (b) The landlord's right to enter the premises for inspection purposes whenever he considers it necessary to do so.

(c) The tenant's right to receive interest on his security deposit at the termination of the lease.

(d) The landlord's right to change outside locks to the residential property when there is a threat to its security.

(e) A prohibition against acceleration of the rent when the tenant breaches the contract.

51. Which of the following does not describe another interest in land?
(a) Option agreement
(b) Agreement for sale
(c) Mortgage
(d) Security
(e) All of the above

52. What are two conditions that represent a temporary interest in land?

_____

_____

53. An option agreement provides for some consideration to hold an offer open for a specific period of time.
(a) True
(b) False

54. A major reason for setting up systems of registering documents related to land transactions was to create an accurate title trail.
(a) True
(b) False

55. Two different systems of registering land transactions are in force in Canada. What are they and how do they differ?

_____

_____

_____

_____

56. The Land Titles System is unique because it:
(a) guarantees the title
(b) is a depository of documents but parties must determine meaning
(c) is evidence of what is recorded
(d) does not effect the title
(e) a and c above

57. In the Land Titles System a central registry prepares a certificate of title which determines interest and guarantees title.
    (a) True
    (b) False

58. Which of the following is not true with regard to leasehold estates?
    (a) Landlord retains reversionary interest in property
    (b) Lessee is entitled to exclusive possession during term of the lease
    (c) Contract law applies
    (d) Must be evidenced in writing (over 3 years)
    (e) Leasehold interests end when property is sold

59. Which of the following is not a type of tenancy?
    (a) Term lease
    (b) Periodic tenancy
    (c) Tenancy at will
    (d) Tenancy in common
    (e) Tenancy at sufferance

60. Periodic tenancy is stipulated to run for a specific period of time.
    (a) True
    (b) False

61. A term lease and a periodic tenancy are different forms of leasehold agreements, which vary in the way they are terminated.
    (a) True
    (b) False

62. A landlord is obligated to provide which of the following conditions?
    (a) Vacant possession.
    (b) Make premises fit for purpose intended.
    (c) Make all repairs as they become necessary.
    (d) Refrain from coming onto the property after lease has begun.
    (e) Consent to a tenant's arrangements to sublet.

63. For which of the following actions by the landlord could a commercial tenant legally withhold rent?
    (a) Failing to repair a leaky roof
    (b) Discontinuing a service that is reasonably related to the tenants continued use and enjoyment of the premises.
    (c) Failing to maintain the premises and fix normal wear and tear.
    (d) Adding a term to the tenancy contract that is not a term dictated by statute
    (e) None of the above

64. Notice to change or terminate a commercial tenancy must be given in:
    (a) one month
    (b) three months
    (c) one clear rental period
    (d) a reasonable time
    (e) none of the above

65. Tenancy at sufferance occurs when a tenant remains in possession after the term of the lease has expired.
    (a) True
    (b) False

66. The obligations of the landlord do not include which of the following unless specified by statute?
    (a) must not interfere with tenant's use of the property
    (b) premises rendered vacant and ready for occupancy
    (c) quiet enjoyment
    (d) clean and in good repair
    (e) termination with proper notice

67. The obligations of the tenant include which of the following?
    (a) pay the rent
    (b) repair undue damage caused by him- or herself
    (c) not disturb other tenants
    (d) not use property for uses other than those for which it was intended
    (e) all of the above

68. A tenant is obliged to:
    (a) make all repairs as they become necessary
    (b) pay the rent at the appropriate time
    (c) insure the premises
    (d) pay the landlord whether or not the property has been destroyed
    (e) allow the landlord to come in whenever he wants

69. A tenant has the right to remove his/her own fixtures before termination of lease.
    (a) True
    (b) False

70. Which of the following statements relating to the obligations of the parties in a residential tenancy are accurate?
    (a) A natural disaster (earthquake, flood, etc.) that destroys the residential premises will excuse each party his or her obligations toward the other.
    (b) In the event that the tenant does not pay his rent, the landlord is prohibited from seizing the tenant's personal possessions to make up for the nonpayment.

   (c) Where the tenant abandons premises that are the subject of a term certain, the landlord is entitled to do nothing and can just sit back and let the rent arrears accumulate until he decides to sue for the entire debt.

   (d) When the landlord breaches material covenants of the lease, the tenant's strongest legal remedy is to withhold the rent until the landlord complies with his obligations.

   (e) If the landlord sells the residential property before the lease expires, then the purchaser will have the same obligations with respect to the security deposit that the landlord originally had.

71. Which of the following may be a remedy available to a landlord when a tenant breaches a lease?
   (a) distress
   (b) rent to others when tenant has abandoned premises
   (c) change the locks
   (d) injunction
   (e) all of the above

72. Which of the following is not normally a remedy available to a tenant when the landlord breaches the lease?
   (a) may sue for injury suffered
   (b) injunction
   (c) withhold rent
   (d) vacate premises and terminate lease
   (e) seek a court order to end the lease

73. Which of the following is not an area usually covered by provincial legislation modifying residential tenancy rules?
   (a) controls on rent increases
   (b) notice of termination periods
   (c) quality of facilities and repair
   (d) security deposits
   (e) maximum rents to be charged

74. When a mortgage is used as a means of borrowing money the lender takes possession of the property used as collateral.
   (a) True
   (b) False

75. In order to raise the money to buy an apartment building, Mr. Jones borrowed $200 000 from Canada Trust and granted a first mortgage on the building. Mr. Jones borrowed another $50 000 from the Bank of Montreal and granted it a second mortgage on the building. Because of a major malfunction in the heating/cooling system of the building several of the tenants refused to pay their rent. As a result Mr. Jones defaulted on the payments to both banks. Which of the following is true?

(a) If, by the mortgage document, Mr. Jones has given the fee simple to the first mortgagee and the equity of redemption to the second mortgagee, he still retains an equity of redemption.
(b) If the first mortgagee obtained an *order absolute* for foreclosure and then sold the building for more than the amount owed, out of the remainder the second mortgagee would be paid first, and the surplus would go to the mortgagor.
(c) If the court granted the first mortgagee Canada Trust an order providing a six month redemption period and the second mortgagee an order of judicial sale and conduct of the sale, Jones could be sure that the land could not be sold until the expiration of the redemption period.
(d) If the first mortgagee had taken no action, but the second mortgagee obtained an order foreclosing the equity of redemption it could take the fee simple free and clear.
(e) If the second mortgagee obtained an order for sale and it was not enough to pay out the claim and the first mortgagee and the second, Jones could rest assured that the second mortgagee would have no right to sue him for the shortfall.

76. Equity of redemption means the mortgagor retains right to redeem after defaulting on mortgage payments.
(a) True
(b) False

77. Mortgagor retains right to redeem even after he/she has failed to make a payment.
(a) True
(b) False

78. Mortgagor can use the right to redeem as security on a second mortgage.
(a) True
(b) False

79. A second mortgage is based on the transfer of the

_____.

80. A mortgagor is obliged to:

(a) _____

(b) _____

(c) _____

81. Mortgages must be registered to obtain priority.
(a) True
(b) False

82. Which of the following is not a remedy of an unpaid mortgagee?
    (a) Action against the mortgagor on his personal promise to pay.
    (b) Contractual right to enter, lease or sell.
    (c) Judicial sale.
    (d) Foreclosure.
    (e) A redemption period.

83. Which of the following is not a remedy available to the mortgagee on default
    (a) Exercise the right to foreclose
    (b) Power of judicial sale
    (c) Take possession
    (d) Sue on the contract
    (e) Exercise the right to redeem against the mortgagor

84. Fawlty is the tenant of an apartment that he rents from O'Hill. Originally they had verbally agreed to a one-year lease to commence on July 1, at a monthly rent of $500. Fawlty has now been in possession of the premises for over a year, but the relationship between O'Hill and Fawlty has begun to deteriorate. O'Hill had noticed that rental rates in the neighbourhood for similar apartments had increased significantly in the last year and he decided that he was giving Fawlty too good a deal. Therefore, on February 13, O'Hill telephoned Fawlty and told him that the rent was going up to $750 per month, effective April 1st.

    Fawlty was quite upset by this development but he didn't know what he could do about it. He started to have some pretty rowdy parties to show his displeasure and eventually the tenants of the other apartments began to complain to O'Hill. O'Hill's reaction was to call Fawlty again on March 3rd and tell him that the rent was to go up to $1000 instead of $750 (even though he knew that comparable rates were closer to $750). There were no similar apartments available in the area and Fawlty did not want to leave because it was close to his work and to most of his friends. Which of the following statements would summarize the relationship between the parties if they resided in your jurisdiction?

Part 1
    (a) O'Hill is entitled to give Fawlty a one-month notice of eviction for "cause."
    (b) O'Hill can say that because the fixed term contract had expired the previous June 30, Fawlty was simply a tenant-at-will and that he could evict him any time he chooses.
    (c) If O'Hill decides to evict Fawlty, he must give him a signed written notice on a government form and specify the reasons and inform him of his rights to dispute.
    (d) If Fawlty's guests drunkenly wreck the landscaping, O'Hill can claim this loss as damages against Fawlty.
    (e) O'Hill may be able to get a court order allowing him to evict Fawlty on even shorter notice than one month.

Part 2

The following statements concern the legal rules that govern O'Hill's rights to increase the rent. Which of them are correct?

(a) O'Hill is limited to a rental increase of 7%.
(b) O'Hill can increase the rent by whatever amount he wants and for whatever reason he chooses so long as he complies with the requirement he give proper notice and it has been at least 12 months since the last increase.
(c) If Fawlty is absent or evading O'Hill, then O'Hill may post the notice on Fawlty's door and Fawlty will be considered to have received notice three days later.
(d) O'Hill must give at least three months written notice.
(e) If O'Hill increases the rent as a way to force Fawlty to leave, he may be liable for Fawlty's increased rent somewhere else for up to 12 months.
(f) If Fawlty doesn't think the rent increase is fair, he can take the matter to arbitration for settlement and the arbitrator can adjust the rent.
(g) If Fawlty doesn't think the increase is fair, he can simply give a months notice and move out.

85. Mr. Grange, the owner of a house, needed money for his business and mortgaged his house to the First National Bank for $75 000. This was not enough to meet his needs and so he took out a second mortgage with the Second National Bank for $50 000 and a third mortgage with the Third National Bank for $25 000. Unfortunately, because there was a change in personnel at the Second National Bank, the interest of the Third National Bank was registered at the land registry office before the mortgage was taken out by the Second National Bank. Other than this all three mortgages were properly registered.

Two events followed: (1) The value of the property in the area where the house was located declined and (2) Mr. Grange's business went sour and he was forced to declare personal bankruptcy. He managed to keep up the payments on the first mortgage, but failed to make the payments on the second and third mortgages and failed to pay the taxes. The First National Bank brought an application to the court for an *order nisi* of foreclosure. The Second and Third National Banks also appeared and both banks applied for a personal judgment against Grange as well as an order for sale. The Second National Bank was given the right to supervise the sale and the property was sold for $100 000 with the court's approval. The amount owing at that time was $74 000 in principle to the First National Bank, plus $10 000 in accrued interest and legal expenses; $49 000 to the Second National Bank plus $5 000 in accrued interest and legal expenses and $24 000 plus $3 000 in accrued interest and legal expenses to the Third National Bank.

At the trial the judge had granted the first mortgagee's request for an *order nisi of foreclosure* and granted a six-month redemption period. This sale took place two months after the *order nisi* was granted and four months before the expiration of the redemption period. Two years after his house had been sold and one year after Grange had been discharged from his personal bankruptcy, he won a provincial lottery of $2 500 000. There was a considerable amount of publicity attached to this and when the officers at the Second and Third National Banks recognized Grange they remembered the considerable amount in claims still outstanding and both sued Grange. Explain the legal positions of all the parties.

Answers to Review Questions

1. b   P. 455   D.1

2. Real property pertains to land and things attached to it whereas personal property is moveable.

          P. 455   D.1

3. e   P. 455   D.1

4. a   P. 455   D.1

5. b   P. 456   D.1

6. e   P. 456   D.1

7. b   P. 456   D.2

8. a   P. 457   D.2

9. b   P. 457   D.2

10. c   P. 459   D.2

11. gratuitous bailment, bailment for value

          P. 457   D.1

12. b   P. 459   D.2

13. Real property refers to land and things attached to it (buildings). Chattels refers to moveables such as cars, books, etc.

          P. 455   D.1

14. b   P. 461   D.1

15. a   P. 461-2 D.1

16. a   P. 462   D.1

17. b   P. 462-7 D.2

18. a   P. 462   D.2

19. a   P. 463   D.1

20. Fee Simple

          P. 462   D.1

21. Landlord and tenant

          P. 463   D.1

22. a   P. 462   D.1

23. a   P. 462   D.1

24. b   P. 462-3 D.2

25. d   P. 462-3 D.2

26. d   P. 465-6 D.1

27. b   P. 463   D.2

28. b, f   P. 462-3 D.2

29. c   P. 462   D.2

30. a   P. 471   D.1

31. b   P. 463, 470   D.1

32. d   P. 464   D.2

33. a   P. 464   D.1

34. b (not an exclusive right)

          P. 464   D.1

35. e   P. 464   D.2

36. a   P. 464   D.1

37. a   P. 464   D.1

38. b   P. 464   D.1

39. a   P. 465   D.1

40. a   P. 464   D.1

41. a   P. 464   D.1

42. a   P. 465   D.1

43. e   P. 465   D.1

44. Interests in land are separated vertically instead of horizontally.

          P. 468   D.1

45. Commercial tenants - vacant possession, quiet enjoyment, major repairs made. When lease is for fixed term tenant is entitled to exclusive possession for that period.

          P. 470   D.2

46. f   P. 471-5 D.2

47. c   P. 475-6 D.2

48. b   P. 465   D.1

49. a   P. 465   D.1

50. Varies with jurisdiction

          P. 477-9 D.2

51. d, e   P. 466-7 D.2

52. Life estates and leasehold estates

          P. 462-3 D.1

53. a   P. 466   D.1

54. a   P. 467   D.1

55. (1) Land Titles System - a guaranteed certificate of title is produced.

(2) Land Registry System - documents pertaining to titles are registered but the parties must search those documents to determine their effect.

       P. 467   D.2

56. e   P. 467   D.2
57. a   P. 467   D.1
58. e   P. 463   D.2
59. e   P. 465, 471-3   D.2
60. b   P. 471   D.1
61. a   P. 471   D.1
62. a, d   P. 473   D.2
63. e   P. 474   D.2
64. c   P. 471   D.2
65. a   P. 473   D.1
66. d   P. 473   D.2
67. e   P. 472-4   D.2
68. b   P. 474   D.1
69. a   P. 475   D.1
70. Will vary with jurisdiction. P. 474-9 D.2
71. e   P. 475-6   D.2
72. c   P. 476   D.2
73. e   P. 477-9   D.2
74. b   P. 479   D.1
75. a   P. 479-488   D.1
76. a   P. 479 480   D.1
77. a   P. 479   D.1
78. a   P. 481   D.1
79. Equity of redemption P. 481 D.1

80. Keep insurance; pay the taxes; keep the property in good repair. P. 483 D.2
81. a   P. 482   D.1
82. e   P. 482-8   D.2
83. e   P. 482-8   D.2

84. In Part 1, (a) would probably be accurate depending on the jurisdiction, because of the noisy parties. (b) is false. A tenancy at will has not been created because of the continued payment of rent. Probably a month-to-month tenancy has been created. (c) is true in most jurisdictions. In (d) the accuracy of this will depend on the jurisdiction. (e) If the noisy parties are bad enough this is likely right, depending on the jurisdiction.

In Part 2 of this question, the accuracy of all of the questions depends on the provincial jurisdiction in which the property is located. P. 469-79 D.3

85. The answer to this question again will depend to some extent on the jurisdiction, but generally the order of priority will depend on the order of registration in a land titles system (and probably in a registrations system as well assuming the registration of the second mortgage was not within the time allowed). Thus the third mortgagee will have priority over the second mortgagee. So the first will recover $84 000, the third will then recover $16 000, the entire amount remaining. The third then becomes a general creditor for the remaining $11 000 of their claim and the second mortgagee becomes a general creditor for the entire $54 000 of their claim. Because of the bankruptcy of the mortgagor Mr. Grange, these claims are ended and upon discharge, Grange is no longer responsible for them and so when he wins the lottery he has no obligation to pay any of these parties. P. 479-88 D.3

Chapter 16

Intellectual Property and Insurance

Learning Objectives

At the end of the chapter you should be able to:

1. Distinguish between personal intellectual and real property.
2. Discuss the goals of legislation protecting intellectual property
3. List the forms of intellectual property and the statutes that regulate them.
4. Outline the purposes and kinds of insurance available to business people.

Key Terms

The following terms are highlighted in the text.

copyright	right for the author or owner to control the use of created work
moral rights	author's right to prohibit the owner from changing original to degrade it
interlocutory injunction	court order to prevent copyright violation before trial
balance of convenience	determination of who will suffer the greatest injury if the copyright violation were allowed to continue
Anton Piller order	court order to seize offending material before trial
permanent injunction	prohibits production, sale or distribution of infringing products - granted at trial
damages	monetary compensation to victim of copyright and other infringements
accounting	court order that any profits made from wrongdoing be paid over to victim
punitive damages	in cases of flagrant violation, money paid to victim in order to punish the offender
patent	government granted monopoly prohibiting anyone but the inventor from profiting from the invention
trademark	symbols or designs associated with a business are protected
passing-off action	prevents someone from misleading the public into thinking it is dealing with some other business when it is not.

industrial design	unique shapes or patterns that distinguish manufactured articles protected
confidential information	private information, the disclosure of which would be injurious to a business
trade secrets	information that gives a business competitive advantage
injurious falsehood	false and misleading information about a company's products
electronic commerce	retail selling using the Internet
spamming	generating and sending unsolicited advertising via the Internet
netiquette	a code of conduct for on-line commercial activities
encryption coding	technological innovations to protect privacy and security on the Internet
digital watermarks	a method of insuring the authenticity of a website
business interruption	insurance to protect holder if business is interrupted
insurance riders	modifications to a standard insurance contract
liability insurance	covers negligence by self or employees
insurable interest	insured would suffer loss if the insured against thing happens.
subrogation	the right of insurer upon payment to take over the rights of the insured in relation to whoever caused the injury
fidelity bond	insurance against an employee's wrongful conduct
surety bond	insurance in case a party to a contract fails to perform

Chapter Outline   Notes

Intellectual Property

The law protects ideas and creative work.

Copyright - the right to copy or reproduce a created work, usually held by the author or artist Copyright can be assigned and holder has complete control over work for author's life plus 50 years. Standard civil remedies available for copyright holder when copyright violated plus some unique to intellectual property.

Patents - a monopoly granted to inventor to produce or sell or otherwise profit from an invention.

Trademarks - any term, symbol or design that identifies a business or product is protected under the federal *Trademarks Act*
- Registration is required for protection

Industrial Designs - a design or pattern that distinguishes a manufactured article is protected by special legislation

Confidential Information - protected at common law when there is a duty not to disclose

Trade Secrets - a kind of confidential information that gives a businessperson a competitive advantage. Wrongful disclosure will be remedied by the courts.

Electronic Commerce

Personal information Protection and Electronic Documents *Act* attempts to regulate privacy interests on the Internet

Law is in developmental stage and Internet users must rely on technology to protect commercial transactions on the net.
- Tort law and Criminal Code may provide some remedies

Insurance

Designed to provide compensation for damaged, lost or stolen property and has been expanded to include non-tangibles

Property Insurance - covers losses to buildings and their contents due to fire

Business Interruption Insurance - covers expenses industrial design act industrial design act incurred when businesses are unable to function because of some unforeseen occurrence

Life and Health Insurance - provides security for dependants after the death of the insured

Liability Insurance - to cover injuries caused by wrongful or careless conduct or damages caused by an employee

There must be an insurable interest and a claimant can only collect to the extent of that interest

Bonding - an employer may bond an employee against that employee's own wrongful conduct

Review Questions

1. What distinguishes intellectual property from personal or real property?

   _____

   _____

2. The purposes of intellectual property law do not include which of the following?
   (a) protect the product of mental effort
   (b) encourage the free flow of new ideas
   (c) give the creator the right to benefit from it
   (d) outline the rights and responsibilities of the inventor and the users of the invention
   (e) prevent people from using the invention

3. Which of the following is not included in intellectual property legislation?
   (a) copyright
   (b) patents
   (c) trademarks
   (d) trade secrets
   (e) industrial designs

4. The term *copyright* refers to the right to copy or reproduce a created work.
   (a) True
   (b) False

5. A new idea about the relationship between cancer and a person's chromosomes is copyrightable.
   (a) True
   (b) False

6. A copyright comes into existence automatically and no registration is required.
   (a) True
   (b) False

7. What significant area is affected by the 1988 amendments to the *Copyright Act*?

   _____

8. Which of the following is/are incorrect with respect to the copyright law of Canada?
   (a) The *Copyright Act* is a federal statute.
   (b) Computer software is not covered under the *Copyright Act*.
   (c) The copyright is created automatically when the author creates the work.
   (d) The copyright protection lasts for 20 years.
   (e) Only the creator of the work can be the owner of the copyright.

9. Which of the following is/are correct with respect to the law of copyright in Canada?
   (a) Even though the copyright law provides for registration this is not necessary to create a copyright.
   (b) The term of the copyright is for the life of the author plus 50 years.
   (c) The work is only protected by the copyright law if it is clearly marked as being copyrighted.
   (d) Copyright protection is restricted to published works.
   (e) An employer may have the right to copyright of a work created by an employee.

10. Copyright extends to the ideas expressed as well as the written form.
    (a) True
    (b) False

11. Which of the following cannot be protected by copyright?
    (a) Literary works
    (b) folklore
    (c) musical compositions
    (d) graphic works,
    (e) computer soft and hardware

12. Writers need to undertake complex legal process to insure the existence of their copyright.
    (a) True
    (b) False

13. A copyright must be registered to gain international protection.
    (a) True
    (b) False

14. Which of the following is false with regard to the copyright law in Canada?
    (a) In general, the purpose of copyright law is to encourage creativity by giving the "author" a monopoly over his work.
    (b) Generally the term of copyright is the life of the author plus fifty years.
    (c) If a computer programmer creates a program for hire, but not as an employee he owns copyright unless he assigns it.
    (d) Joint ownership of copyright is prohibited by the *Copyright Act*.
    (e) None of the above

15. List and describe four of the remedies that are available when there has been an infringement of a copyright.

    (1) _____

    (2) _____

    (3) _____

    (4) _____

16. Matt, Sarah and Rob worked together on a student project which required that they create a computer program to aid a finance company keep track of its efforts in bill collecting. Because Ms. Jannes, the president of the company, had been in the business for twenty years, the students knew she would be an invaluable aid if they decided to market the program. The students also felt that before the program could be marketed, a manual should be written and none felt qualified to do that. The students have asked you how they should arrange their affairs legally for their best advantage. Which of the following is false with regard to their legal rights?
    (a) The copyright arises automatically when the work is created.
    (b) The copyright in the computer program does not have to be registered under the federal *Copyright Act* but there are some advantages in doing so.
    (c) Only unique works with significant literary or scientific merit can be copyrighted.
    (d) If the students employ someone to write a manual, copyright in the manual will belong to the students as employer.
    (e) The students have a right to enter into a licensing agreement with Ms. Jannes which could give her the right to market the program in Canada for a period of time.

17. The creator owns the work except where there is an agreement with employer or publisher.
    (a) True
    (b) False

18. The copyright holder has complete control over the work for author's life plus 75 years.
    (a) True
    (b) False

19. Copyright infringements do not include which of the following?
    (a) selling and distributing
    (b) performing or broadcasting
    (c) copying for private study and research
    (d) using brief quotations
    (e) c and d above

20. What impact do the amendments to the *Copyright Act* had in terms of penalties to violators of the *Act*?

_____

21. For patent protection, an invention must have which of the following characteristics?
    (a) It must be something new
    (b) It cannot have been in use by others
    (c) It must be a concrete thing that can be constructed
    (d) It must have unique qualities
    (e) All of the above

22. Patent law is distinguished from copyright in that it protects the idea and theory behind the invention as well as the invention itself.
    (a) True
    (b) False

23. The only way to create a patent is to register the invention with the Patent Office.
    (a) True
    (b) False

24. Patent law provides for the disclosure of information about new inventions.
    (a) True
    (b) False

25. Which of the following is incorrect with respect to patent law in Canada?
    (a) A patent is only effective when registered or applied for.
    (b) The first person to obtain registration is entitled to the patent.
    (c) The patent protects the idea rather than the work itself.
    (d) The protection given under patent law is for 20 years.
    (e) If another person obtains a patent and you can show that you were using the process or invention before the patent was granted you will not infringe on that patent if you continue to use it.

26. Which of the following is false with regard to patent registration?
    (a) the first to apply has priority
    (b) in order to ensure protection, application must be made in other jurisdictions
    (c) monopoly over invention runs for 20 years
    (d) patent law protects information about how to build the invention
    (e) gives the patent holder exclusive rights to manufacture and sell the invention

27. Trademarks protect terms, symbols, or designs that identify a product or company.
    (a) True
    (b) False

28. The federal court only applies the trademarks statute and cannot apply civil remedies.
    (a) True
    (b) False

29. Civil remedies available in a provincial court action include which of the following:
    (a) an order giving the custody of infringing products to the owner of the trademark
    (b) imprisonment
    (c) injunction, damages and accounting
    (d) fine
    (e) a and c above

30. Which of the following is/are incorrect with regard to the law of trademarks?
    (a) As soon as you have created a distinctive symbol or design that identifies a business, that is a trademark and protected under the act. No registration is required.
    (b) Even though someone else has developed a distinctive design or symbol that is identified with their business, you are entitled to use it as long as you are the first to have it registered.
    (c) You can't use the word "Royal" in a trademark without permission.
    (d) Even if you have not registered your trademark you may still be able to sue a competitor at common law if they are deceiving your customers into thinking they are dealing with you.
    (e) The period of protection for a trademark is 15 years and is renewable.

31. What is an *Anton Piller* order and when would it be available as a remedy?

    _____

    _____

32. When a trademark is registered it gives protection for a period of 50 years.
    (a) True
    (b) False

33. Protection under the *Industrial Design Act* lasts 5 years and is renewable.
    (a) True
    (b) False

34. Which of the following is not true with respect to an industrial design which can be registered under the *Industrial Design Act*?
    (a) it must be a unique shape, pattern or ornament
    (b) it makes a manufactured article distinct in some way
    (c) any distinctive product can be registered and protected for a period of five years
    (d) the item can be similar to some product already on the market
    (e) the product must be original and not a copy

35. What do trade secrets and confidential information have in common?

_____

_____

36. Confidential information is treated like personal property because when it is disclosed the owner of the information has lost something of value.
    (a) True
    (b) False

37. A trade secret is confidential information that creates a competitive advantage.
    (a) True
    (b) False

38. Which of the following is correct with respect to the law of confidential information?
    (a) This area of law is governed by the federal *Confidential Information Act*.
    (b) When an employee has disclosed certain confidential information to a competitor the appropriate remedy is to obtain an injunction against that employee
    (c) An *Anton Piller* order is an order by the court requiring the person profiting from the use of the confidential information to pay over those profits to the victim of the breach of confidence.
    (d) An employee's obligation not to disclose trade secrets does not end with that employment.
    (e) A victim must choose between suing for wrongful disclosure of confidential information and infringement of copyright, and cannot pursue both claims at the same time.

39. Which of the following is true with regard to the law of trade secret/breach of confidence?
    (a) Trade secret protection is seldom used because it is governed by a difficult-to-understand federal statute.
    (b) The subject matter protected by the law of trade secret is set out in the provincial trade secrets act.
    (c) A person cannot be accused of wrongful disclosure of confidential information if it is no longer confidential.
    (d) An *Anton Pillar* order is an order of the court requiring a person who stole and used a trade secret to make an accounting of all the profit realized from its use.
    (e) None of the above

40. In which of the following ways can an employer protect him- or herself from having trade secrets disclosed?
    (a) disclosure may be prohibited by contract in a restrictive covenant
    (b) non-disclosure agreement in employment contract
    (c) copies of information should be marked "Confidential"
    (d) employees should be told what is confidential and how to treat it
    (e) all of the above

41. The following list contains descriptions of various types of property. Which of them would be protected by the laws governing intellectual property?
    (a) a mark used by a person for the purpose of distinguishing his wares or services from those of others
    (b) compilation of secret information which is used in one's business and gives an advantage over competitors
    (c) a written, original musical work
    (d) a certification mark on a cheque
    (e) all of the above

42. List and briefly describe four common kinds of insurance.

    (1) _____

    (2) _____

    (3) _____

    (4) _____

43. Insurance provides compensation for
    (a) damaged, lost, or stolen property
    (b) life,
    (c) liability
    (d) business interruption
    (e) all of the above

44. The purpose of insurance is to reduce the cost of loss by spreading the risk.
    (a) True
    (b) False

45. Which of the following would make a person a co-insurer of his/her own property?
    (a) when two insurance policies are taken out on the same property
    (b) when a person over-insures his/her property
    (c) when a person under-insures his/her property
    (d) when there is no insurance on the property
    (e) b and c above

46. Joe insured a house that was used by a local motorcycle gang and Joe anticipated that it might be damaged. If it did burn down, in which of the following situations would he be able to collect all of the insurance?
    (a) Joe had no interest in the house.
    (b) Joe didn't own the house but his wife did.
    (c) Joe owned the house but had a large mortgage on it.
    (d) Joe and a partner each owned 50% of the house through a tenancy-in-common arrangement.

47. Business interruption insurance covers lost profits and expenses of bringing a business back into operation after it has gone into receivership.
    (a) True
    (b) False

48. Life insurance provides for dependants and/or business associates after death of insured.
    (a) True
    (b) False

49. Health, medical, and disability insurance:
    (a) covers not only property loss but any injuries associated with that loss
    (b) covers loss of income from a business that is closed down
    (c) covers health care expenses
    (d) provide income for disabled worker
    (e) c and d above

50. Liability insurance covers injuries caused by negligence of self or employees and applies only when insured is at fault.
    (a) True
    (b) False

51. Bonding is a form of insurance that protects employers and others from the wrongful acts of their employees.
    (a) True
    (b) False

52. Which of the following is correct with respect to the law of insurance and bonding?
    (a) When a person causes damage on another person's property he can be assured that he will not have to pay for the damages if the owner has insurance.
    (b) If a person causes injury to another through his wrongful conduct, he can be assured that he will not have to pay for the losses if he was bonded.
    (c) For a person to claim on an insurance contract he must demonstrate that he has an insurable interest in the subject matter of the insurance.
    (d) If a person does not keep her insurance coverage on her house high enough compared to the value of the property there is a danger she will be classed as a co-insurer and will not be able to realize the entire coverage in the event of a fire.
    (e) None of the above

53. Joe, a basement experimenter, invented a laser-based cell stimulator that seemed to be successful in the treatment of skin cancer. In May 1989 he recorded the details of his invention in a paper and took it to Sam's Complete Assistance for Marketing Ltd. (Scam for short). Sam wasn't sure just how valuable this invention was and took the paper to his brother George, a world famous scientist, researching in this area to get his opinion. George took the paper, successfully duplicated Joe's efforts to create a

similar machine and used extensive parts of Joe's paper in writing his own article to be published in a medical journal. George also registered the invention on Sept, 10, 1989. Sam stalled Joe while waiting for a response from his brother. He told Joe that he didn't think that the invention was very original or valuable. Joe was very discouraged until he read the paper, written by George in the medical journal and recognized the parts of the paper he had written. He became very angry, especially when he learned that George had entered into a deal with Blue Chip Pharmaceuticals Ltd. to develop a treatment based on the invention and had received a signing payment of $10 000 000 from that company as well as a right to royalties. Explain the legal position of the parties indicating any legal recourse Joe might have.

54. Joe owned a house and his friend Sam came over to visit. Sam brought some flowers to give to Joe as a practical joke. As he presented those flowers to Joe he pulled a string causing a flare to go off, frightening Joe. Joe dropped the flowers and the flare caused his furniture to catch on fire. The fire got out of control and the whole house burned down. The total loss was $104 000 including the costs of staying in a motel, but fortunately, Joe had a good fire insurance policy with coverage of $125 000. His friend also had liability insurance in excess of that amount. The house was worth $100 000 and the land a further $50 000 but Joe had taken out a mortgage on the property for $50,000. Actually Joe was a 50% shareholder in a successful printing business, Ace Printers Ltd. For tax purposes Joe had put the house in the name of Ace. He had taken out the insurance policy in his own name, however. Explain the legal position of the parties including any arguments that the insurance company might use to reduce or eliminate their liability. How would your answer be different if the insurance company after being sued by Joe denied liability but upon further pressure agreed to pay Joe $30 000 to settle while still denying any liability on the claim?

Answers to Review Questions

1. Intellectual property deals with ideas, information, or creative works.

    P. 493   D.2

2. e   P. 492   D.2

3. d   P. 507   D.2

4. a   P. 494-5 D.1

5. b   P. 495   D.1

6. a   P. 496   D.1

7. The new act imposes stronger penalties, sets up a copyright board but most important covers computer programs under copyright protection.

    P. 495   D.1

8. b, d, e P. 494-6 D.2

9. a, b, e P. 495-7 D.1

10. b   P. 495   D.1

11. b   P. 495   D.2

12. b   P. 496   D.1

13. a   P. 496   D.1

14. d   P. 494-7 D.2

15. (1) Injunction - a court order to stop the offending conduct. (2) Damages - the offending party is order ed to pay monetary compensation to the victim. (3) An *Anton Piller* order - where the offending subject matter and other evidence is seized. (4) An accounting - where the offending party is ordered to pay over to the victim any profits he made because of the infringement.

    P. 498-9 D.2

16. c   P. 495-6 D.2

17. b   P. 496   D.1

18. b   P. 497   D.1

19. e   P. 497-8 D.2

20. The penalties have been significantly increased.

    P. 499   D.1

21. e   P. 500   D.1

22. a   P. 500   D.1

23. a   P. 501   D.1

24. a   P. 501   D.1

25. e   P. 501   D.2

26. b   P. 501   D.2

27. a   P. 502   D.1

28. b   P. 503-4 D.1

29. e   P. 503-4 D.2

30. a, b P. 503-4 D.2

31. An *Anton Piller* order is an order by the courts to seize the goods and associated evidence that is infringing on the intellectual property rights of the person applying for the order. It is given *ex parte* and so the court must be convinced that there is clearly an infringement, that the person applying is suffering losses due to the infringement and that surprise is needed to protect the evidence.

    P. 498-9 D.1

32. b   P. 503   D.1

33. b   P. 505   D.1

34. d   P. 504-5 D.2

35. Trade secrets are a particular kind of confidential information which if disclosed will give a competitor a competitive advantage.

    P. 505-7 D.1

36. a   P. 506   D.1

37. a   P. 508   D.1

38. d   P. 508   D.2

39. c   P. 508   D.2

40. e   P. 508   D.2

41. a, b, c P. 495, 502, 507 D.2

42. (1) Property insurance provides protection against damage to property.

    (2) Liability insurance provides coverage against people suing the insured for negligence etc.

    (3) Life and health insurance provides coverage against losses due to death or illness of the insured.

(4) Business interruption insurance provides coverage if for some reason your business is forced to close down because of some event such as the premises being destroyed by fire. Business interruption and property insurance complement each other.

P. 513-5 D.2

43. e   P. 512   D.2

44. a   P. 512   D.1

45. c   P. 513   D.2

46. c   P. 513   D.2

47. b   P. 513   D.1

48. a   P. 513   D.1

49. e   P. 514-5   D.2

50. a   P. 515   D.1

51. a   P. 519   D.1

52. c, d   P. 519   D.2

53. Sam has a duty of confidentiality and when he gave that paper to his brother he breached that duty. George, on the other hand, infringed Joe's copyright protection when he copied extensive parts of Joe's paper and had it published under his own name. While Joe could not claim the patent at this time, he could sue Sam for damages because of the breach of confidentiality and George for an accounting to pay over any profits he made by selling the invention to Blue Chip Pharmaceuticals. This would amount to the $10 000 000 payment and any future royalties paid.

P. 506-7,
497-8

54. Joe would be in a position to claim against the insurance company, but only for the amount of the loss of $104 000, not the face value of the policy. The mortgage outstanding on the property would not affect the extent of Joe's insurable interest because even after the fire he still has to pay it back. Joe only having a 50% interest in the company that owns the house would have an impact however. It is clear now that Joe's interest in the company that owns the property is enough of a relationship to provide for an insurable interest, but he only owns half of that company and so he has only an insurable interest to the extent of half of the value of the property. In these circumstances Joe will only get $52 000 from the insurance company, but can then turn to his friend and sue him for the rest. The insurance company will also be subrogated to Joe's rights in relation to the $52 000 they have paid out and will be able to sue Joe's friend who caused the fire for the rest. Of course, Joe's friend will report this to his insurance company and they will pay Joe the remaining $52 000 and pay Joe's insurance company the other $52 000. If the insurance company settled the court action for $30 000, denying all liability, they would lose their right to subrogation and Joe would not only get that $30 000 but would be free to sue his friend for the entire amount of the loss. His friend's insurance company would then pay out to Joe a further $104 000 and Joe would come out ahead.

P. 513,
515-7

Research and Study Aids

Primary Legal Sources

Primary legal sources are reports of national and provincial laws as established through cases heard in the courts and statutes passed by governments. They include:

Law Reports	Federal Regulations
Federal Statutes	Provincial Regulations
Provincial Statutes	Municipal By-laws
Official Gazettes	

Reported Cases are accounts of cases heard in Canadian and other courts and reported in legal volumes published periodically. Besides outlines of the cases they provide interpretations of the law and the reasoning behind the decisions. Not all cases tried in the law courts are published - only those that are important enough to affect future cases. The reports of cases in most Canadian jurisdictions are now available on the Internet very shortly after the case is heard. They can be found on federal and provincial government websites or you can access them through www.acjnet.org. The print versions are eventually compiled into bound volumes such as the Dominion Law Reports (D.L.R.), or the *British Columbia Law Reports.* (B.C.L.R.). Publishers specializing in court reports now offer reports in CD ROM with services that continually update them.

Legal citations follow any reference to a case and enable the reader to find the published account of the case in a variety of case reporting publications. A standard format of abbreviations and punctuation is used. An example follows:

Cadbury Schweppes Inc. v. FBI Foods Ltd. (1994) 93 B.C.L.R. (2d) 318 (B.C.S.C.); 138 D.L.R. (4th) 708 (B.C.C.A.); 167 D.L.R. (4th) 577 (S.C.C.)

The first section sets out the names of the plaintiff (s) and the defendant(s) or at the higher levels, the appellant and the respondent. In this example, Cadbury Schweppes Inc. is the plaintiff company that brought the action against the defendant, FBI Foods. The year that the decision was passed down follows and is enclosed in either round or square brackets. When round brackets are used, the volume containing the case is one of a series (e.g. Volumes 1 - 39) and only the volume number is required to find the case. In this case it is reported in Volume 93 of the British Columbia Law Reports Second Series. When square brackets are used around the year it indicates that the volume containing the cited case must be located by reference to the year the decision was rendered. The page number on which the case can be found (318, in the example) follows the name of the volume. Usually the name of the court that heard the case is added at the end of the citation, enclosed in brackets. In our example B.C.S.C. stands for the British Columbia Supreme Court When the case has been reported in more than one place, each source is separated by a semi-colon. This case then went to the British Columbia Court of Appeal and is reported in volume 138 of the Dominion Law Reports Fourth Series at page 708. (Note: a list of abbreviations commonly used in case citations follows.) This case also was appealed to the Supreme Court of Canada and the report of that hearing can be found in Volume 167 of the Dominion Law Reports Fourth Series at page 577. If the name of a case is known, but no citation is available, the Supreme Court of Canada Reports Service provides a cumulative index of cases tried in the Supreme

Court. Provincial reports provide similar indexes. In most instances of case citations in the text, just the last court hearing the case is referred to. And now that most cases can be found on-line, the referencing has become even simpler. Usually the citation refers to the name of the case, the date and the court hearing the matter. To locate a case on line refer to the section that follows entitled How to Brief a Legal Case.

Statutes are laws enacted by federal and provincial parliaments (also called legislation, acts or bills). Current federal and provincial statutes are now available on-line in most jurisdictions. Go to the provincial government website and click on legislation or statutes. In order to find printed versions of legislation, most libraries will carry current compilations of federal or provincial statutes referred to as:

Statutes of Canada: compilation of all statutes passed by the federal government in a particular year (published annually).

Revised Statutes of Canada : compilation of federal legislation, updated to include amendments to previously passed statutes. This is not published annually but is periodically revised (last revision 1985). Each of the Provinces and the Territories issue bound copies of all the acts passed in a session of the legislature. They are issued in print periodically as *Revised Statutes* of their respective provinces.

Annotated Statutes are arranged under individual statutes, one section at a time. They briefly summarize legal case decisions and provide references for locating case reports, e.g., *Canada Statute Annotations* , R.S.C.; Federal Court of Canada Service.

Other Aids

Legal Dictionaries *The Canadian Law Dictionary* (Can.), *Dictionary of English Law* (Brit.), *Black's Law Dictionary* (Amer.)

Legal Directories *Canadian Directory of Public Legal Information*, *Canadian Law List*, *Canadian Parliamentary Guide*

Computer Data Bases These are accessible to the users of some libraries upon request. Computer searches can be conducted for reports on cases dealing with a particular subject matter and complete texts of statutes, e.g., *Revised Statutes of Canada, Supreme Court Reports, All Canada Weekly Summaries*. Libraries with this service will provide a list of the particular materials available through this system.

Legal Resource Centres Located in most major centres across the country, legal resource centres provide a valuable educational service to the public. Many have libraries containing complete sets of law reports and statutes. All provide information services.

Internet Websites This has become an invaluable source of legal information and has become an efficient way of disseminating information about the law to the general public. The following is a list of general purpose sites that also provide a search service when looking for information on a particular legal topic.

> Access to Justice Network www.acjnet.org/ - Provides access to legislation, court reports, people and organizations, publications, databases and discussion forums on justice and legal issues.
>
> Canadian Legal Information Centre www.wwlia.org/ca-home.htm A non-profit corporation based in Victoria British Columbia providing legal information
>
> Canadian Legal Resources on the WWW www.mbnet.mb.ca/~psim/can_law.html. A list of resources on Canadian law and government
>
> Virtual Canadian Law Library and Supreme Court of Canada Reports www.lexum.umontreal.ca/index_en.html
>
> Osgoode Hall Law Journal www.osgoode.yorku.ca Canadian legal documents online.

Hieros Gamos-Law and Government www.hg.org/ Comprehensive international law and government site
Canada: Ministry of Justice www.canada.justice.gc.ca
Canadian Bar Association www.cba.org

Citation Abbreviations

A.E.R.	All England Reports (English)
All E.R.	All England Reports (English)
Abr.	Abridgment; Abridged
B.C.L.R.	British Columbia Law Reports
B.C.R.	British Columbia Reports
B.L.R.	Business Law Reports
C.B.L.J.	Canadian Business Law Journal
C.C.C.	Canadian Criminal Cases
C.H.R.R.	Canadian Human Rights Reporter
C.L.L.C.	Canadian Labour Law Reports
Can. B.A.J.	Canadian Bar Association Journal
Can. Bar Rev	Canadian Bar Review
D.L.R.	Dominion Law Reports
F.C.	Federal Court Reports (Canada)
M.P.R.	Maritime Provinces Reports
N.B.R.	New Brunswick Reports
Nfld. & P.E.I.R.	Newfoundland and Prince Edward Island Reports
N.S.R.	Nova Scotia Reports
O.A.R.	Ontario Appeal Reports
O.L.R.	Ontario Law Reports
O.R.	Ontario Reports
O.W.N.	Ontario Weekly Notes
Osgoode Hall L.J.	Osgoode Hall Law Journal
R.R.	Revised Reports
R.S.A	Revised Statutes of Alberta
R.S.B.C.	Revised Statutes of British Columbia
R.S.C.	Revised Statutes of Canada
R.S.M.	Revised Statutes of Manitoba
R.S.N.B.	Revised Statutes of New Brunswick
R.S.Nfld.	Revised Statutes of Newfoundland
R.S.N.S	Revised Statutes of Nova Scotia

R.S.O.	Revised Statutes of Ontario
R.S.P.E.I.	Revised Statutes of Prince Edward Island
R.S.Q.	Revised Statutes of Saskatchewan
S.C.R.	Supreme Court Reports
UBC L. Rev.	University of British Columbia Law Review
U.T.L.J.	University of Toronto Law Journal
W.L.A.C.	Western Labour Arbitration Cases
W.L.R.	Western Law Reports
W.W.R.	Western Weekly Reports

How to Use Legal Cases

The legal case study is a method used in law schools to help students learn case law. One approach requires students to find the reports of significant legal cases, summarize the information in the reports and prepare to convey the essential elements of a case to the class. After hearing a case argued in their court, judges write a report of all the proceedings. The report contains the names of the parties in the case, a summary of the facts leading up to the court case, the names of the lawyers for each side; a list of all the precedent cases the lawyers used to support their clients' positions. The report then gives the judge's decision in the case and the reasons for the decision. Court reports are often long and complex documents, and it requires considerable effort to extract the essential information and to clearly and succinctly summarize it. Once a case report is "briefed," a student can use, the arguments, decision, reasons and ratio to illustrate how legal principles are applied to facts, how the courts use precedent cases and how the law develops. The cases used in the textbook have all been 'briefed' from original court reports and it is important that you be able to find relevant cases, summarize court reports, organize that information and store it for future reference.

How to Find a Court Report

Before the Internet, legal researchers had to go to a university law library or to the courthouse library to find the reports of cases which were published in series of volumes for each year, such as the Dominion Law Reports or the Western Weekly Reports. Court reports in most jurisdictions are now readily available on line and you can access them by going to the provincial websites, for example. www.courts.gov.bc.ca. You can access all provincial and federal courts from www.acjnet.org. The Supreme Court of Canada reports are available at www.lexum.umontreal.ca/csc-scc/. They are filed according to the court making the decision, ie. the Supreme Court of the Province, or the Court of Appeal and then by date with the most recent decisions appearing first. Most sites allow you to search for a case by date, the case name or the subject matter of the case. If you are looking for a case for which the decision was rendered in October of 1999 by the Supreme Court of Canada, you would click on the third volume of 1999 and find a list of all the cases heard by the court during that period. If you know the name of at least one of the parties, put the name in the search function and it may be possible to locate it that way. If you are searching for any case on a particular topic, professional negligence for example, you could type those words into the search box and a list of all related cases will be brought forward and then you can investigate them individually.

How to Read a Court Report

I have selected a case from the Supreme Court of Canada website to illustrate how to read, organize and summarize the report. The entire report is 17 densely packed pages and rather than reproduce the whole report here, I will copy only those pages or the headnotes that are essential to the brief. For the full report, you can go to the website at www.lexum.umontreal.ca, click on Volume 3, 1999 and at the bottom of the first page you will find the case citation which you can open to view the full report, the first page of which appears as follows.

British Columbia (Public Service Employee Relations Commission) *v.* **BCGSEU**

The British Columbia Government and Service Employees' Union *Appellant*

v.

The Government of the Province of British Columbia as represented by the Public Service Employee Relations Commission *Respondent*

and

The British Columbia Human Rights Commission, the Women's Legal Education and Action Fund, the DisAbled Women's Network of Canada and the Canadian Labour Congress *Interveners*

Indexed as: British Columbia (Public Service Employee Relations Commission) *v.* **BCGSEU**

File No.: 26274.

1999: February 22; 1999: September 9.

Present: Lamer C.J. and L'Heureux-Dubé, Gonthier, Cory, McLachlin, Iacobucci, Major, Bastarache and Binnie JJ.

ON APPEAL FROM THE COURT OF APPEAL FOR BRITISH COLUMBIA

Civil rights - Sex - Employment - Adverse effect discrimination - Forest firefighters - Women having more difficulty passing fitness test owing to physiological differences - Whether fitness test a bona fide occupational requirement - Test to be applied - Human Rights Code, R.S.B.C. 1996, c. 210, s. 13(1)(a), (b), (4).

Most of the civil cases that are heard by the Supreme Court of Canada now deal with some aspect of the Charter of Rights and Freedoms. If you are looking for more business oriented cases, you would likely find more examples by searching the court website in your province. The federal websites focusing on the Federal Court, Federal Court of Appeal and to s lesser extent the Supreme Court of Canada will also have some business case references. By reviewing the first page of this report we can see that the parties in dispute are the British Columbia Government and Service Employees' Union and the Government of British Columbia as represented by the Public Service Employee Relations Commission. The list of parties also includes intervenors. These are individuals or groups who have an interest in the issue and decision and are willing to support either of the parties in the matter. This is the long formal title of the case. The next line indicates how it is usually referenced or indexed. The File No. refers to the court docket and the date indicates the day the matter was heard followed by the date this report and the decision was made public.

The justices of the Supreme Court hearing the case are listed next. In this case all nine members of the court heard the case. The next line in capital letters indicates that the case is being appealed from the decision made in the BC Court of Appeal. The italicized terms are keywords describing the legal questions raised in the case and also suggest the words that might be used to search for this case. The first few pages of a report constitute the headnotes containing the essential information of the case. After the headnotes you will find the complete version of the report containing a more detailed review of the facts, arguments and reasons. We include here the headnotes of the case as they appear on the Supreme Court of Canada website.

How to Brief a Court Report

We use the information from the headnotes to create a sample brief. From this page we can extract the first two elements of a Case Brief.

1. **The Parties: The appellant is the British Columbia Government and Service Employees' Union and the respondent is the Public Service Employee Relations Commission.**

2. **Case History: The BC Court of Appeal reviewed a decision of the Public Service Employee Relations Commission and it is this decision that is being appealed to the Supreme Court of Canada. [It is important to note in this particular case that the appellant Union has gone to the court asking it to review the decision of a commission or administrative tribunal. See Chapter 3 of the text for a more detailed description of how judicial review is initiated.]**

The second page of the report contains a very brief description of the facts of the incident that led to the case and the legal issues that are in question.

The British Columbia government established minimum physical fitness standards for its forest firefighters. One of the standards was an aerobic standard. The claimant, a female firefighter who had in the past performed her work satisfactorily, failed to meet the aerobic standard after four attempts and was dismissed. The claimant's union brought a grievance on her behalf.

Evidence accepted by the arbitrator designated to hear the grievance demonstrated that, owing to physiological differences, most women have a lower aerobic capacity than most men and that, unlike most men, most women cannot increase their aerobic capacity enough with training to meet the aerobic standard. No credible evidence showed that the prescribed aerobic capacity was necessary for either men or women to perform the work of a forest firefighter safely and efficiently. The arbitrator found that the claimant had established a *prima facie* case of adverse effect discrimination and that the Government had not discharged its burden of showing that it had accommodated the claimant to the point of undue hardship. The Court of Appeal allowed an appeal from that decision. The narrow issue here was whether the Government improperly dismissed the claimant. The broader legal issue, however, was whether the aerobic standard that led to her dismissal unfairly excluded women from forest firefighting jobs.

Held: The appeal should be allowed.

The facts and issues are followed by the single line that tells us what the Supreme Court decided. By saying that the appeal should be allowed, the Court reverses the decision of the BC Court of Appeal and decides in favour of the appellant.

This leads us to the next three elements of the brief. The expanded discussion of the facts and issues appears later in the report and should provide additional information for the brief.

3. **The Facts: Tawney Meiorin, a forest firefighter for the Province of British Columbia, lost her job How long had she had the job) for failing a new series of tests the Government had adopted for forest fire fighters.**

4. **The Issues: The main issue in this case is whether the Government improperly dismissed Ms. Meiorin from her job as a forest firefighter. The broader legal issue is whether the aerobic standard that led to Ms. Meiorin's dismissal unfairly excludes women from forest firefighting jobs. For, if due to physiological differences between men and women, women are less able to meet the physical standard, the effect may be to exclude qualified female candidates on the basis of gender, thereby violating the entrenchment of affirmative action in section 15 (2) of the Charter.**

The next section of the report summarizes the reasons for the decision in the case, again these are dealt with in much more detail later in the report.

The conventional approach of categorizing discrimination as "direct" or "adverse effect" discrimination should be replaced by a unified approach for several reasons. First, the distinction between a standard that is discriminatory on its face and a neutral standard that is discriminatory in its effect is difficult to justify: few cases can be so neatly characterized. Second, it is disconcerting that different remedies are available depending on the stream into which a malleable initial inquiry shunts the analysis. Third, the assumption that leaving an ostensibly neutral standard in place is appropriate so long as its adverse effects are felt only by a numerical minority is questionable: the standard itself is discriminatory because it treats some individuals differently from others on the basis of a prohibited ground, the size of the "affected group" is easily manipulable, and the affected group can actually constitute a majority of the workforce. Fourth, the distinctions between the elements an employer must establish to rebut a *prima facie* case of direct or adverse effect discrimination are difficult to apply in practice. Fifth, the conventional analysis may serve to legitimize systemic discrimination. Sixth, a bifurcated approach may compromise both the broad purposes and the specific terms of the *Human Rights Code*. Finally, the focus by the conventional analysis on the mode of discrimination differs in substance from the approach taken to s. 15(1) of the *Canadian Charter of Rights and Freedoms*.

A three-step test should be adopted for determining whether an employer has established, on a balance of probabilities, that a *prima facie* discriminatory standard is a *bona fide* occupational requirement (BFOR). First, the employer must show that it adopted the standard for a purpose rationally connected to the performance of the job. The focus at the first step is not on the validity of the particular standard, but rather on the validity of its more general purpose. Second, the employer must establish that it adopted the particular standard in an honest and good faith belief that it was necessary to the fulfilment of that legitimate work-related purpose. Third, the employer must establish that the standard is reasonably necessary to the accomplishment of that legitimate work-related purpose. To show that the standard is reasonably necessary, it must be demonstrated that it is impossible to accommodate individual employees sharing the characteristics of the claimant without imposing undue hardship upon the employer.

It may often be useful to consider separately, first, the procedures, if any, which were adopted to assess the issue of accommodation and, second, the substantive content of either a more accommodating standard which was offered or alternatively the employer's reasons for not offering any such standard.

Here, the claimant having established a *prima facie* case of discrimination, the burden shifts to the Government to demonstrate that the aerobic standard is a BFOR. The Government has satisfied the first two steps of the BFOR analysis. However, the Government failed to demonstrate that this particular aerobic standard is reasonably necessary to identify those persons who are able to perform the tasks of a forest firefighter safely and efficiently. The Government has not established that it would experience undue hardship if a different standard were used.

The procedures adopted by the researchers who developed the aerobic standard were problematic on two levels. First, their approach was primarily a descriptive one. However, merely describing the characteristics of a test subject does not necessarily allow one to identify the standard minimally required for the safe and efficient performance of the job. Second, the studies failed to distinguish the female test subjects from the male test subjects, who constituted the majority of the sample groups. The record therefore did not permit a decision as to whether men and women require the same minimum level of aerobic capacity to perform a forest firefighter's tasks safely and efficiently.

Assuming that the Government had properly addressed the question of accommodation in a procedural sense, its response that it would experience undue hardship if it had to accommodate the claimant is deficient from a substantive perspective. There is no reason to interfere with the arbitrator's holding that the evidence fell well short of establishing that the claimant posed a serious safety risk to herself, her colleagues, or the general public. The Government also claimed that accommodating the claimant would undermine the morale of the workforce. However, the attitudes of those who seek to maintain a discriminatory practice cannot be determinative of whether the employer has accommodated the claimant to the point of undue hardship. If it were possible to perform the tasks of a forest firefighter safely and efficiently without meeting the aerobic standard, the rights of other forest firefighters would not be affected by allowing the claimant to continue performing her job. The order of the arbitrator reinstating the claimant to her former position and compensating her for lost wages and benefits was restored.

The final sentence of this section tells us the effect of the decision. The brief might summarize these reasons even further as follows.

5.   **Decision: The order of the arbitrator (Public Service Employee Relations Commission) is restored and Ms. Meiorin can return to her job with compensation for her losses.**

6.   **Reasons: The key Charter sections relevant to yielding gender parity are sections 15 (1) and (2) and section 28.**

Justice McLachlin pointed out the need to interpret human rights legislation purposefully in order to consider the effects of systemic discrimination. There are three elements in the Court's approach to determining that the Government's prima facie discriminatory standard was not a bona fide occupational requirement:

(1)   **the employer had not adopted the standard for a purpose rationally connected to the performance of Ms. Meiorin's job;**

(2)   **the employer had not adopted the particular standard in an honest and good faith belief that it was necessary to the fulfillment of a legitimate work related purpose; and**

(3)   **that the standard was not reasonably necessary to the accomplishment of a legitimate work-related purpose. That is, the employer did not demonstrate that it would be impossible for it to accommodate individual employees sharing the characteristics of Meiorin because of an imposition of undue hardship on the employer.**

McLachlin points out the benefit of establishing a unified approach (such as the three step test applied above) towards all equality judicial interpretation so that human rights analysis and Charter analysis would serve to protect an equally high standard of nondiscrimination.

The final element of the brief is taken from the **_Ratio Decidendi_** of the court report. This is where the judges state the law as it is established by this case. It is the part of the case that is binding on all other courts in the judicial system when they deal with cases that have similar facts. This also suggests what impact the decision will have on future cases.

7.   **Ratio: Removing a discriminatory standard to create a nondiscriminatory workplace is not reverse discrimination.**

The balance of the court report lists the cases that the justices referred to in coming to their decision as well as the applicable Statutes. The on-line version provides links to all of the cases to facilitate further research. The report includes a list of the academic writings consulted by the justices. The list of the names of the lawyers acting for the parties appears next and an indication that Justice McLachlin prepared this report. The remainder of the report which can be found on the Supreme Court website provides a more detailed breakdown of the facts, issues and reasons and will assist students in understanding the case.

Cases Cited

Referred to: *Ontario Human Rights Commission and O'Malley v. Simpsons-Sears Ltd.*, [1985] 2 S.C.R. 536; *Ontario (Human Rights Commission) v. Borough of Etobicoke*, [1982] 1 S.C.R. 202; *Caldwell v. Stuart*, [1984] 2 S.C.R. 603; *Brossard (Town) v. Quebec (Commission des droits de la personne)*, [1988] 2 S.C.R. 279; *Central Alberta Dairy Pool v. Alberta (Human Rights Commission)*, [1990] 2 S.C.R. 489; *Saskatchewan (Human Rights Commission) v. Saskatoon (City)*, [1989] 2 S.C.R. 1297; *Large v. Stratford (City)*, [1995] 3 S.C.R. 733; *Canada (Human Rights Commission) v. Toronto-Dominion Bank*, [1998] 4 F.C. 205; *Canada (Human Rights Commission) v. Taylor*, [1990] 3 S.C.R. 892; *Griggs v. Duke Power Co.*, 401 U.S. 424 (1971); *Commission scolaire régionale de Chambly v. Bergevin*, [1994] 2 S.C.R. 525; *Law v. Canada (Minister of Employment and Immigration)*, [1999] 1 S.C.R. 497; *Canada (Attorney General) v. Levac*, [1992] 3 F.C. 463; *Large v. Stratford (City)* (1992), 92 D.L.R. (4th) 565; *Saran v. Delta Cedar Products Ltd.*, [1995] B.C.C.H.R.D. No. 3 (QL); *Grismer v. British Columbia (Attorney General)* (1994), 25 C.H.R.R. D/296; *Thwaites v. Canada (Armed Forces)* (1993), 19 C.H.R.R. D/259; *Canadian National Railway Co. v. Canada (Canadian Human Rights Commission)*, [1987] 1 S.C.R. 1114; *Insurance Corp. of British Columbia v. Heerspink*, [1982] 2 S.C.R. 145; *Zurich Insurance Co. v. Ontario (Human Rights Commission)*, [1992] 2 S.C.R. 321; *Robichaud v. Canada (Treasury Board)*, [1987] 2 S.C.R. 84; *Andrews v. Law Society of British Columbia*, [1989] 1 S.C.R. 143; *Eldridge v. British Columbia (Attorney General)*, [1997] 3 S.C.R. 624; *Bhinder v. Canadian National Railway Co.*, [1985] 2 S.C.R. 561; *Central Okanagan School District No. 23 v. Renaud*, [1992] 2 S.C.R. 970; *R. v. Cranston*, [1997] C.H.R.D. No. 1 (QL).

Statutes and Regulations Cited

Canadian Charter of Rights and Freedoms, s. 15(1).

Canadian Human Rights Act, R.S.C., 1985, c. H-6, s. 15(2) [am. 1998, c. 9, s. 10].

Human Rights Act, S.Y. 1987, c. 3, s. 7.

Human Rights Code, R.S.B.C. 1996, c. 210, ss. 3, 13(1)(a), (b), (4).

Human Rights Code, R.S.O. 1990, c. H.19, s. 24(2).

Human Rights Code, S.M. 1987-88, c. 45, s. 12.

Authors Cited

Canada. Canadian Human Rights Commission. *The Effects of the Bhinder Decision on the Canadian Human Rights Commission: A Special Report to Parliament*. Ottawa: The Commission, 1986.

Crane, M. C. "Human Rights, *Bona Fide* Occupational Requirements and the Duty to Accommodate: Semantics or Substance?" (1996), 4 *C.L.E.L.J.* 209.

Day, Shelagh, and Gwen Brodsky. "The Duty to Accommodate: Who Will Benefit?" (1996), 75 *Can. Bar Rev.* 433.

Etherington, Brian. "Central Alberta Dairy Pool: The Supreme Court of Canada's Latest Word on the Duty to Accommodate" (1993), 1 *Can. Lab. L.J.* 311.

Lepofsky, M. David. "The Duty to Accommodate: A Purposive Approach" (1993), 1 *Can. Lab. L.J.* 1.

McKenna, Ian B. "Legal Rights for Persons with Disabilities in Canada: Can the Impasse Be Resolved?" (1997-98), 29 *Ottawa L. Rev.* 153.

Messing, Karen. *One-Eyed Science: Occupational Health and Women Workers.* Philadelphia: Temple University Press, 1998.

Messing, Karen, and Joan Stevenson. "Women in Procrustean Beds: Strength Testing and the Workplace" (1996), 3 *Gender, Work and Organization* 156.

Molloy, Anne M. "Disability and the Duty to Accommodate" (1993), 1 *Can. Lab. L.J.* 23.

Pentney, William. "Belonging: The Promise of Community - Continuity and Change in Equality Law 1995-96" (1996), 25 C.H.R.R. C/6.

Phillips, Paul, and Erin Phillips. *Women and Work: Inequality in the Canadian Labour Market*, rev. ed. Toronto: James Lorimer & Co., 1993.

Watkin, Kenneth. "The Justification of Discrimination under Canadian Human Rights Legislation and the *Charter*: Why So Many Tests?" (1993), 2 *N.J.C.L.* 63.

Yalden, Maxwell F. "The Duty to Accommodate - A View from the Canadian Human Rights Commission" (1993), 1 *Can. Lab. L.J.* 283.

APPEAL from a judgment of the British Columbia Court of Appeal (1997), 37 B.C.L.R. (3d) 317, 94 B.C.A.C. 292, 152 W.A.C. 292, 149 D.L.R. (4th) 261, [1997] 9 W.W.R. 759, 30 C.H.R.R. D/83, [1997] B.C.J. No. 1630 (QL), allowing an appeal from a decision of a Labour Arbitration Board (1996), 58 L.A.C. (4th) 159, allowing a grievance and reinstating the employee with full compensation. Appeal allowed.

Kenneth R. Curry, *Gwen Brodsky*, *John Brewin* and *Michelle Alman*, for the appellant.

Peter A. Gall, *Lindsay M. Lyster* and *Janine Benedet*, for the respondent.

Deirdre A. Rice, for the intervener the British Columbia Human Rights Commission.

Kate A. Hughes and *Melina Buckley*, for the interveners the Women's Legal Education and Action Fund, the Disabled Women's Network of Canada and the Canadian Labour Congress.

The judgment of the Court was delivered by

McLACHLIN J. -

A Brief in Brief

The following are the essential elements of a brief:

1. The Parties Plaintiff (the party suing) and Defendant (the party being sued) or in an appeal case, Appellant (the party appealing a lower court's decision) and Respondent (the other party in the original action). At trial level, the name of the plaintiff is usually placed first. An appeal is initiated by whichever party is dissatisfied with the decision in the original case and in some jurisdictions the order of the parties' names is changed if the defendant is the appellant. Often only a reading of the facts will distinguish the parties accurately.

2. Case History It is important to know which court is hearing the action. It is also important to know what prior courts the case has been heard in and who won and lost Is the case at the first trial stage or has it been appealed to a higher court? Often a judge will refer to comments made at a lower level court and so the reader must be aware of any prior court action in the case.

3. The Facts Included in this section are all the facts that affect the position of the parties and, therefore, the outcome of the case. This is the account of what happened to give rise to the dispute between the parties.

4. The Issues (a) Main Issue, and (b) Secondary Issues. The issues are questions that the court must answer before it can make a decision in the case.

5. The Decision/Holding This is the decision of the judge or the outcome of the case.

6. Reasoning/Comment The judges reasons for the decision..

7. Ratio Why the case is important and what precedent it sets.